D1447947

Plain Cooking

Plain Cooking

LOW-COST, GOOD-TASTING AMISH RECIPES

BILL RANDLE

Recipes edited by Nancy Predina

Photographs by Perry Cragg

QUADRANGLE/THE NEW YORK TIMES BOOK CO.

Some of the materials in this book have previously appeared in privately printed publications and the several Sun Newspapers in Cleveland, Ohio.

 For information, address: Quadrangle/The New York Times Book Co., 10 East 53 Street, New York, N.Y. 10022. Manufactured in the United States of America. Published simultaneously in Canada by Fitzhenry & Whiteside, Ltd., Toronto.

Book design: Rita Naughton

LIBRARY OF CONGRESS CATALOGING IN PUBLICATION DATA

Randle, Bill, 1923–
Plain cooking; low-cost, good-tasting Amish recipes.

1. Cookery, Mennonite. I. Title.
TX721.R19 1974 641.5 74-77952
ISBN 0-8129-0492-3

Man does not live by bread alone.

Deuteronomy 8:3

Contents

Foreword

For the past thirty years I have spent most of my time as a disc jockey for radio and television in Detroit, Cleveland, and New York. I was fortunate enough to be closely associated with the careers of many of the biggest name music stars of the era, ranging from Johnnie Ray and Tony Bennett to Mantovani and Elvis Presley. My years in the music business brought me high visibility, a sometimes extraordinary income, a string of race cars, airplanes, show horses, and houses in various parts of the world.

Like many people who are locked into high income, ego massaging careers, I found myself constantly questioning the values I lived with. Radio and television purport to be licensed for the benefit of the "public interest, convenience, and necessity." In reality they are game preserves for sophisticated verbal manipulators and exploiters of bottom-line mass tastes. Success in such a field, while it is gratifying economically, poses enormous ethical and intellectual problems for the performer.

As a seeker of a more satisfying life style, I have been drawn, as a participant-observer, to hundreds of religious services. At various times I have listened to, lived with, recorded, and actively joined in with West Virginia snake handlers, Hare Krishna street people, shouting black storefront revivalists, native American peyote chewers, Shaker meditators, flagellant New Mexico Penitentes, intellectual Baha'i practitioners, wealthy Catholic Pentecostals, Jesus Only mountain fundamentalists, Unitarian discussion groups, campus Jesus Freaks, and dozens of other deviations from the American big-city religious organizations.

In a similar way, I started visiting the Amish communities as a folklore collector. My primary interest was in recording the church services of rural Amish held in their own houses. During the following years I recorded many such services, both Old Order Amish and the more liberal "splinter" congregations. In the course of my collecting I got to know many Amish on a first name basis and, slowly but surely, I began to feel at home whenever I visited an Amish community. Most of the Amish I have met through the years have been warm and friendly although there are some, not few in number, who are quite aloof and simply do not care to mix with the "English" or "Yankee."

When I first started to visit the Amish I was struck by the simplicity of their food. They grew almost everything that they served on the table. It was good tasting, plain, home cooking with an emphasis, of course, on their German and Swiss rural heritage. The portions were large, the flavor excellent. It was truly low cost, high quality eating.

All societies change through time, but the process of change is much slower in folk groups like the Amish who live in small communities. I have eaten hundreds of meals in private homes, on small and large farms, and in dozens of local family restaurants, and the quality of Amish cooking has stayed first class. There has been, however, some change in content and preparation of meals.

When I started seriously collecting "plain" recipes a decade or so ago, many of the Amish had already changed their kitchens from cast-iron coal stoves to more modern and convenient equipment. There is nothing masochistic about the Amish farmer or housewife. If it is possible within the tenets of their religion to use an ingredient or a technique that saves time and effort, well and good. While the range of accepted adaptation, from the strictly orthodox sects to the more liberal "Beachy" and Mennonite groups, is quite wide, it is safe to say that no Amish family lives exactly the way it did fifty years ago.

As the society changed in subtle ways through time, so has the average Amish family's approach to food. While there are many who still prefer the old-style, heavier Pennsylvania Dutch and traditional items, there are at least as many who use contemporary dishes.

Some meals, like the Sunday church dinner of Swiss cheese, bologna, pickles, beets, homemade bread, and jelly, are fairly standard. In the cold of winter a family having church at their house will serve a classic hot Amish bean soup, homemade bread with apple butter or jelly, cheese, pickles, apple snitz pie, and coffee. A big Sunday church lunch is often baked chicken, mashed potatoes and gravy, homemade noodles, pork and beans, potato salad, home baked bread, and a panoply of desserts including tapioca pudding, butterscotch delight, angel food cake, apple pie, and coffee. The Amish *love* sweet things. Don't we all.

We all, as individuals and groups, want to maintain our special myths. In the case of the Amish, the myths are largely perpetuated by outsiders. The legends of the groaning tables of the Pennsylvania Dutch have been told and retold. The story of the "seven sweets and seven sours" grows with each telling, largely by tourists who patronize the multitude of "Dutch" restaurants in the Lancaster, Pennsylvania, area. Such foods and exotic "hex" signs are singular and entertaining aspects of the Amish story, but only some of these popularly known aspects are true.

There are some meals that are truly traditional and almost ritualistic in the Amish areas. The Amish do make and enjoy scrapple, shoofly pie, Lebkuchen, Dutch potatoes, sweet and sour cabbage, apple butter, stink case, chow chow, apple dumplings, snitz und knepp, three-bean salads, rivel soup, German chocolate cake, date-nut pudding, sliced green tomato pie, canned steak, and quince honey.

They also eat an Amish-style pizza, sloppy joes, yumazetti, meat loaf, pot roast, fried chicken, pancakes, doughnuts, and casseroles by the dozen. Many of the contemporary meals reflect the realities of everyday living in propinquity to towns and small shopping centers. Supermarkets in the Amish areas do a thriving business with their horse-and-buggy customers as well as with the "English" trade. The Amish use fresh foods when they are handy and practical, canned when necessary or convenient. Why not? Life is not all berrying, potato digging, manure shoveling, and hoeing and raking. Even the Amish have adapted themselves to supermarket shopping and quick availability of specific food items. However, the Amish still maintain gardens to provide most of their daily food needs.

Amish women spend a lot of time cooking, baking, and canning. A really fine cook develops a reputation far and wide since church dinners and other communal cooking chores bring her work to the attention of everyone in the community. "Visiting" by friends and relatives also spreads the word. Sunday visiting is the major social activity of all the Amish, and good food, of course, is a big part of such visiting.

Amish women preserve all kinds of food. Alma Kaufman, former columnist for the Cleveland *Plain Dealer*, writes of rows of fried pork chops and steaks encased in lard-filled crocks, waiting for guests to arrive. Hams and slabs of bacon are cured. Sausages are smoked. Chicken and meat loaf are generally served to visitors. The Amish like their meat well-done. Hundreds of jars of fruits and vegetables are put up. Potatoes are stored and cheeses and apple butter are always ready. Graham cracker pudding is so common it is called Amish pudding, and special date-nut pudding and other "delights" and "surprises" are famous Amish dishes.

Puddings and cakes are standard Amish desserts and the pies are numerous and legendary. Items like a vanilla pie top off special meals. While shoofly pie and knepp are well known in some areas, in others they are seldom seen. Meat, whether butchered professionally or at home, is now often kept in freezer-storage lockers. Grape arbors are frequently seen in Amish country; part of the crop is used for winemaking. There are some Amish and Mennonites who make beer as well as hard liquor.

Many of the recipes in this book come from individual cooks and bakers I have met—persons like the remarkable Mrs. Roman Miller of Berlin, Ohio, and her daughter Betty. A few are from the Shaker cooks I recorded in 1960 in Maine and New Hampshire. Some are from Der Dutchman restaurant in Walnut Creek, Ohio. A good many are from the advertisements I took inviting recipes over the years in the *Budget*, the Amish newspaper. Others are from friends I made through the various radio programs I did on the Amish and their food practices on New York's WCBS from 1961 to 1965 and Cleveland's WERE between 1965 and 1972.

Through the past eight years, private editions of these and similar recipes have circulated in the Cleveland area (as well as other Amish communities) and have brought forth individual comments and changes based on personal experience and trial-and-error experimentation. I have eaten most of the dishes presented here, many of them in Amish kitchens.

Where do they originally come from? Most of them, though credited in the text to the individual who contributed them, are the products of many minds and sources, orally transmitted or written down, continually changing from the numerous, ephemeral originals. There are those who are interested only in an "authentic" and "pure" folk tradition and a collection of such memorabilia. Without equivocation, that is *not* what I have tried to do here. There are "modern" as well as "old-time" recipes because both reflect the realities of the present as a preservation of the past.

One of the most exciting things about doing this book was the testing of the various recipes. Over a period of several months this year we had almost 2000 volunteer cooks and bakers involved in a massive program of trying out a total of more than 1000 "plain cooking" recipes. In every case a comprehensive testing form was used by our small army of housewives.

Any cookbook, of course, should be used as much as possible by the owner. With this in mind, I thought it only sensible to have as testers the kind of everyday folk who were actually going to *use* these recipes. The Amish and Mennonite and other "plain" cooks have no problems; they grow up with a background that gives them the expertise and skills that make kitchen magic an ordinary thing. But I am well aware that many women are not completely involved these days in such kitchen activities and we had to make sure that everything in this book could be easily prepared by almost anyone from the newest young married to the most sophisticated expert.

Obviously we could not include every recipe tested. Space and cost factors precluded that. In no sense were we trying to produce a definitive cookbook. As a social scientist, I recognize that such a work is far beyond me. I am sure that the future will see an encyclopedic, scholarly, and "pure" compendium of Amish cookery that will be the last word. I will certainly buy a copy when it comes out.

However, our several thousand "average experts" provided us with an excellent sounding board. As a result, I have included in the back of this book the names of the people who so enthusiastically participated in our final collection. To those others whose comments and efforts are not recognized individually in these pages, let me say "Thanks!" I mean it sincerely and unequivocally—without you we could not have done this book.

The individuals listed actually made and analyzed the recipes included. In most cases each recipe was tested at least two times by different people before its final selection. The names are listed alphabetically; each person made an equal contribution.

The sociological and historical information in the preceding essay has come from many sources: magazine and newspaper articles, the lecture notes from my classes in American Folk Culture at Columbia University in the early sixties, and my own observations of the Amish. While no direct attributions have been made because of the style of this book, I have also culled information from several excellent academic works which the reader may also wish to explore: *Our Amish Neighbors* by William I. Schreiber (University of Chicago Press, 1962); *Amish Society* by John A. Hostetler (Johns Hopkins Press, 1963, 1968); *The Amish Year* by Rollin C. Steinmetz and Charles S. Rice (Rutgers University Press, 1956); *The Amish People* by Elmer Lewis Smith (1958).

The photographs by Perry Cragg illustrating this book speak for themselves. They were taken over almost half a century and reflect the involvement of an internationally recognized photographer in the collective life of a people. Cragg's pictures appeared in a wide range of publications from suburban weekly newspapers and huge dailies to specialized books and magazines. He won numerous prizes for his work, particularly his intense portraits of the Amish and Mennonite "plain people."

Perry Cragg died in March, 1970, after a lingering illness. His friend Peter Bellamy spoke these words at his simple funeral service: "We may hardly doubt that his affectionate soul will roam the rolling Ohio farmlands of the gentle Amish and visit the hearts of those to whom he was faithful in good times and in bad times."

The varied collection of "plain cooking" recipes are simply dishes that taste good, fill you up, and frequently have high nutritional value.

Bill Randle
Cleveland, Ohio
May, 1974

Plain Cooking

The Amish in America

A TOUGH-MINDED PEOPLE

It is truly unfortunate that through the years there has been a commercialization and almost deliberate perpetuation of the folklore of the so-called "Pennsylvania Dutch." Newspaper features, magazine articles, and even a Broadway show (*Plain and Fancy*) picture these vital people as a group of quaintly dressed ladies in bonnets and shawls and bearded men with wide-brimmed black hats clip-clopping along Midwestern back roads in horse-drawn buggies, every once in a while showing up at an apple butter festival or the Hershey Antique Auto Show to entertain the tourists.

The simple fact is that the Amish are a tough and vital group who live in America side by side with other Americans. While it is true that they have clustered in certain areas of the country (Ohio, Pennsylvania, Indiana, Michigan, Illinois, Iowa, and Virginia) because of the early migration of their families to those areas, it is also true that they have competed economically and socially with a highly industrialized and technological society that has so far been unsuccessful in crushing their individuality, fragmenting their culture, or destroying their way of life.

This in itself is an extremely important and valuable contribution by the Amish to this country. They do not live in a vacuum, insulated from the general population, and they are forced to maintain their special life style against what would seem on the surface to be hopelessly overwhelming odds. Yet it is quite true that the Amish have been able to thrive under the impact of our mechanized society's pressures and grow in numbers and economic influence. In a similar way, the Hutterites of the Dakotas have been able to compete with agricultural "factories in the field" operated by huge corporations and not only persist but often economically dominate their local areas.

The Amish and similar groups do not maintain themselves by rigidly uncompromising patterns of behavior, in spite of the myths. They are able to survive because they are willing to work hard at maintaining what they believe to be the right way to live. When their religious rights were threatened beginning in the early 1930s they fought back and, after a series of legal battles stretching over a forty-year period, they finally prevailed.

The *Wisconsin v. Yoder* decision recently ruled that Amish children can legally leave school at age 14 or after the eighth grade has been completed. This removes the younger Amish from the potential seduction of the secondary school systems, eliminating the major threat to Amish culture, the loss of the young people to the "world." The Amish generally feel that they can compete with the secular society on any other level, and with their children available to them from age 14 they are now secure in the knowledge that their ways will persist through time against outside influences and pressures.

The Amish are far from perfect people, either in a religious or a social sense. Again, the myths and folklore consistently portray this folk group as completely honest, kind, dedicated to the land, hard working, nose-to-the-grindstone religious fanatics. Most Amish are indeed hard working and honest but there are those who are slick and quick to take advantage as well.

Amish young people can be wild and rowdy, quick to anger, and rough in a back-of-the-tavern or back-of-the-barn fight. Sometimes Amish girls get pregnant before they get married. Bundling and courtship among the Amish result in the same kind of tolerance of premarital sex as has become the general community standard in America. Amish parents have the same ability to be ignorant of their children's real behavior as any other American parents.

While some Amish stick to the old ways more fervently than others, the ties between them, even with the deviation from the norm, are far greater than the differences. The Amish, all orders, really do maintain high standards in their work. They are painstaking in their labor and craftsmanship and they make things that do not fall apart in a few months or years. When an Amishman builds a barn or lays brick for a house or makes a kitchen cabinet, it is first quality work and his name and reputation stand behind it.

The Amish are not blind to the economic advantages of developing the natural resources of the land. In the past few years they have opened their farm areas to exploitation by mining interests and natural gas companies. The major difference between this exploitation and similar practices elsewhere is that they do not allow the companies to rape the land and destroy the soil. Millions of tons of coal have been mined and hundreds of natural gas wells are in operation with minimal damage to the environment. This *is* a major difference.

The only way the differences between the Amish and majority American culture can be explained is by examining how the Amish came to this country, where and why they settled, how their communities grew and prospered, and what changes took place through time. Such a profile of the Amish, compacted though it is by space requirements and the limited scope of this book, should give the reader a better understanding of how these recipes and foodways came to be.

HISTORICAL BACKGROUND

When I first studied the Reformation and the subsequent development of Protestant sectarianism I was most fascinated by the Anabaptists, "that group of strangely devoted and extremely brave fanatics who faced the tortures of the spirit and the flesh with a firmness and integrity that defies belief." Their stories are told and retold in the contemporary Amish communities and forge a link with the historical past that is permanent and unbreakable. The pervasive impact that their religion has on the daily lives of the Amish is inescapable. Religious beliefs and customs are with them from the cradle to the grave and it is an awesome thing indeed.

Amish history begins with priest Menno Simons, who left his medieval church order in 1536 to become the leader of a stricter, more disciplined group, the Mennonites, already in conflict with both established state and religious authorities. Jacob Ammann, from whom the Amish derive their name, split with the new Mennonites a century and a half later over an even more strict adherence to primitive Christian doctrines. The "Amish," from 1693, became a separate people and deliberately removed themselves from the temptations and corruption of the world around them.

Due to constant persecution they became farmers and maintained their families and religious identity during the years of religious and economic turbulence that shattered medieval society and fragmented empires. In the mid-1600s, after the horrors of the Thirty Years War, thousands of the Amish and Mennonites came to America, many of them brought by William Penn.

The flood of Swiss and German immigrants from the Palatinate and other impoverished European areas flowed into Pennsylvania and dominated areas that are today known as "Pennsylvania Dutch" counties. Berks, Lancaster, Bucks, Lehigh, York, Northampton, and a dozen other limestone-fertile areas were populated and enriched by the industrious German-speaking farmers.

Clusters of families spread out and claimed the soil from the forests. They were pioneers in the best sense, opening new areas, clearing the land, planting, and harvesting. By 1776 half of Pennsylvania's population came from the German states. Many thousands were Amish or Mennonite, some were bond servants working out their passages, and all were farmers and craftsmen.

After the American Revolution the Amish and Mennonites moved in an almost direct westward line from their Pennsylvania base. Hundreds of Amish followed pioneer church members to Ohio, Indiana, Illinois, and Iowa areas of the Western Reserve. By 1808 the first of ultimately thousands of Millers moved into the Sugarcreek section of Ohio, expanding through the years into Stark, Tuscarawas, Wayne, and Holmes counties to become the largest Amish family group in the largest Amish area in the world.

Joe Miller opened up the Indiana territory in 1840 and contemporary Amish settlements in LaGrange, Noble, and Elkhart counties date from that time. Illinois had numerous Amish by 1850; Iowa had a fair Amish homesteading cluster by 1846. Later, Amish people moved to Kansas, Nebraska, Arkansas, Oregon, Colorado, Montana, the Dakotas, Idaho, and Oklahoma with their Mennonite brethren. There were Amish in the Virginias, Kentucky, Maryland, and New York. By 1962 there were Amish church members in twenty states, including Florida. There were also Amish in Canada, Mexico, and other parts of Latin America.

Middlefield, Ohio, is the center for an Amish community that numbers over four thousand. In 1886, banker Joe Rose financed Holmes County Amishman Samuel Weaver in the purchase of a farm in the area. The Parkman–Middlefield Road was the geographical magnet that drew Amish settlers from other Ohio Amish communities and from Pennsylvania as well. By the early 1920s the Amish were the major economic factor in this booming rural area a few miles from Cleveland.

A similar story can be told of many other Amish centers. Hartville, Ohio, is a thriving Amish community in Stark County. It dates from 1905 when several Amish families moved in and became the nucleus of a major church district, subsequently splitting into several new districts as the families prospered and grew. On the other hand, new Amish districts like New Glarus, Wisconsin, were settled when the Amish left established areas in 1964 because of conflicts with state authorities over educational requirements for their children. They reflect the continuing Amish desire to be separated from the state in matters that they feel directly affect their ability to maintain their religious integrity.

So the history of the Amish in America has been one of continuous growth, both economic growth and increase in population. There are now nearly sixty thousand Amish in America, and their numbers are increasing more rapidly than any other group with the exception of the Hutterites of North and South Dakota. Like the Amish, the Hutterite brethren are descendants of the Anabaptists. The Hutterites are religious communitarians, holding all land in common and working in a communal economic system, unlike the Amish who are independent entrepreneurs.

AMISH BELIEFS

The Amish generally adhere to the Biblical injunction "Be not conformed to this world." They have historically kept their lives apart from the populations of the countries and states in which they have lived. As a "chosen people" they renounce "the Devil and the world with all its wicked ways." Their interpretation of the Bible is a literal one and they are strict fundamentalists in their beliefs and practices, conforming to a New Testament ideal.

Even though rules of behavior are not written down but passed along orally, the firmness of their traditions and the persistence of their life style and religious tenets do not permit extensive change. "The old ways are the best ways" is their motto and, if as in the case of bundling, this proves to be slightly impractical in modern times, it is unfortunate. No stone can be cast at the past behavior of God-fearing and honest Amish who practiced such ways a century or more ago. It would be unthinkable for a contemporary Amish preacher to accuse a previous generation of wrong or sinful ways.

Whatever criticism there is within the religious community is kept internal, not broadcast to the world. This kind of isolation, with the losers in the unfortunate position of being "shunned" by the rest of the group, seriously inhibits any tendencies toward radical change. The list of taboo behavior is long and well known. Deviation is punished by the feared "meidung" or "miting" excommunication from the church which keeps anyone so castigated from any association with other members of the church. This applies to husbands, wives, children, parents, and other relatives, and such a weapon, having hard economic and psychological consequences, is a powerful deterrent and a harsh punishment.

Amish religious beliefs provide social and economic relations with the "world." There is no buying or selling or economic activity of any kind on Sunday. While the Amish participate in all aspects of day-to-day business with the "English," they do not become their partners, nor do they often borrow or owe money for services or goods.

The Amish never marry outsiders. They refrain from holding public office and generally vote only when it is an issue that specifically affects them, such as school bond issues. They have a firm tradition of personal commitment to the principle of brotherly love and consider themselves to be defenseless Christians. They refuse to take oaths of any kind and are conscientious objectors in time of war. They do not accept welfare or other state systems of family aid and, since 1965, have been exempted from the provisions of the Social Security program. Previously they paid into the programs but did not accept any money at age 65 and above.

The Amish feel, according to their deepest beliefs, that mutual aid is the personal responsibility of every member of the community. Not to help a neighbor in need is as cardinal a sin as pride. When money is lent to an individual or family in need, no interest is charged. While collections in Amish churches are only taken twice a year, there are always funds for widows, permanently disabled people, victims of fire and natural disasters, and other emergencies. In most cases such aid comes directly from the community.

Notices and letters read:

> We wish to thank our friends and neighbors for the quilts, comforters, bedding, the many letters, prayers and deeds of kindness, for the people that helped us in every way with eats and to rebuild our home. Also for the Fire Department's help. [Sugarcreek, Ohio]

> We wish to express our thanks and appreciation for the help, donations and food during the barn fire, cleaning up and rebuilding. [Lancaster, Pennsylvania]

Even the Amish cannot take care of their own in case of extraordinary emergencies. An example of public interest and Amish acceptance of worldly aid took place in August, 1973 when a drunk driver smashed into the buggy of an Amish family near Ashland, Ohio. Rosie and Harvey Yoder were seriously injured in the accident and required extensive surgery and long-term hospitalization. Publicity in the Cleveland *Plain Dealer*, the *Budget*, and local television news stories flooded the Yoder family with contributions. By Rosie's 13th birthday in February, 1974 over $61,000 had been donated, equalling the cost of medical care to that time and assuring the child of every medical treatment necessary. Much of the money was contributed by Amish people throughout the country.

AMISH MEN

An Amishman becomes a full fledged member of the church and the district community any time after the age of sixteen when he decides to stop shaving, join the church, and get married. Amish bachelors are not common because they are unable to hold church offices and are not considered to be active and contributing members of the community. When an Amish youth makes his decision to join the church it is a final one and he, for all practical purposes, leaves "worldly" things behind. His family and the church district in which he settles and works become the primary and dominating factors in his life.

While almost all Amish are farmers to some degree, in the last ten years many of the Amish men have turned to other kinds of work. Only about fifty percent of the working Amish now devote all their time to farming. Most do maintain small farms even if they are gainfully employed in some other line of work. Farming and agricultural work is still the central motif in the lives of most Amish in America.

This will probably continue in the years to come, even though Amish lands are being exploited for natural gas and coal as well as truck farming and dairy products. The Amish shift with the times and the markets for their goods. Many Amishmen now depend on the great cities nearby for a market for their eggs, produce, and milk. This economic dependence has resulted in some major changes in the typical Amish farming operation.

Even though the contemporary Amish farmer tends to be far behind the huge American conglomerate farms that are almost totally mechanized, he still uses farm implements and technology that would have been absolutely proscribed a generation ago. Some Amish use diesel engines, sell milk to regional milk distributors who control coolers and modern pasteurizing equipment, develop and sell hybrid seeds for grain, use chemical fertilizers and advanced soil technology, operate threshing machines, own gas-powered corn shuckers, and utilize power from tractors to grind corn and cut lumber. They are fairly quick to adopt new and better techniques that do not flagrantly violate local church rules. The Amish boy who gets a corner of a garden to tend and a pig or goat of his own at age five learns to operate within the rules set by his own community. He generally learns to farm successfully.

The Amish pay cash for everything except land. Today, buying a farm takes more cash than many of the younger people can raise. As a result, bankers cooperate with responsible people in the Amish settlements and often loan money for farm mortgages. In recent years the cost of farm acreage has skyrocketed in most farm areas, and many of the younger Amish have been squeezed out of the market. Many Amish have moved to Canada and South America where land is cheap and available.

In some cases where local customs did not allow for technological change, the Amish community met the challenge head on. In the mid 1950s, Amish dairy farmers in Middlefield, Ohio were faced with a state law requiring the cooling of Grade A milk to 55° for home consumption, a rule that was impossible for the Amish to meet since such refrigeration requires electrically controlled cooling tanks. Thousands of acres in the area were involved in dairy farming and land costs had zoomed due to the pressure of huge suburban land deals.

The Amish dairy farmers organized, brought in a Swiss-cheesemaker named Hans Rothenbuler, and formed a cooperative to absorb their production of what was classed Grade B milk. Rothenbuler developed a high quality Swiss cheese that became nationally famous and turned an emergency program into a multimillion dollar industry, not only using millions of gallons of milk but also employing many local Amish in the plant.

Amish who are not full time farmers work in a wide variety of occupations. Many of them work in factories. There are Amish in rubber companies, plastics plants, machine shops, buggy works, pallet making, road construction, harness shops, plastering, making furniture, railroad work, trailer manufacturing, bricklaying, and farm implement sales. Others are working in sawmills, as lumberjacks, watchmakers, seed salesmen, weavers, printers, blacksmiths, and veterinarians. There are Amish butchers, day laborers, bakers, shoemakers, tanners, and leatherworkers, cabinet makers, manure haulers, and dynamite blasters. Some Amish build dams, breed and train horses, cover coin-machine routes, mill flour, operate cider presses, work in grain elevators, and own small stores. A considerable number of Amishmen are carpenters. Some are teachers.

Amish workers are thorough, highly skilled, and conscientious at their jobs. When Amish construction workers were laid off because they would not replace their own hats with the hardhats required by federal law, employers protested the loss of their best workmen. A U.S. Department of Labor exemption (on religious grounds) allowed the Amish to return to the jobs wearing their traditional black broadbrims. Similarly, the government has ruled that Amish do not have to be involved in workmen's compensation or insurance benefits. The United Steel Workers and other unions have given the Amish special permission to work in union shops without joining the union.

Some of the Amishman's work is recreational. Many are vernacular architects who use carpentry manuals to build their own homes. Roman Miller designed and built the addition to his home that serves as one of the major Amish-owned restaurants in Ohio. In Stuart's Draft, Virginia, where many Amish work in the production of the famous hams, farming is both for fun and profit. Hunting and fishing, in combination with trapping mink, beaver, and muskrat, provides food for the dinner table and extra cash for the family.

Many Amish are regulars during the Michigan and Pennsylvania deer hunting seasons and often work as guides for beginning hunters. Some Amish are professional hunters and recreational areas experts. Martin Miller is the Parkman River Pines Camping Club manager in Ohio. He directs the complete operation including hunting, fishing, hiking, camping, and backpacking on this beautiful Grand River glacial terrain. His assistant is a younger Amish outdoorsman, Moses Troyer.

Numerous Amish are horse traders and trainers. At least one Amish-bred horse became a famous trotter earning a small fortune for his owners after being taken from behind a plow and trained to harness racing. Many of the horses owned by the Amish are of show horse quality. My own Blu-Fox Farms was started in 1968 from breeding stock and stallions from the large herd of Devan Morgans in Wilmot, Ohio, in the heart of the Amish country. And the Amish build the sturdiest, best looking barns in the horse country.

A barn raising is regarded as recreation for the entire Amish community. Recently two major firms tried to move an old barn to the Burton, Ohio historical village, but with no success. Finally the local Amish, about forty men and women, dismantled the original barn, moved it several miles, and rebuilt it piece by piece in one day. Big iron pots of beef and noodles tended by the women provided the food for the barn raising "bee," and the forty-foot beams, braces, split wood blocks, wooden pegs, and bent cross sections went up like magic.

Such barn raisings are frequent events and derive from a pioneer tradition. Since the Amish have no insurance, good neighbors become the insurance company in case of fire or storm damage. The communal effort is a major holiday and workmen bring their own saws, hammers, chisels, hatchets, iron tipped pikes, and other tools, and whole families join in. There have been serious accidents and some deaths from falls during barn raising festivities.

Amish farmers also breed farm animals, butcher hogs and cattle, and build bird houses on tall stilts, gravel driveways and buggy turnarounds, and participate in a hundred other necessary, sometimes communal, activities peripheral to daily farm work.

Amish men wear black, blue, or gray denim work clothes and heavy shoes or boots. Their pants are baggy and have no pockets or fly. They have broadfall fronts, commonly known as "barndoor britches," that button at the sides with an underpiece across the waist. The Amish do not often wear belts, but suspenders are common. The work pants are frequently patched. Long, tight underdrawers with trapdoor bottoms are standard.

Work clothes are fastened with hooks and eyes among the Old Order Amish; some more modern districts now use zippered jackets in the winter. Because of the severity of winters in most Amish populated states, several layers of work clothing is common; jackets and sweaters are worn under an outer jacket or, sometimes, an overcoat. Shirts are plain and, if homemade, have no collars, but many Amish wear regular store bought work shirts. Broadbrimmed black hats are worn except in school, church, Sunday meetings, and court appearances. Caps are never worn.

Amish hats find their way out of the community from time to time. The late Bobby Darin wore Amish made clothes and doffed a black Amish beaver in at least one movie. Bob West, a Cleveland radio director and movie maker, used an Amish hat on the star of a recent motion picture. Paul Stookey, of Peter, Paul and Mary, was also intrigued by a similar fur felt, high crown hat, wearing it at a recent concert. Grandfather hats and Bishop hats have the highest crowns.

Since the black hats get very dusty in the summertime, many Amish wear straw hats most of the time. Little boys wear flat, round black hats with long pants and straight black jackets.

Dress-up clothing worn by Amish men is usually covert cloth or woolen worsted fabric cut in a style similar to the Nehru jackets popularized by Johnny Carson and designer Pierre Cardin. There are no lapels or pockets, the neck is high cut with no collar. The jacket is straight, and the bottom is either curved or square cut. Fastenings are hooks and eyes. A sleeveless, lined vest is usually worn. Pants are more closely cut than work clothes but have the same broadfall front. Wide suspenders are sometimes worn and shirts are solid pastels—greens, yellows, and blues. Plain white shirts are worn much of the time.

The Amish wear no jewelry, but many carry pocket watches. I have collected Ball and Howard watches for many years and have often traded the Amish such watches for wooden farm implements, ox yokes, old tools, and similar things. In a trade, the Amish will inevitably pick out a silver watch with a train engraved on the back. Many Amish men wear glasses, always with metal rims.

The Amish hair style is taken from a Biblical quotation (Leviticus) "Ye shall not round the corners of your heads." It is worn long and over the ears, sometimes in bangs, usually roughly trimmed. I have seen Amish men with hair falling practically to their shoulders. Years ago, when Amish teen-agers wanted to go "English" on a Saturday night they had to put up their hair beneath caps to disguise themselves. In the last ten years, Amish teen-agers and men have looked pretty much like everybody else as to hair. When the Beatles made their first appearance in America there were thousands of comments made on radio and in the press about their hair. My reply was simply, "I've got a lot of friends in Ohio and Indiana who have been wearing their hair like that for nearly two hundred years."

The Amish man is a patriarch. He exercises the options of such a role, but I have found he generally respects the wishes of his wife and members of the family in every instance that is not strictly a church matter or one of personal principle. He is a provider, an arbiter, a father, a husband, and mostly a fair man in his dealing with his community and the world.

AMISH WOMEN

Amish women are hard workers. They start when they are small children and by the time they get married they have picked up all of the essential housekeeping and farming skills that make them such a valuable economic asset in the Amish community. Homemaking and child bearing are the only roles that give Amish women status in what is essentially a patriarchal society. Women, while they are certainly respected, are secondary to Amish men in almost every aspect of their daily lives. Anyone who has spent any time with the Amish, however, is quite aware that many strong Amish women dominate their husbands.

Unmarried Amish women have had a rough time in past years. The only single women, except for adolescent girls, are widows and spinsters. Divorce, desertion, or separation are unheard of. Most of the single women "work out" as domestics, often in other Amish homes. In recent years some of them have been employed in hospitals and small factories located near the Amish farm areas, increasing their economic status to a point where they have been more generally accepted. However, the Amish ideal is still to marry early and have a big family.

Families with twelve or more children are not uncommon, although eight or nine is more of an average Amish family group. The Amish birth rate is far higher than the U.S. average. Since children are highly valued and join the labor force early there is almost no reported birth control; such practices are not discussed by the Amish. It is true, however, that varying Amish communities have differing ideas as to maximum family size. Whether such ability to control family size in different parts of the country is due to abstinence or some kind of folk birth control practices is not apparent.

Raising her large family is the major job of the Amish housewife. Most of her work takes place in and around her house and farm. The typical Amish woman is a mother, gardener, seamstress, cook, dishwasher, and full time domestic. She does everything from noodle-making, scrubbing floors, butchering chickens, canning, and quilt-making to darning and mending, hoeing the garden, making bread, milking the cows, and mowing the lawn. She makes soap, varnishes, pares fruit, peels potatoes, and hooks rugs.

The woman runs the house but the man controls the money; no waste or extravagance is tolerated. Occasionally a woman will become so well known as a specialist that she is able to spend most of her time doing just that. One of the best-known tailors in the Ohio Amish communities was a Mrs. Yoder, near Berlin. She made suits for most of the young Amishmen in the Holmes County districts and her family life and income were primarily organized around her tailoring skills.

In a similar way Mrs. Roman Miller, the famous Amish home-style cook, started out with a part-time restaurant that grew to a nationally known place serving thousands. Her simple food is so appealing that reservations are now taken months in advance. I have been there on Saturdays when up to five hundred people have been turned away.

So it is possible, even within the fairly rigid Amish heirarchy, to permit and reward deviations that benefit the family economically, just so long as they do not threaten the overall family structure. In cases where there have been sharper splits with Amish custom and tradition there have been more dramatic examples of changes in the roles of women in the communities. I have seen "Beachy" Amish women driving, doing assembly and inspection in factories, working in libraries, and doing many types of jobs that would be anathema to the Old Order groups. Some of these women use gas lawn mowers, have electrical appliances, and are less conservative in their clothing styles. They are easy to spot, too, for they often go without the traditional white cap.

An Amish woman always wears a dainty cap that fits neatly over the back of the head, encasing the "bun" formed by hair parted in the middle and braided. It is the standard hair style for all Amish and many Mennonite women. The caps are made of fine net, organdy or muslin. An Amish married woman always wears a white cap.

An Iowa "kapp," as shown in John Hostetler's *Amish Society,* is very plain with a few simple pleats around the brim. Pennsylvania head pieces have fewer pleats and an overhanging nape section with an angled tie. Ohio caps have both side pleats and a series of longer top pleats and seams that cover the headgear. Indiana caps are the most complicated of all; side pleats and furrows of top seams that must require hours to iron properly.

Amish women dress much in the style of their original European culture. The bonnets worn by most Amish women are similar to Shaker bonnets. The high button shoes once required of all Amish go back to the days when high button shoes were standard footwear. Since high button shoes are no longer available, even to the Amish, they wear plain black shoes.

The idea, however, that Amish women are drab and nondescript because they wear old-style clothing is a mistaken one. It is true that dresses are well below the knee, but they are often brightly colored. Their dresses and pretty blouses may be of peacock and powder blue, pink, lemon yellow, peach, red, aqua, rose, navy, and green. Even oranges, purples, and plums are found in aprons and neckerchiefs. There are, of course, simple grays and blacks worn as well as more colorful garb. Heavy black and gray shawls are common outerwear for Amish women.

The colors must be solid, not patterned, and one piece dresses are worn with various cape and over-the-shoulder attached capelike cloths. Different styles and colors are closely followed to designate married women and single girls. All of the garments are held in place by straight pins or simple fastenings. None use zippers.

The Amish women are fantastic housekeepers. Their floors are usually hardwood, without carpets or rugs, although you may find some hand-hooked or -braided small rugs in the parlor or spare room. Floors, scrubbed on hands and knees, shine. Furniture is plain. There are odd chairs and benches, wooden cradles, handmade corner cupboards, bentwood rockers, and heavy tables in almost all Amish homes.

The kitchen is the center for Amish family life. The kitchen table is where everybody eats. Sometimes there is oilcloth on the table, most often it is bare. There is no table linen although cupboards sometimes have inside shelves draped with folded paper napkins. Regular dishes are plain heavy china, sometimes picked up at an auction. Utensils are usually stainless steel, never silver. Some families have brightly-colored dishes and other pretty things displayed even though "pride and vanity" are outlawed. Painted tomato cans and clay pots are placed on window sills, a riot of flowering plants inside brightening up the kitchen. Occasional embroidered pieces are also colorful and charming.

Plain single blind draped curtains, blue or green, are found in many windows, but a large number of the older families have no curtains at all.

The stricter families have historically used coal stoves and kerosene or oil lamps. Propane and natural gas, some of it produced on Amish farmland, is now used by more liberal Amish districts. Thousands of mantels burn in gas lit homes along main and back-country roads. Gas stoves and ovens abound, and there are even homes with central heating systems here and there. But fine quilts filled with wool and heavy blankets and comforters are depended on more than heating plants.

There are plenty of outhouses as part of the country landscape, although many families have added more sophisticated plumbing in recent years. Tub baths, once common and sometimes communal, have been in many cases replaced by fixed bathtubs and showers as water systems have been developed that are acceptable to the various groups. Clothing is hand washed and sun and wind dried summer and winter.

There is little time for back fence gossiping and coffee-klatching in the Amish woman's day. She makes her own clothes (except for shoes and simple underwear) and also makes work clothes for the men in the family as well as all the children's clothing. She is a sometime barber and doctor, bandaging up the cuts and abrasions that are everyday problems on a working farm. She is constantly mending and fixing around the house; there is always something to be done.

It would be a serious mistake, however, to think that there is not a lot of joy and happiness in an Amish home because of the constant work and never ending responsibilities built into raising such large families in severe surroundings. Most Amish women love flowers, and there are always patches of colorful geraniums and marigolds, mixed with nasturtiums at times, decorating Amish lawns. There are apple-paring parties and auctions, town trips and visits, church Sundays and family reunions, barn raisings to cook for, and weddings galore. There are Amish women who play baseball and frisbee with enthusiasm and great style. At the other extreme Amish mothers read Bible stories in German to their little children with great reverence and feeling.

Amish women do not use cosmetics. They usually don't have to. The rosy red cheeks of the Amish and their fine clear skin, often freckled, needs no enhancing. They are naturally good looking people, vigorous and healthy women playing roles prescribed for them by tradition, maintained by perseverance, and apparently more than satisfying their needs for a complete and dedicated life.

EDUCATION

The Amish believe that education of their children in public school past the eighth grade is contrary to their religion. The values at the root of American secondary education are in direct variance with Amish values and life styles. Accordingly, most of the Amish have historically resisted sending their youngsters to school after the eighth grade in the sincere belief that they would endanger their own salvation and that of their children. After a series of early legal problems and extensive mass moves from hostile areas, the Amish in combination with interested civil libertarians became the storm center of the landmark school case *Wisconsin v. Yoder*. The case involved Jonas Yoder, Adin Yutzy, and Wallace Miller of Green County, Wisconsin. The children involved were Vernon Yutzy, 14, Frieda Yoder, 15, and Barbara Miller, 15. The Supreme Court decided in favor of the Amish; and the several opinions stated that Amish children compared favorably with the general population academically and received equal educational benefits and that compulsory education past the eighth grade was only recently mandatory in the United States. The court went on to say that the Amish community was a highly successful social unit within the larger American society and affirmed that both the First and Fourteenth amendments protected the Amish in their educational rights. The court concluded by saying that a way of life that is odd or even erratic but interferes with no rights of others is not to be condemned because it is different.

The Amish had earlier fought opposition in various ways. For example, when local school officials tried to enforce state laws, the

Amish voted them out of office. However, they finally developed their own school system, a series of tuition-supported parochial schools with Amish teachers under the direction of their own school boards. There are now more than 200 such schools administered by such Amishmen as Uriah Byler, a carpenter. Since 1951, Byler has headed a two-county school system in Ohio with more than twenty Amish schools. He has written *School Bell, Ringing,* a manual for Amish teachers, and also a United States history textbook. Byler believes that an Amish teacher is a counselor, an umpire, and a psychologist as well as a disciplinarian and taskmaster.

Most of the Amish schools are one-room brick buildings; a few newer ones are larger. Some have outhouses and wood and coal stoves. Children sometimes come to school barefoot, even in winter. They are seated in rows of grades one to eight with the first grade reciting first. Attention is paid to oral drills, recitation, and spelling; there is also a considerable emphasis on mathematics. German and religion are also taught. One or two teachers, usually unmarried girls, handle the entire eight grades, and are paid from $175 to $400 a month. The atmosphere is a relaxed one and children wander around and ask questions. The relationship with the teacher is personal. Recess is a privilege and children play games like "rabbit." School is important to the Amish, and children are expected to do well. The school year is 160 days long with time allowed for plowing, spring planting, and outside work.

Byler's philosophy reflects the sincere desires of the Amish to maintain an equitable place in American society even though they are "a peculiar people." He says, "We are grateful for living in a country where we may worship as our conscience dictates, where private and parochial schools are tolerated, where we may live in peace with our fellow men who have the common sense to respect the wishes of a minority."

AMISH GIRLS

Adolescence, for a young Amish girl, is a work-filled and serious time. Her training is focused on homemaking. The ideal is to make a good marriage, have children, be a good wife and mother, and maintain the family and church traditions. From about twelve years of age, most of her time is spent in preparing herself for these tasks. She changes her dress style from that of a little girl to a young woman. She becomes aware of boys, much as non-Amish teen-agers do.

Of course, young Amish girls have a lot of fun, too. They are open and quite gregarious within the family group and there is keen competition with the boys in the family in both social and economic arenas. While Amish boys in a family tend to try to dominate their sisters, they are well aware that their sisters' friends may well be the girls they want to date, and they act accordingly.

Amish girls accompany their mothers on the visits that are such an important part of everyday recreation and enjoyment. They learn to cook, sew, and help out in church dinners, socials, sewings, and showers. They attend "sings," "barn blasts," "frolics," and parties and play baseball, "rabbit," hand-clapping games, and join in play party events that are really pairing off situations. Here they are able to talk, joke, sing, visit, and get to know the boys better.

There is a lot of undercover meeting after girls get a "steady." Girls from 14 to 16 are generally dating one or two boys regularly. Couples often are paired off at wedding dinners and special events.

The announcing of the wedding is "published" in church two weeks before the celebration. Advance arrangements are made by a deacon who asks the father of the bride-to-be for permission to marry. Since the family has agreed already to the match, such a request is strictly a formality.

The youth lives at the home of his "fiancée" from the time the wedding notice is published until the ceremony itself. No fancy cards are sent; all invitations are requests in person by the groom. He selects the two best men, his bride picks the bridesmaids. Weddings are sometimes Tuesday but usually Thursday, and are held in November and December, due to the time available because of the weather. Older people, widowed and remarrying, do not adhere to these end-of-year wedding months.

Girls usually have filled hope chests, and dowries consist of quilts, furniture, farm equipment, and infrequently land. All items are practical and identified with starting a new family life. Weddings are usually held at a friend's house and all gifts and dowry items are collected at the bride's family's house.

The wedding itself is an impressive affair. No parents are allowed at the wedding ceremony. The services last several hours and clearly spell out the serious and permanent responsibilities of each marriage partner. During the preliminary preaching the couple is instructed privately in their roles as man and wife in the Amish community and then in public they take their simple vows.

After the wedding everybody goes to the bride's house where the dinner is served. The couple sits at a special table. Other tables are loaded with dozens of pies and cakes, desserts, chickens, hams, beef, and extraordinary dishes. There are silent prayers and then hearty eating. Hymns and other singing are part of all Amish weddings. The last song performed after an Amish wedding is a simple folk song, "Good Friend."

The couple spend several weeks or more after the ceremony in visiting throughout the Amish communities where they have friends and relatives. They are honored guests everywhere during this period. All Amish families brace themselves for such visits, joyfully, of course, during December, January, and February. A recent item in an Amish paper read,

> Newlyweds Daniel and Ruth King were Monday night supper guests with me. Most of the newlyweds are about finished with their visitings and ready to settle down in their own home.

AMISH BOYS

The conflict between the old and the new is the source of an underlying tension in all Amish communities. The various splits that have resulted in new-persuasion Amish groups have almost always had their origin in some quite minor aspect of daily life. Through the years Amish have debated the use of the automobile, rubber tires on tractors, the use of electricity, and numerous other technological changes in basic farming. At the same time the underlying fear has been that such technological change (especially radio, phonograph records, and television with their emphasis on "worldly" things) will result in the Amish youth losing their identity with the older ways.

That such fears are well grounded is evidenced in the high rate of Amish youth leaving the parent church districts and either going "English" or turning to the more hospitable Mennonite churches or "Beachy" and other liberal Amish splinter groups. Nearly twenty percent of the younger Amish apparently have done just that in recent years. How much of the loss is due to the pull of the world against the strict Amish way of life is apparent in even a superficial look at Amish youth who live near major population centers.

Many of the young Amish boys either own or drive automobiles. They themselves cannot be punished for this deviation from regular Amish life styles because they are not yet baptized. There are hundreds of hidden phonographs and battery operated tape players in bedrooms, barns, and buggies, stashed out of sight. The number of transistor radios must be in the thousands. Amish youngsters generally like hillbilly music and country favorites like Johnny Cash, Faron Young, Jack Greene, Bill Anderson, and Porter Waggoner.

There are many young Amish musicians. I have recorded several groups during the last ten years that play country music well. The Pennsylvania musicians and singers are more traditional and feature square-dancing with down-home fiddle and guitar playing, but I have found highly skilled pop country pickers and players in Ohio and Indiana who are up to date and know all the current hits. Where the old-time bands will play hoe down and dance tunes like *Bile Them Cabbage Down,* the hipper Amish youth play Flatt and Scruggs-type fast tunes and the sentimental popular country hits like *The Green Green Grass of Home.*

There is quite a bit of drinking among the younger Amish. Barn dances and "frolics" are almost always the scene of heavy beer drinking and local taverns in predominantly Amish communities are often cited for selling beer to such minors. There have been street fights and buggy and car accidents as a result of teen-age drinking by local Amish in Lancaster, Pennsylvania, Shipshewana, Indiana, and Middlefield, Ohio during the past few years. Rowdyism and antisocial behavior, frowned upon by the parents and church members, is generally taken care of within the Amish community itself.

Amish boys will "show off" by dressing within the cultural mode but adapting the style to suit themselves. For example, the standard Amish black broadbrimmed hat is worn by many Amish boys cowboy style, and the standard baggy pants and boots are often replaced by tighter, lean black Levi-like pants, a style approximating the Amish youth's concept of the Western gunfighter image.

There are indications that most young Amish go through a trial period of "sowing wild oats" and even discriminate among themselves if any of their members does not go along. The heckling of the quieter Amish teen-agers by the rougher ones is similar to the pattern found in any contemporary suburban milieu. Amish kids who do not smoke, dance, drink, and hang around are often subjected to the harassment and derision of their peers.

AN AMISH AUCTION

The Amish love auctions. They flock to them for bargains, to meet family and friends, to see what others are buying, and to gossip. There are hundreds of auctions every year in Amish areas and they are always well attended. The auction and farm or house sale is a major recreational activity and has, through the years, become a ritualistic event.

The Amish look for bargains but they buy only what they need.

They generally do not sell land, except to each other, but they often buy land at farm or estate sales, paying top dollar for the best acreage. Farm equipment and machinery sales draw hundreds of Amishmen looking for spike harrows, corn huskers, Burch walking plows, stainless steel double wash vats, milk can racks, brooder houses, pig palaces, self feeders, and countless other useful pieces of "farm stuff."

They bid on brood cows "due to start freshening," 12-gauge shotguns, 2,000 bales of hay, light and heavy butcher sows, copper wall candle holders, a "taffic safe" mare, baby beds, "42 cows, milking age," cane-bottom chairs, oil lamps, a top boar, appliances, shoats and pigs, a box wagon, a silo of corn ensilage, and old clocks.

The competition is fierce on a "2 year old bay road horse, broke single and double," a No. 80 cobber, a Holstein cow "heavy Springer coming in with third calf," glassware, "pigs by the head," tools, an ironing board, "back to farm" calves, a child's rocker, road carts, feeder cattle, and new and used furniture of all kinds. Buyers come and go for "market toppers"—No. 2 light hogs, gas cans, a standardbred driving mare, sinks, bells from India, Depression glass, open heifers, bred heifers, and old heifers. There are seekers of Weller and Roseville pottery, heavy stoneware and china, fishing equipment, "a sorrel mare in foal," old books, the *Ausbund* (the Amish hymnal), good-choice medium-light and thin calves, a brass kettle, "first cutting hay by the bale," a wooden ice box, "a good herd in nice condition," a "four stall slatted calf pen," and a violin (for a beginner).

The Amish mix with the English at the sales and auctions and there are spirited contests for the old painted country furniture the Amish themselves now want back after getting rid of it years ago. They have become antique oriented, and primitive wooden implements, old tinware, ox yokes, and brass harness fittings are just a few of their wants. A sharp eye can clue an experienced auction goer to an upcoming wedding, based on purchases by an eligible Amishman at a sale.

The auctions and sales have venerable histories and some of them—Farmers' Night Sales and the Charm Auction—have been followed by generations. The signs say "Register Early and Get a Good Number," "Good Clean Consignments Welcome," "Livestock to Sell—Livestock to Buy," "Eggs Must Be in by 12:30," and "Come Prepared to Pay Cash."

The auctioneers are stars and have a spiel and style that is passed down through the generations. A rap with the cane, a subtle or broad joke, a little "noodge" at the right time in the bidding—all are a part of the scenario as the residue and memories of one life pass into new hands, ready to be used again.

CHURCH

The Amish go to church every other Sunday. It is a day of rest and contemplation. It is also a busy day for children and women in Amish communities. Farm chores have to be taken care of, great quantities of food have to be prepared and served. Men, women, and children come together to worship.

There are Amish who have regular churches. Simple in design and not large in structure, these churches house many of the liberal and splinter Amish groups that, through time, have left the mainstream of Orthodox Amish tradition. The churches have electric lights and central heating. There are rows of traditional pews and benches.

The majority of the Amish, however, have church at home. Each Amish home is, in a sense, a church. And each church member in a district (an area delineated by the travel distance that a buggy can easily cover in combination with a number of families living within such a radius) is expected and required to have a church meeting when it is his turn. When the Sunday comes the Amish home is opened to as many as a hundred, often more, members. They come early (church starts between 8:00 and 8:30 A.M.) and stay late (visiting and supper take time, you know).

When it is time, each group enters the main house designed so that doors open wide between rooms to accommodate large numbers. There is a strict procedure for entering and seating determined by seniority and sex. The Amish are a patriarchal people—the select, older, and ordained are first in line, both in church and at the dinner tables after.

Backless wooden benches line the rooms. There are occasionally a few rockers for very old or handicapped church members. It is not unusual, either, to see a chair or two for visiting ministers, the bishop, and similar heirarchical figures. Amish ministers are nominated for the position by members of the church (when there is an opening) and a new minister is chosen by chance (a slip in a Bible selected at random from a table) from the nominees. It is a lifetime job and there is no pay.

Amish services are characterized by slow, dirgelike hymns sung in unison by the entire group. The hymns are generally selected from the *Ausbund* and always include the "Hymn of Praise" ("'S

Lobg'sang"). There are two sermons, a short introductory one and a long and intense main effort. In addition there is group kneeling, silent prayer, scripture reading, testimonials, a benediction, and various church announcements.

There is considerable freedom during an Amish service. While small children are expected to attend, they sometimes wander or, more often, fall asleep. There is a restlessness and shifting about as the benches get harder to the seat. The average Amish church service is about four hours long. The sermons are emphatic about suffering and tribulation and relate the tortures of the faithful during the Anabaptist period, as do the hymns.

After preaching comes the Sunday dinner. The early menu was the famous Amish bean soup and a few assorted cold cuts and snacks, but more recent times have seen the Sunday church meal expand to be more complete. Austerity has yielded to convenience and mutual consent, and Amish women bake and cook with the housewife of the day to fill the tables with food. The food is eaten in shifts by the church members; again, heirarchy determines when the members eat. Table settings are minimal, and plates and cups are generally communal.

There is a lot of visiting in the afternoon and, again, a lot of singing. There have been instances of lawn evangelism in Amish areas with more contemporary singing and preaching, a kind of missionary effort that derives from more modern tendencies among the younger Amish. There are German versions of songs like "What a Friend We Have in Jesus" and some English hymns as well.

MEDICAL CARE

The Amish are fanatical about good medical care, and it is one of the few areas of their lives where frugality does not play a part. They spare no expense for the best care available. Of course there are the perhaps apocryphal stories of the Amish husband who waits until the last minute to call the doctor, gambling that the baby will come before the doctor, which lowers the fee about thirty percent. Few Amish, however, ignore obvious medical problems and they are receptive to all modern medical practices including immunization.

An Amish woman writes simply of preventive medicine:

> Nothing serious wrong with us, and no Dr. there. As we get older we get more aches and pains. For example, like an older fence. The fence is serviceable if we keep it in repairs. But it's much better to check it in the spring before we turn our cattle out, than let them break through a

few times. Then we have a hard time to keep them in. So with our body. If we once develop arthritis or other ailments, they are hard to get under control, especially after we're old. A stitch in time saves nine.

When special treatment that involves long distance travel is required the Amish are not deterred. The Mayo Clinic and other world-renowned research centers have often had Amish clients. The unusual Amish genetic deformity, six-fingered dwarfism, is generally handled by specialists and involves amputation of fingers, corrective cosmetic surgery, and complicated operations for the commonly related heart abnormalities.

There are many folktales of "powwowing" and faith healing in every county where there are Amish people. Much of it is only folklore, but some of the persistent rumors are based on the fact that there is a mainstream of pure folk tradition that surmounts the outsider's quaint idea of the spells and charms of "hex" doctors. The current interest in witchcraft and demonology, as evidenced by the success of *The Exorcist,* has brought many young people to the study of the Amish underground lore, part of which traces back directly to Albertus Magnus. The Amish, of course, absolutely believe in the existence and malevolence of the Devil.

There are some individuals in every Amish community who are almost legendary in their ability to handle the sick and emotionally unstable. The "laying on of hands," anointing, and other special healing practices may be based solidly on a folk awareness of the extremely important roles that kindness, attention, interest, personal closeness, and touching play in some psychosomatic illnesses.

The range of illness among the Amish is about the same as in the general American rural population, although there seems to be a much higher incidence of work-related accidents (probably due to primitive farming techniques) and minor problems like bed-wetting. Thousands of Amish youngsters, for example, are plagued by this nocturnal and embarrassing involuntary habit.

Mental illness exists in all Amish areas but there is more of a tendency for the Amish to maintain and integrate the emotionally disturbed person in the family than is generally true of most Americans. Depression and anxiety are the most common difficulties. Severely disturbed people, as psychotics and schizophrenics, are admitted to state and private hospitals for treatment since the Amish are aware that they cannot control such extreme behavior in even the most sympathetic home environment. The suicide rate among the orthodox Amish groups may be slightly higher than other Americans in rural areas.

Typical illness and accidents among the Amish are reflected in the following series of news items, gathered in the course of one week in February, 1974.

> Lydia Blucker is home from the hospital again and found out she has a big ulcer, anemia, and sugar diabetes.
>
> Owen, son of Harvey Schrock, suffered a concussion. He had hit his head several times and didn't think it serious until all at once he had such awful headaches.
>
> Walter Beach's 11-year-old Richard had the painful misfortune of breaking his left arm while scooting down a snowy bank. He has to work twice as hard with his right arm now.
>
> Jonas Hochstetler had the misfortune of hurting his eye when he was putting up a clothes line and the nail somehow flew out and hit him in the eye. He saw the doctor Friday evening.
>
> Mrs. Dan Schmucker got up through the night and kicked against something and her foot is cracked or badly sprained.

In addition to good doctors, fine hospital and clinic care, some folk medicine, and personal concern and involvement, the Amish sincerely believe in prayer as an answer to ill health. Typical is the note of Sarah Stooltzfuss: "Let us keep on praying for the sick and afflicted among us."

OLD PEOPLE

Old people have a very important place in Amish society. They are listened to, loved, respected, and cared for when they are too old to take care of themselves. In many respects all Amish communities are dominated by the older men and women. Tremendous power is vested in the church leaders and they use the power to maintain the traditions and strengthen the family within the system.

There is another side to the role of old people, however, that is just as important as the power they obviously have and use. It is the kind of gentleness and understanding that younger Amish have in dealing with their own grandparents and other old people they know. There is a real closeness between the very young and the very old, a beautiful thing to see. A caring and caring for, based on love and understanding.

Letters and notes from Amish and other plain people about their older family members and friends are quite revealing.

Mother seems more like herself again and eats by herself at times. We have her out on a wheelchair part of each day. She receives some mail the last while from old friends and cousins whom she usually remembers. Her look out of the eyes and her smile assures us that she really does, even tho' she says very little.

Grandmother Coblentz' visitors the past week were Jake Slabaugh and his daughters from Holmes County, Levi D. J. Miller and Dan Miller, John M. Miller and wife Clara from Geauga County, and his brother Andy, and Alfred Rabers. Grandma slept nearly all the time we were there.

Wednesday was open house for Fannie H. Byler in her home for her 80th birthday. 200 guests attended.

Some of the young folks sang for Sam W. Bender Sunday. Mrs. Bender has not been able to get away all winter.

[Part of a letter] Now Manass is an old man but still pretty good, is able to get around a bit with the aid of a walker, and is a bit hard of hearing, but what can you expect, in six more years he will be 100 years old. His first wife died some years back and left Manass a widower, but at the good old age of 83 he married the second time, to a widow that was 72 at the time, that was ten years ago.

Visits are of most importance in the lives of old folks and the little remembrances of birthdays and special events are expected and much appreciated. Relatives and neighbors visit and spend time talking to and reminiscing with the aged in the "doddy" house. "We visit the widow of Em D. Yoder (Lizzie), 85, about every week as she is glad for company and mail."

It is noticed when regular church goers are not there.

Our oldsters were not all in church. Moses Borkholder is having more pains off and on and Mrs. Eli N. Miller was also not present. . . . Susie Borntrager has lost a leg and a toe off the other foot. She also has poor circulation and is on the wheel chair a lot at home and cannot travel to church.

Senility is accepted and discussed quite openly. It is not frightening to the children or a problem to the family to which the older people belong. "Aunt Alice Hochstedler remains about the same, her mind being badly mixed up at times." Sometimes, however, it is necessary to institutionalize older people when there are no other family members to maintain a home.

This past Wednesday, the 13th, was the day of the sale on the Shannauer farm, selling all the farm tools and household goods, which had been on this farm for many years. This farm had been in the Shannauer name for a long time, but was recently sold. The aged Shannauers, Kurt and Nettie (brother and sister), are now both in an old people's home. Only Kurt was able to be at the sale for a little while. This sale drew many people including a lot of antique buyers, who paid some amazing prices for some of the items.

DEATH

Death is not a bitter end to the Amish people. Death is a fact and is accepted as such. It is discussed, anticipated, and not feared since the Amish are convinced that they are a "chosen people" and will "reign forever in the Kingdom of Heaven." The Amish are human, however, and there is a great sadness and sense of loss when someone in the particular family or church district passes away. The community is diminished and the death affects everyone.

There is a clinical approach to the facts of life and death on the part of most Amish and it is reflected in their descriptions of such occasions. "Mrs. Miller died very suddenly on Monday. She had done her washing and it was dinner time but she wanted first to rehang the wash when she fell over and was instantly gone."

While death is a hard fact, the Amish funeral is a big occasion. There can be as many as a thousand people at a wake of a well-known preacher or bishop. The body is presented in a bare room, simply clothed, placed on a table or in a casket on sawhorses. Caskets are plain, squared off boxes, generally with no handles. Family and friends sit around the body on straight-backed chairs. There are no flowers.

If there are many people at a wake, cold meats, vegetables, pickles, and desserts are served to all. If it is a small group, hot food is served.

The funeral itself is a quietly impressive and serious affair. Services are preached by a number of ministers. "Tuesday was the funeral of Miss Bena Miller held by Minister Neil M. Hershberger from Delaware and Bishop Dan Schlabach in the large house and Bishop David E. Yoder and Wayne E. Yoder in the small house."

After the services the body is carried in a high-sided wagon, used as a hearse, to the burial area. This can be a small cemetery with plain markers but often is on the grounds of the family. A long line of buggies slowly follows the burial wagon and the final interment is brief and plain: the body is lowered into the ground and a group of close friends and relatives fill in the gravesite.

> Bishop Sam Roth of Lisbon died of a heart condition. Funeral was last Monday. It was a big funeral and people showed their respects to a bishop who was well liked far and wide.
>
> Tuesday was the funeral of widow Lizzie, third wife of Henry B. Miller, age 81. Was bedfast almost two years.
>
> The funeral of Mrs. Emanuel Schrock was largely attended on Wednesday. Approximately 420 people attended including many relatives and friends from the surrounding counties and different states. Her age was 69 yr. 5 mo. and 18 days. Survivors are her husband, three sons and six daughters, 69 grandchildren, and one great grandchild.

Even with the acceptance of the inevitability of death of older people, the death of a child is an especially painful event to the Amish. Their obituary poems, a part of the folk tradition, reflect this sentiment. The poem for Naomi Smoker began:

> God came for dear little Naomi,
> January eighth, nineteen seventy-four,
> To take her up to Heaven,
> She was a little over four.

The Photographs of Perry Cragg

Perry Cragg "brought his great artistry and sensitivity to give a comprehensive picture of a whole culture."

Yousuf Karsh, 1972

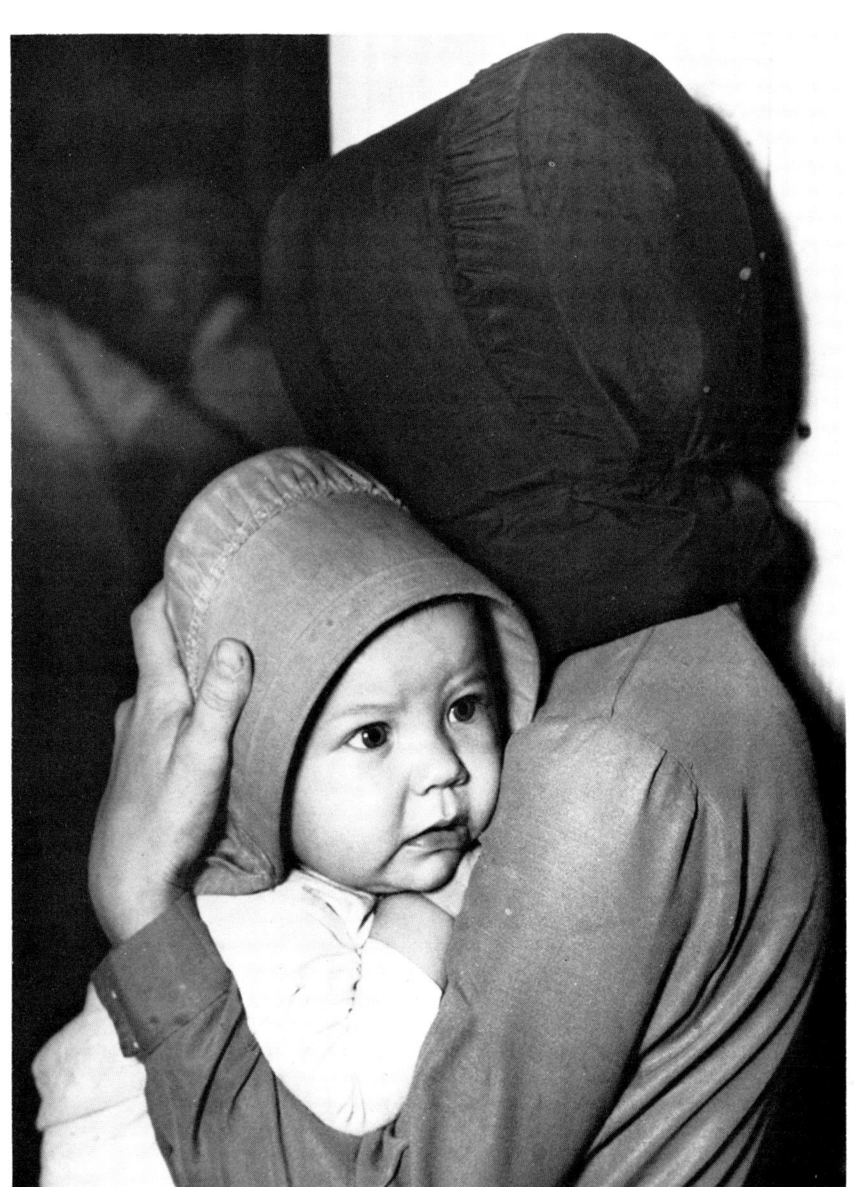

SALE
WEDNESDAY, JULY 26
35 HD. HOLSTEIN COWS
HOWARD McELROY
NOW AVAILABLE
FRANK BODNAR

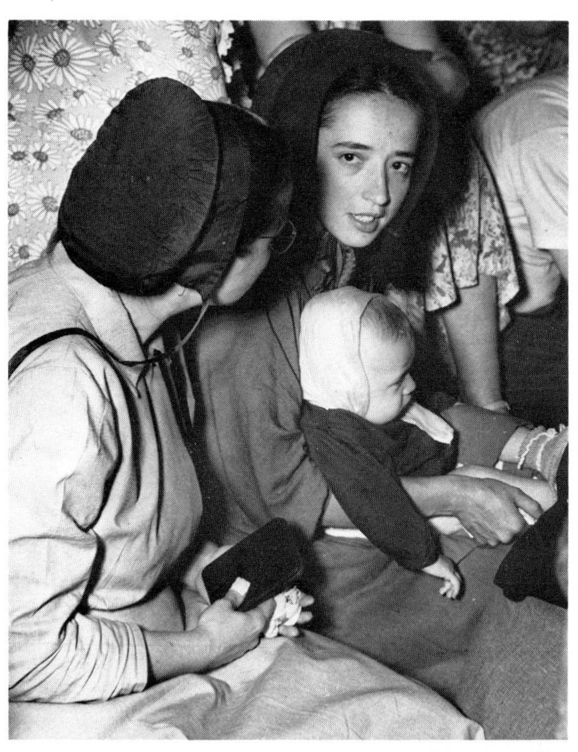

Plain Cooking Recipes

Soups and Stews

Amish soups can be and often are a meal in themselves. Hearty and filling, they make good main dishes as well as fine openings for a meal. In preparing these soups, Amish women often make their own noodles (a good noodle recipe is in the next section) and are famous for their rivels, similar to dumplings about the size of a large grain of rice.

AMISH BEAN SOUP

There is nothing more traditionally Amish than this simple classic.

1 cup dried beans of your choice
1 teaspoon salt
4 tablespoons butter
1 quart milk
2 slices stale bread

Soak the beans overnight, then cook in salted water until soft (about 2½ hours). Drain. Melt the butter, add the beans, and mix well. Add the milk and bring to the boiling point, then remove from the stove.

While the mixture is cooling, cut the stale bread into 1-inch cubes. Add the cubes, which should absorb liquid, but not to the point of dryness, to the slightly cooled bean-milk mixture (don't stir—it will get mushy), and serve at once.

Serves: 4 *Mrs. Christ Jay Miller*

GRANDMA'S MILK (OR RIVEL) SOUP

A favorite soup, especially loved by Amish children.

1 quart milk
3/4 teaspoon salt
1 medium-sized egg
1/2 cup all-purpose flour
1 1/2 tablespoons cream

Heat the milk to the boiling point in the top of a double boiler, then add salt. Make rivels by rubbing the egg and flour and cream together, best done by cutting through the mixture with two forks. When the rivels are about the size of cherrystones, drop into the hot milk. Keep the milk at the boiling point for 3 to 5 minutes.

Serves: 4

Mrs. Andy Yoder
Apple Creek, Ohio

BEAN RIVEL SOUP

"The rivels are great. Try them in chicken broth."

1 cup all-purpose flour
1/4 teaspoon salt
1 egg, beaten
3 1/2 cups milk
1 teaspoon sugar
1/2 cup cooked navy beans

To make the rivels, combine the flour, salt, and beaten egg and blend with two forks until the mixture is crumbly.

Add the milk to the sugar in a saucepan and bring to a boil, then turn down the flame and add the rivels. Cook slowly for about 10 minutes, then add the cooked navy beans. The rivels will look like cooked rice.

Serves: 4 to 5

Mrs. John Kurty

CREAM OF POTATO SOUP

"Very nice tasting, not too thick."

4 large stalks celery, green top included, chopped
2 medium onions, chopped
1 1/2 cups cubed potatoes
3 1/2 cups chicken broth
Dash of paprika
2 cups milk
1 tablespoon butter
Salt and pepper

Combine the celery, onions, and potatoes in a saucepan with 2 cups of the chicken broth and add a dash of paprika. Simmer pot 30 minutes, then add the remaining chicken broth, milk, and butter. Heat without boiling, add salt and pepper to taste, and serve.

Serves: 8 *Mrs. Cornelius E. Miller*

WHITE SOUP

"The sour cream gives it a subtle difference."

1 quart water
Pinch of dried dill weed
2 cups trimmed fresh green or wax beans, cut into 1-inch lengths
5 medium-sized potatoes, peeled and cubed
1 pint thick sour cream
1/2 cup all-purpose flour

Heat the water with the dill in a 5- or 6-quart kettle. Add the fresh green or wax beans and the cubed potatoes. When the potatoes and beans are tender, add the sour cream and the flour. Bring to a boil, then simmer a bit. Add salt and pepper to taste and serve.

Serves: 6 *Mrs. Leroy Mualert*

OLD-FASHIONED POT PIE

A full-flavored, hearty, and filling dish.

1/2 cup milk
2 eggs, beaten
2 1/2 cups all-purpose flour
1/4 teaspoon baking powder
2 medium potatoes, peeled and sliced
1 cup diced celery
1 quart chicken or beef broth
1 teaspoon salt
Pinch of pepper

Make up a dough by combining the milk, eggs, flour, and baking powder. Roll thin and cut into 1-inch squares.

Add the potatoes and celery to the broth in a saucepan, season with salt and pepper, and bring to a boil. When the broth does begin to boil, add your dough, each square separately, and keep the liquid at a boil while adding. When all the squares have been added, cook on low heat for 10 to 15 minutes, stirring occasionally.

Serves: 5 *Mrs. Eli Schlabach*

CORN AND BEEF SOUP

The beef flavor is augmented by the corn; you can thicken this and serve it over toast.

2 tablespoons butter
1 pound beef, cubed
1½ quarts water
1 tablespoon salt
2 carrots, chopped
1 onion, chopped
2½ cups fresh, whole-kernel corn

Heat the butter in a pot and brown the beef, then add the water and salt and let cook slowly for 1 hour. Add the carrots, onion, and corn to the soup and let simmer 1 hour more.

Serves: 6

Ruth Shetler
Smithville, Ohio

TOMATO SOUP

This is a really well-seasoned soup; "it stays with you."

2 quarts chopped tomatoes
1 large onion, chopped
1 sweet pepper, chopped
2 stalks celery, chopped
4 whole cloves, tied in cheesecloth
1 quart tomato juice
¼ cup sifted all-purpose flour
¼ cup granulated sugar
1 teaspoon salt
¼ cup water

Place the chopped vegetables, the cloves, and tomato juice in a large kettle. Cook until tomatoes are soft, then remove the cloves and force the mixture through a sieve. Return to the kettle.

Sift together the flour, sugar, and salt. Gradually add a little water, stirring constantly until a smooth paste is formed. Slowly add to the hot tomato mixture, stirring constantly.

Serves: 6

Susie Swartzentruber

CHILI SOUP

Amish kids love this.

4 tablespoons butter
2 pounds ground beef
1 onion, chopped
1 cup all-purpose flour
1 quart tomato juice
1 teaspoon chili powder
1 teaspoon paprika
2 one-pound cans kidney beans
1 quart water

Heat the butter in a large kettle and brown the meat, onions, and flour in it. Add the tomato juice, chili powder, paprika, kidney beans, and water and continue to cook for 30 minutes.

Serves: 8 to 10

Mrs. Leroy Coblentz

HOMEMADE VEGETABLE SOUP

"My mother-in-law's favorite soup."

1½ pounds beef, cubed
1 soup bone
1 large can tomatoes
3 stalks celery, chopped
½ medium head cabbage, cut up
½ cup raw rice
Salt and pepper to taste
1 teaspoon granulated sugar
1 large onion, chopped
6 to 8 carrots, cut up
5 medium potatoes, cut up
½ teaspoon celery seed

Cover the beef and bone with water and simmer for about 1½ hours, then remove the bone and add the remaining ingredients. Cook for another 30 minutes, or until the rice and vegetables are tender. Stir frequently to prevent sticking or burning on the bottom.

Serves: 10

Margaret Africa

TRAMP SOUP

"Really a hearty potato soup flavored with sausage." A good one-dish meal on a busy day.

4 cups peeled, diced potatoes
1 cup water
1/2 large onion, diced
Salt and pepper to taste
1 tablespoon butter
2 cups canned, drained, and cut-up sausage or 3/4 pound fresh sausage, fried in small patties
1 1/4 cups milk
1 1/2 teaspoon all-purpose flour

Cook the potatoes with water and onion till nearly tender, then add salt, pepper, and the butter. Add the sausage and let cook thoroughly, then add 1 cup of milk. Combine the flour with the remaining milk, add to the soup, and stir until slightly thickened. Serve hot.

Serves: 6

Mrs. Eli E. Miller
Middlefield, Ohio

CHILLY DAY STEW

A very filling, nonmeat stew; there are dozens of similar recipes, Amish style.

1 carrot
4 onions
4 cups peeled, diced potatoes
2 tablespoons raw rice
2 tablespoons raw macaroni
1 teaspoon salt
1 pint cream

Into a large saucepan of rapidly boiling water, chop the carrot. While it is cooking, peel and chop the onions, then add them to the saucepan. Add the potatoes, and over them sprinkle the rice, macaroni, salt, and more water, if necessary, to cover. When ready to serve, add the cream and let heat through, but do not boil again. Serve with croutons, crackers, or hot toast.

Serves: 6

Crist K. Byler

BEEF STEW

"A traditional and good-tasting beef stew."

4 tablespoons margarine
1½ pounds beef, cubed
1 cup diced onion
½ cup all-purpose flour
8 large potatoes, peeled and cubed
2 cups cut-up carrots
2 cups fresh peas
1 cup tomato juice
Salt and pepper to taste

Heat the margarine in a large saucepan and brown the beef and onion with the flour. Add the potatoes, carrots, tomato juice, and enough water to cover. Season and cook for 1 hour, or until the vegetables are soft. Ten minutes before serving, add the peas.

Serves: 8

Mary Jo Hilty
Berne, Indiana

Casseroles

The Amish make more casseroles than any other main dish. They use the casserole form to get the most out of their meat supplies, and ground beef is a constant in these recipes. The emphasis is on economy but the wide variety of other ingredients makes for great diversity in the dish that reaches the table. Homemade noodles, a staple in all Amish cookery, is the first recipe in this section.

NOODLES

The Amish often make their own noodles from scratch. Here is a standard Amish noodle recipe. The egg whites left over are about the right amount for an angel food cake.

6 egg yolks
6 tablespoons water
3 cups all-purpose flour

Beat the egg yolks together, then add the water and beat until well combined. Stir in the flour to make a dough about as stiff as can be worked with. Divide into 4 balls and roll each very thin. As you finish them, lay each sheet separately on a cloth so they won't stick together. Turn them over to dry evenly then lay them on top of each other. Roll up in a bundle and cut. (A meat slicer will do this well.)

Makes: At least 1 pound *Mrs. Raymond Weaver*

MOCK TURKEY

"Use beef instead of poultry—good company fare."

2 pounds ground beef
4 tablespoons butter
Salt and pepper
2 ten-and-one-half-ounce cans condensed cream of chicken soup
1 cup condensed cream of celery soup
1 quart milk
1 loaf of bread, cut into cubes

Heat the butter in a flameproof casserole and brown the ground beef. Add salt and pepper to taste, then mix in the soups, the milk, and the bread. Bake, uncovered, at 350 degrees for 45 minutes.

Serves: 6

Mrs. John N. Schlabach

GROUND BEEF CASSEROLE

"The biscuit top here is very nice, broken up into the casserole."

2 tablespoons butter
1½ pounds ground beef
½ cup chopped onions
1 eight-ounce package cream cheese, softened
1 ten-and-one-half-ounce can condensed cream of mushroom soup
¼ cup milk
1 teaspoon salt
¼ cup catsup
1 can baking powder biscuits

Heat the butter in a large saucepan and brown the ground beef and onions. Drain off the pan drippings and set aside.

Combine softened cream cheese, soup, and milk in a 2-quart casserole and add the salt, catsup, and ground beef. Bake uncovered, at 375 degrees for 10 minutes, then place the biscuits on top and bake for 15 to 20 minutes longer, or until brown.

Serves: 6 to 8

Mrs. Willis Coblentz
Sara Raber
Mrs. Moses J. E. Miller

HUNGRY BOY'S CASSEROLE

A standard Amish low-cost dinner. The beans extend the meat and give it a very different flavor.

2 tablespoons butter
$1^1/_2$ pounds ground beef
1 cup chopped celery
$^1/_2$ cup chopped onion
$^3/_4$ cup water
$^3/_4$ cup tomato paste
1 teaspoon salt
1 teaspoon paprika
1 one-pound can pork and beans

Biscuit Topping

2 teaspoons baking powder
$^1/_2$ teaspoon salt
$1^1/_2$ cups all-purpose flour
4 tablespoons butter or margarine
$^1/_2$ cup milk, approximately

Heat the butter in a flameproof casserole and fry the beef, celery, and onion until the vegetables are tender. Drain off the pan drippings and set aside.

Combine the water, tomato paste, salt, and paprika. Setting aside 1 cup, combine the rest with the beef mixture. Add the beans and set to simmer while you prepare the biscuits.

Sift together the flour, baking powder, and salt. Cut in the butter or margarine and add enough milk to make a stiff dough. Roll out, spread with a few spoonfuls of the meat mixture, then roll up and cut into 1-inch pieces. Put on top of the remaining meat mixture, pour the reserved tomato paste mixture over the top and bake at 425 degrees for 30 minutes.

Serves: 6 to 8 *Elva J. Yoder*

POOR MAN'S DISH

This distinctive-tasting dish can be enhanced even more by the proper seasoning. "Makes a large dish, and very tasty when meat is so expensive."

1 pound ground beef
1 onion, chopped
$^1/_8$ teaspoon garlic salt
1 one-pound can tomatoes
1 one-pound can kidney beans, drained
Salt and pepper
1 teaspoon gravy concentrate

Heat the butter in a frying pan and brown the ground beef and onion. Add the garlic salt, tomatoes, and kidney beans. Season with salt and pepper and simmer for 30 minutes. Stir in the gravy concentrate and serve.

Serves: 6 to 8

Nancy J. Eicher
Sugarcreek, Ohio

SIX-LAYER CASSEROLE

A colorful and economical casserole.

1 pound browned sausage or raw ground beef
1½ cups sliced potatoes
1 cup sliced carrots
1 cup diced onions
2 cups chopped tomatoes, juice included
½ cup raw rice
1½ teaspoons salt
1½ tablespoons granulated sugar

Alternate layers of meat, vegetables, and rice, making sure the rice isn't the top layer or it will dry out. Sprinkle the salt throughout the layers and the sugar on top. Cover and bake for 1½ to 2 hours in a 350-degree oven, adding extra liquid as necessary to prevent excessive drying out.

Serves: 6

Mrs. Wayne Kornhaus
Orrville, Ohio

HAMBURGER CASSEROLE

A basic Amish meat and potato dish.

2 tablespoons butter
1 pound ground beef
6 medium potatoes, peeled and diced
1 ten-and-one-half-ounce can vegetable soup, diluted
1 teaspoon salt
¼ teaspoon pepper

Heat the butter in a skillet and brown the ground beef. Drain off the pan drippings and set aside.

Dice the potatoes and place them in the bottom of a greased 2-quart casserole. Add the ground beef, pour the vegetable soup over, and add salt and pepper. Bake in a 350-degree oven for 1½ hours.

Serves: 6

Maryann Hostetler
Topeka, Indiana

BEEF AND POTATO CASSEROLE

"This has a light bacon-y flavor."

2 slices bacon
4 medium potatoes, peeled and sliced thin
1 teaspoon salt
1/4 teaspoon pepper
2 tablespoons butter
1 medium onion, chopped
1/2 pound ground beef
1 ten-and-three-quarter-ounce can spaghetti sauce

Cook the bacon until crisp and browned, then remove from the pan, crumble, and set aside.

Add the potatoes to the bacon grease, cover, and cook slowly for 10 minutes. Sprinkle the potatoes with the salt, pepper, and the reserved crumbled bacon and place in a greased shallow casserole.

Melt the butter in the pan the potatoes were cooked in, add the chopped onion and ground beef, and brown. Pour the mixture over the potatoes, then pour the spaghetti sauce over all and bake, uncovered, at 350 degrees for 30 minutes.

Serves: 4 to 6

Mrs. Joe E. Hershberger
Millersburg, Ohio

THREE-LAYER DINNER

An easy-to-make, down-to-earth ground beef, potato, and cabbage recipe.

1/2 small head cabbage
1 1/2 cups diced raw potatoes
1/2 pound ground beef
1/2 cup milk, more if necessary
Pinch each salt and pepper

Shred the cabbage and put half of it in the bottom of a greased 1 1/2-quart casserole. Next add half the potatoes, then half the ground beef, and season with salt and pepper. Add another layer of cabbage, one of potatoes, and a final one of ground beef, then pour over the milk and bake, covered, at 350 degrees for 2 hours, adding more milk if necessary.

Serves: 4

Mary Stutzman
Blountstown, Florida

BEEF AND CORN SHEPHERD PIE

A layered casserole with a fluffy potato topping.

2 tablespoons cooking oil
1 pound ground beef
2 teaspoons minced onion
1 eight-ounce can cream-style corn
1 teaspoon Worcestershire sauce
2 teaspoons salt
2 teaspoons minced fresh parsley
1/8 teaspoon pepper
2 cups mashed potatoes
4 eggs

Heat the cooking oil in a skillet and sauté the beef and onion until lightly browned. Add the corn, Worcestershire sauce, 1 1/2 teaspoons of the salt, the parsley, and pepper; mix lightly, then put in an oblong 2-quart baking dish.

Spread the potatoes over the meat mixture. Beat the eggs with the remaining 1/2 teaspoon salt and pour over the potatoes. Bake in a 400-degree oven for 30 minutes, or until brown.

Serves: 4

Mrs. J. J. Pitts
Blountstown, Florida

HAMBURGER CRUNCH

A creamy casserole whose crunchy texture is provided by chow-mein noodles.

1/2 pound ground beef
2 tablespoons butter or margarine
1 small onion, cut up
1/2 ten-and-one-half-ounce can condensed chicken soup
1/2 ten-and-one-half-ounce can condensed mushroom soup
1/4 cup water
1/4 cup raw rice
2 tablespoons soy sauce
Pinch of pepper
1/2 cup chow-mein noodles

Fry the ground beef in the butter until it loses its red color. Add the cut-up onion, and fry for 5 minutes longer.

In a greased 1 1/2 quart casserole combine the chicken and

mushroom soups, water, rice, soy sauce, and pepper. Stir in the beef and onion mixture and bake in a 350-degree oven for 50 minutes, then sprinkle with the chow-mein noodles and bake for 5 minutes longer.

Serves: 4

Laura Swartzentruber
Virginia Beach, Virginia

NUTTY NOODLE CASSEROLE

"A neat blending of the smooth texture of soup with the crunchy texture of nuts and chow-mein noodles."

2 tablespoons butter
1 pound ground beef
1/2 cup chopped onion
6 black olives, pitted and chopped
1/2 cup shredded sharp cheese
1/2 ten-and-one-half-ounce can condensed cream of mushroom soup
1/2 cup milk
4 ounces cooked noodles
1/2 teaspoon salt
Pinch of pepper
1/2 five-and-one-half-ounce can chow-mein noodles
2 tablespoons chopped nuts

Heat the butter in a flameproof casserole and brown the meat and onion. Add the olives, cheese, soup, and milk, then stir in the cooked noodles, salt, and pepper. Bake, covered, in a 350-degree oven for 30 minutes, then top with the chow-mein noodles and nuts and bake for 15 minutes more, uncovered.

Serves: 6

Mrs. John H. Hochstetler
Stoneboro, Pennsylvania

HAMBURGER CASSEROLE

"Rich and creamy, good tasting."

2 tablespoons butter
1 pound ground beef
1/2 cup chopped onion
4 ounces fine noodles
1/2 ten-and-one-half-ounce can condensed cream of mushroom soup
1/2 ten-and-one-half-ounce can condensed chicken noodle soup
1/2 cup sour cream
1 eight-ounce can peas
1/2 cup buttered bread crumbs

Heat the butter in a skillet and brown the ground beef and onion. Cook the noodles according to package directions, then drain. Mix the beef and noodles together, then stir in the mushroom soup, chicken noodle soup, sour cream, and peas. Place in a greased 2-quart casserole, top with the buttered bread crumbs, and bake at 350 degrees for 45 minutes.

Serves: 6

Esther Shetler
Middlefield, Ohio

BAKED NOODLES

Serve this to guests with a simple salad.

4 ounces wide noodles
Salt
1 pound ground beef
1 small onion
2 tablespoons butter
1/4 teaspoon pepper
1 ten-ounce package frozen peas
1 cup catsup
1 cup water
1/2 cup bread crumbs, browned in butter

Cook the noodles in salted water until soft (about 10 minutes), then drain and set aside. Fry the ground beef and onion in the butter till brown, and season with 1 teaspoon salt and the pepper. Cook the frozen peas for 3 minutes, then drain. Combine the peas, meat, catsup, noodles, and water in a 2-quart casserole. Top with the browned bread crumbs and bake, uncovered, at 325 degrees for 30 minutes.

Serves: 4 to 6

Ada Miller

YUMAZETTI

Far and away the most popular new Amish quick dinner. There are hundreds of variations and dozens of spellings: Yumma Zetta, Yumzetti, Yummy Zetta, and on, and on . . .

8 ounces wide noodles
Salt
1 1/2 pounds ground beef
2 tablespoons butter
1/4 teaspoon pepper
1/2 cup diced celery
1 ten-and-one-half-ounce can condensed cream of chicken soup
1 six-ounce can tomato paste
1/2 pound Cheddar cheese, grated

Cook the noodles in salted water until soft (about 10 minutes), then drain and set aside.

Brown the meat in the butter and season with 1 teaspoon salt and the pepper. In a 2-quart casserole, put in a layer of noodles, then one each of meat, celery, soup, tomato paste, and cheese. Repeat until all the ingredients are used, ending with a layer of cheese, and bake, uncovered, at 350 degrees for 1 hour.

Serves: 6 *Mrs. David Troyer*

JUNK DISH

"Well known to every Amish family."

2 tablespoons lard
1½ pounds ground beef
1 large onion, chopped
4 ounces egg noodles
1 sixteen-ounce can whole-kernel corn
1½ cups water
2 ten-and-one-half-ounce cans condensed tomato soup
½ cup grated Cheddar cheese
Salt and pepper to taste

Melt the lard in a deep frying pan and brown meat and onion well. Meanwhile, cook noodles according to package directions and then drain. Combine all the ingredients except the cheese and pour into a buttered casserole. Top with the grated cheese and bake at 350 degrees for 15 minutes, or until the cheese is nicely browned.

Serves: 8 to 10 *Ruth Stutzman*
Blountstown, Florida

TEXAS HASH

"A blend of beef, onion, tomato, and green pepper, extended to feed an entire family with the addition of spaghetti."

2 large onions, sliced
2 green peppers, chopped fine
2 tablespoons shortening
1 pound ground beef
1 cup cooked, drained spaghetti
2 cups chopped tomatoes, fresh or canned
1 teaspoon salt
1 teaspoon pepper

Fry the onion and green pepper slowly in the shortening until the onion is yellow. Add the ground beef and continue frying until browned, then stir in the spaghetti, tomatoes, salt, and pepper. Place in a greased $1^1/_2$ quart casserole, cover, and bake in a 375-degree oven for 45 minutes.

Serves: 6

Mrs. Monroe N. Byler
Middlefield, Ohio

PENNSY SUPPER

An excellent casserole for kids.

6 frankfurters, sliced thin
4 medium potatoes, peeled, cooked, and diced
2 tablespoons minced onion
4 tablespoons soft butter
1 teaspoon prepared mustard
1 cup cooked peas
1 ten-and-one-half-ounce can condensed cream of mushroom soup
Salt and pepper to taste

Combine all but $^1/_4$ cup of the sliced frankfurters with the remaining ingredients in a $1^1/_2$-quart casserole. Toss well, then dot on the remaining frankfurter "pennies." Cover, and bake at 350 degrees for 25 to 30 minutes.

Serves: 4

Mrs. Christ Bontrager

YANKEE FRANKS AND NOODLES

"A one-dish stove-top casserole with franks, gravy, and noodles."

2 tablespoons butter or margarine
1 pound frankfurters, halved lengthwise
$^1/_2$ cup chopped onion
Salt and pepper to taste
1 ten-and-one-half-ounce can condensed cream of celery soup
$^1/_2$ cup chopped canned tomatoes
$^1/_2$ cup milk
4 ounces wide noodles, cooked
$^1/_2$ teaspoon dried basil
2 tablespoons chopped fresh parsley

Heat the butter in a skillet and brown the frankfurters, then add the onion and cook until tender. Add salt and pepper, then stir in soup, tomatoes, milk, noodles, basil, and parsley. Heat through, stirring occasionally.

Serves: 4 to 5 *Mrs. Harvey Bowman*

SCALLOPED POTATOES AND FRANKFURTERS

Potatoes in cream sauce, made more nourishing with meat.

8 medium potatoes, peeled and sliced
1 quart milk
2 tablespoons all-purpose flour
1/2 pound frankfurters
Salt and pepper

Put the potatoes in a large saucepan, add a little water, and bring to a boil. Steam for 10 minutes. Meanwhile, in a small saucepan bring the milk to a boil, stir in the flour, and allow to thicken slightly.

Drain the potatoes, and combine with the sliced frankfurters in a 2-quart casserole. Pour the milk over and season to taste. Bake 1 hour at 350 degrees.

Serves: 6 *Mrs. Moses E. Miller*
Conewango Valley, New York

LIVER LIMA BEANS

A unique way to serve liver, this is a standard Amish dish.

3/4 pound dried lima beans
1/2 pound beef liver
2 cups sliced or chopped onion
2 tablespoons butter or margarine
2 cups chopped tomatoes, fresh or canned
1 teaspoon salt
1/4 teaspoon pepper
1/4 teaspoon paprika

Bring the beans to a boil in 2 quarts water, then turn off the heat and let soak for 1 hour. Drain, then cover with fresh water and cook for 45 minutes. Drain.

Parboil the liver for 5 minutes, then dice and fry, along with the onions, in the fat. Combine the beans, liver, onion, and tomatoes in a greased 2-quart casserole and season with the salt, pepper, and paprika. Bake at 350 degrees for 30 minutes.

Serves: 4 to 6

Alvin K. Fisher
Gordonville, Pennsylvania

AMISH DELIGHT

A steak casserole.

2 tablespoons butter
1/2 pound beefsteak, cubed
8 ounces noodles, cooked
1 ten-and-one-half-ounce can condensed cream of mushroom soup
1 ten-and-one-half-ounce can condensed cream of chicken soup
2 cups fresh, whole-kernel corn
1/2 pound Cheddar cheese, chopped fine
Buttered bread crumbs

Heat the butter in a flameproof casserole and brown the steak cubes on all sides. Add the noodles, soups, corn, and cheese and mix well. Top with buttered bread crumbs and bake for 1 hour at 375 degrees.

Serves: 4

Mrs. Emanuel M. Beachy

CAMPERS' CASSEROLE

"Outdoorsy dish for indoor serving."

1 five-ounce jar dried beef
3/4 cup chopped onion
2 tablespoons bacon drippings
8 ounces elbow macaroni
3 tablespoons butter or margarine
3 tablespoons all-purpose flour
2 cups milk
3/4 cup grated Cheddar cheese
Pepper

Cut up the dried beef. Reserving 1/4 cup for topping, brown the remaining beef, along with the onion, in the drippings. Drain and set aside. Cook the macaroni according to package directions, then drain and set aside.

Melt the butter in a saucepan, stir in the flour with a whisk, and blend together. Add the milk all at once and simmer, stirring constantly with the whisk, until the sauce thickens. Add the cheese and stir until melted.

Combine the dried beef mixture, the macaroni, pepper, and cheese sauce and pour into a greased 2-quart casserole. Top with the reserved 1/4 cup dried beef and bake in a 300-degree oven for 45 minutes.

Serves: 6 to 8 *Anna Mae Miller*

HOMEMAKER'S HOLIDAY CASSEROLE

"A hot dog, noodle, and cheese dish for everybody."

8 ounces elbow macaroni
1 tablespoon chopped onion
1 ten-and-one-half-ounce can condensed cream of mushroom soup
1 cup milk
1 tablespoon chopped green pepper
1/2 teaspoon black pepper
1/4 cup grated Cheddar cheese
1/2 pound frankfurters, sliced; or 1 seven-ounce can luncheon meat, cubed; or 1 seven-ounce can tuna, flaked with a fork

Cook macaroni according to package directions, then drain and set aside. Combine the onion, soup, milk, green pepper, and black pepper in a saucepan. Add the cheese and cook over low heat, stirring occasionally, until the cheese is melted. Combine the drained macaroni with the cheese sauce, then pour half of the mixture into a 1 1/2-quart casserole. Cover with half the frankfurter slices. Add the remaining macaroni and sauce and top with the balance of the frankfurters. Bake at 325 degrees for 15 minutes.

Serves: 4 to 6 *Mrs. Ben Coblentz*

BUSY DAY CASSEROLE

"Pretty good lunch meat and potato chip dish."

1 twelve-ounce can luncheon meat
2 tablespoons butter
1 small onion, chopped
1 sixteen-ounce can peas
1 ten-and-one-half-ounce can condensed cream of mushroom soup
2 cups crushed potato chips

Cut the meat into 1-inch cubes. Melt the butter in a flameproof casserole and brown the onion, and then add the meat and brown lightly. Add the peas and soup, stir to mix, and spread the potato chips on top. Bake at 350 degrees for 20 to 25 minutes.

Serves: 4

Mrs. Jonas Schrock

RAINY DAY DINNER

"This is ideal for the working woman, as it is easy, quick, and good."

1/2 pound any left over meat
3 medium potatoes, peeled and cubed
1 cup cooked elbow macaroni
3 carrots, chopped
3 beef bouillon cubes
2 cups water
Salt and pepper to taste

Combine all the ingredients in a large saucepan and cook for about 1 hour and 15 minutes.

Serves: 4

Mrs. David Hostetler
Kenton, Ohio

CORN PATCH LUNCH MEAT BAKE

"One of the best tasting simple family dishes; doesn't taste like canned lunch meat usually does."

8 ounces noodles
Salt
1 twelve-ounce can whole-kernel corn, drained
1 can cream of vegetable soup
1 twelve-ounce can luncheon meat, diced
3/4 cup milk
Pepper to taste
1/2 cup grated Cheddar cheese

Boil the noodles in salted water until tender (about 10 minutes), then drain and pour into a 9-inch casserole. Combine the corn, soup, and luncheon meat and mix with the noodles. Add the milk, 1 teaspoon salt, and pepper, and top with the cheese. Bake 30 minutes at 350 degrees.

Serves: 4 to 6

Verne E. Wenger
Chambersburg, Pennsylvania

SNITZ AND KNEPP

The traditional apple and ham casserole, with fluffy dumplings.

Snitz

2 cups dried apples
1½ pounds smoked ham, cubed
2 tablespoons brown sugar

Knepp

2 cups all-purpose flour
3½ teaspoons baking powder
½ teaspoon salt
1 egg, beaten
2 tablespoons butter
⅓ to ½ cup milk

Wash the apples, cover with water and soak overnight. Cover the ham with water and cook for 3 hours, then add the apples, their soaking water, and the brown sugar and cook for 1 hour longer.

Sift the flour, baking powder, and salt together, then add the eggs, butter, and enough milk to make a stiff batter. Drop by spoonfuls into the ham and apples, cover, and cook for 10 to 15 minutes. Don't lift the cover until ready to serve.

Serves: 8

Mrs. Pauline Burger
Baltic, Ohio

INSTANT RICE AND HAM CASSEROLE

Ham strips in a neatly flavored bed of rice.

3/4 pound cooked ham, cut into strips
2 tablespoons cooking oil
1 ten-and-one-half-ounce can condensed onion soup
1 1/2 cups instant-type rice
2 tablespoons chopped fresh parsley
4 to 6 stuffed green olives, sliced

Sauté the ham in the cooking oil for a few minutes, then stir in the soup. Add the rice and simmer for 5 minutes. Stir in the parsley, add the olives, and serve.

Serves: 4

Mrs. Wayne Kornhaus
Orrville, Ohio

SCALLOPED POTATOES AND HAM

Creamy baked ham and potatoes.

5 medium potatoes, peeled and sliced thin
1 cup cubed ham
1 teaspoon salt
1 1/2 teaspoons all-purpose flour
2 teaspoons butter
2 1/2 cups milk

Place half the potato slices in a greased 1 1/2-quart casserole. Add a layer of half the ham, then sprinkle on half the salt and flour. Add the remaining potatoes, then the remaining ham, salt, and flour. Dot the top with butter, pour over the milk, and bake, covered, in a 400-degree oven for 1 hour 15 minutes.

Serves: 4

Mrs. Roman H. Miller
Millersburg, Ohio

HAM AND POTATO SCALLOP

"This is a nice church pot-luck supper."

5 cups peeled, thinly sliced potatoes
1 pound cooked or canned smoked ham, cut into 1/2-inch cubes
1/4 cup chopped green pepper
1/2 cup chopped onion
1 ten-and-one-half-ounce can condensed cream of mushroom soup
1/4 cup milk
Pinch of pepper
1 tablespoon butter or margarine
Fresh parsley for garnish

Place the potatoes, ham, green pepper, and onion in a 2-quart casserole. Combine the soup, milk, and pepper and pour over. Dot the top with butter and bake, uncovered, at 350 degrees for 1 hour, then cover and continue baking for 45 minutes, or until the potatoes are done. Garnish with parsley and serve.

Serves: 4 to 6

Mrs. Paul Garber
Dundee, Ohio

HAM ROLLS

Good-tasting ham rolled in a biscuit dough and topped with cheese.

2 tablespoons soft butter
1 1/2 tablespoons prepared mustard
1 cup ground ham
2 cups all-purpose flour
4 teaspoons baking powder
1/2 teaspoon salt
1/4 cup lard
3/4 cup milk

Combine the butter and mustard with the ground ham and set aside. Sift together the flour, baking powder, and salt. Cut in the lard until the mixture resembles fine crumbs, then add the milk to make a soft dough. Roll out 1/4 inch thick and spread with the ham mixture. Roll up like a jelly roll and cut into 1 1/2-inch slices. Place, cut side down, in a greased baking pan and bake at 425 degrees for 15 to 20 minutes.

Serves: 4

Mrs. Mike Miller

PORK CHOP–POTATO SCALLOP

"Fine flavor, because as the chops bake the fat bakes into the potatoes."

2 tablespoons butter
4 pork chops
1 package instant scalloped potatoes
Salt and pepper to taste
1 teaspoon instant onion
$^{1}/_{4}$ teaspoon garlic salt

Heat the butter in a skillet and brown the pork chops on both sides. Prepare the scalloped potatoes as directed on the package and season with salt and pepper. Put a layer of half the potatoes in the bottom of a $1^{1}/_{2}$-quart casserole. Add the pork chops in a single layer, then top with another potato layer, and top with the instant onion and garlic salt. Bake at 375 to 400 degrees for 1 hour.

Serves: 4

Dorothy Miller

PORK CHOPS AND POTATOES

"Packed with a fine flavor, and very filling."

6 medium potatoes, peeled and sliced very thin
1 ten-and-one-half-ounce can condensed tomato soup
1 onion, sliced
6 pork chops

Put a layer of half the potatoes in a greased $2^{1}/_{2}$-quart casserole. Pour over half the soup, then add the remaining potatoes. Pour over the remaining soup, cover with the onion slices, and place the pork chops on top. Bake at 325 degrees for 1 hour.

Serves: 4 to 6

Mrs. Leroy Weaver
Dundee, Ohio

BEAN-SAUSAGE CASSEROLE

"A good meal to make when getting home late from work."

1 sixteen-ounce can lima beans, drained
1 ten-and-one-half-ounce can condensed cream of mushroom soup
1/4 cup milk
1/2 pound smoked sausages
3 cups buttered bread crumbs

Combine the lima beans and cream of mushroom soup, in a 1 1/2-quart casserole, then stir in the milk and mix well. Pan-fry the sausages and add both sausages and drippings to the bean mixture. Stir well, top with buttered bread crumbs, and bake at 325 degrees for 30 minutes.

Serves: 4 to 6

Mrs. Kenneth Gerber
Massillon, Ohio

SAUSAGE, POTATOES, AND "BUTTONS"

A typical Amish boiled dinner.

1 pound sausage
2 quarts water
6 cups peeled, cubed potatoes
2 cups all-purpose flour
1 teaspoon baking powder
Salt
1 egg, beaten
1/3 to 1/2 cup milk
Pepper

Cook the sausage in the 2 quarts water for 1 hour, then add the potatoes and cook until tender (from 20 to 30 minutes). Sift together the flour, baking powder, and 1/2 teaspoon salt, then add the egg and enough milk to make a batter the consistency of a stiff cake batter. Drop by spoonfuls on top of the sausages and potato cubes and cook, covered, for 15 minutes or more. Add salt and pepper to taste and serve.

Serves: 4

Mrs. Cornelius Miller
Apple Creek, Ohio

OLD-FASHIONED DRESSING

"Not overly moist, but chewy and light flavored."

1/4 pound butter or margarine
10 slices bread, cubed
1/2 cup chopped raw chicken
1 cup chopped celery
1 cup chicken broth
3 eggs, beaten
1/2 cup milk
3/4 teaspoon parsley flakes
Salt and pepper to taste

Brown the butter in a skillet, then add the bread cubes and toast. Add the chicken and celery. Put the broth in a bowl and add the eggs and milk. Add the egg mixture to bread; there should be enough liquid to soak up bread. Season with parsley flakes, salt, and pepper, and mix well, then turn into a greased 10-inch casserole and bake, uncovered, for 30 minutes at 350 degrees.

Serves: 6

Mrs. Henry Petersheim
Oakland, Maryland

AMISH DRESSING

This is a standard main-course casserole.

2 tablespoons all-purpose flour
1 cup evaporated milk
1 egg
3 large carrots, diced
2 large potatoes, diced
1/2 cup diced onion
1 cup diced celery
1 loaf bread, cubed and toasted
1/2 teaspoon dried sage
1 teaspoon salt
Pinch of pepper
3 cups diced raw chicken
1 cup chicken broth
4 tablespoons butter or margarine

Combine the flour, milk, and egg in the top of a double boiler and cook over simmering water until thickened. Meanwhile, combine the carrots, potatoes, onion, celery, bread, sage, salt, pepper, and chicken, then pour the broth and white sauce over the chicken mixture.

Melt the butter in a flameproof 2-quart casserole, then add the chicken mixture and fry until brown. When brown, bake for 1 hour at 350 degrees.

Serves: 10 to 12

Barbara Miller
Topeka, Indiana

CASHEW NUT DRESSING OR STUFFING

The cashews really give this a different texture.

4 packages bread cubes
1 quart chopped celery
1/2 cup chopped onion
1 pound fresh bulk sausage, fried and fat reserved
2 cups chicken broth
2 cups chopped raw chicken
1 pound cashew nuts
4 ten-and-one-half-ounce cans condensed cream of mushroom soup
2 thirteen-ounce cans evaporated milk
Salt and pepper to taste

Mix all the ingredients lightly but thoroughly in a 2-quart casserole, seasoning according to your own preference. Bake, uncovered, in a 300-degree oven until all the dressing is hot clear through. (In large amounts like this, one needs to gently lift the outside and bottom layers toward the center so it heats evenly and thoroughly.)

Serves: 25

Mrs. Edison Snyder

SCALLOPED CHICKEN

A layered chicken and bread casserole.

1/4 cup rendered chicken fat or butter
1 quart bread cubes
Giblets from the chicken, chopped
3/4 cup all-purpose flour
6 cups chicken broth
Diced, cooked meat from 1 chicken
Salt and pepper to taste

Melt the fat or butter in a pan, add the bread cubes and chopped giblets, and mix. Set aside while you make the gravy. Gradually blend the flour into the broth. Bring to a boil, and add the chopped chicken and salt and pepper to taste.

In a greased casserole, place a layer of bread dressing on the bottom, add the chicken and gravy, and place another layer of dressing on the top. Bake, uncovered, at 350 degrees for 45 to 50 minutes.

Serves: 6 — *Mrs. Daniel Troyer*

SCALLOPED CHICKEN WITH MUSHROOM SAUCE

Bread crumbs, chicken, and soups incorporated into a casserole.

3 eggs, beaten
2½ cups bread crumbs
Diced, cooked meat from 1 chicken
3 cups chicken broth
1 ten-and-one-half-ounce can condensed cream of mushroom soup

Add the beaten eggs to 2 cups of the bread crumbs, then add the chicken and chicken broth and stir to combine. Place the mixture in a greased 2-quart casserole and pour the mushroom soup over. Sprinkle with the remaining ½ cup bread crumbs and bake, uncovered, at 350 degrees for 45 minutes, or until browned.

Serves: 6 to 8 — *Laura Miller*
Baltic, Ohio

SCALLOPED CHICKEN AND MACARONI

A chicken and macaroni casserole that has been extended to feed more by the addition of beans.

6 tablespoons butter or margarine
6 tablespoons all-purpose flour
1 teaspoon salt
¼ teaspoon pepper
3 cups chicken broth
3 cups chopped, cooked chicken
3 cups cooked shell macaroni
2 cups cooked navy beans
½ cup buttered bread crumbs

Melt the butter, then blend in the flour, salt, and pepper. Gradually add chicken broth and cook, stirring constantly, until the mixture thickens. Combine with the chicken, macaroni, and beans in a 2-quart casserole, then sprinkle with the buttered bread crumbs and bake 30 minutes at 375 degrees.

Serves: 6 to 8

Mrs. Dan J. Shetler
Kalona, Iowa

CHICKEN SUPREME

"This is pepped up with cheese, and has a crunchy bread-crumb crust."

Diced, cooked meat from 1 chicken
2 tablespoons all-purpose flour
1½ cups chicken broth
½ pound Cheddar cheese, grated
2 cups cooked macaroni
1 teaspoon salt
¼ teaspoon pepper
1 cup buttered bread crumbs

Mix the chicken meat with the cooked macaroni and set aside. Make a gravy by stirring the flour into the chicken broth and cooking until thickened. Stir the cheese into the gravy, then mix with the meat and macaroni. Put into a 2-quart casserole or baking pan, season with salt and pepper, and cover with the buttered bread crumbs. Bake, uncovered, at 350 degrees for 25 minutes, or until bubbly.

Serves: 6 to 8

Mrs. Obed J. Miller
Westphalia, Kansas

CHICKEN AND NOODLE CASSEROLE

A bread crumb topping is tasty with chicken and noodles in a creamy sauce.

2½ cups chicken broth
1 cup water
8 ounces noodles
2½ cups diced, cooked chicken
2 ten-and-one-half cans condensed cream of mushroom soup
Salt and pepper to taste
1 cup bread crumbs, browned in 4 tablespoons butter

Put the broth in a saucepan and dilute with the water. Bring to a boil, add the noodles, and simmer for 10 minutes. Remove from the heat and add the chicken, cream of mushroom soup, and salt and pepper to taste. Put in a 2-quart casserole and cover with the buttered bread crumbs. Bake, uncovered, at 300 degrees for 45 minutes, or until brown and bubbling.

Serves: 6

Emma Hershberger
Millersburg, Ohio

CHICKEN IN A BLANKET

"This has a nice, subtle flavor."

1 tablespoon melted butter
½ teaspoon salt
½ teaspoon chopped fresh parsley
2 cups peeled, sliced potato
½ cup water
2 cups chopped, cooked chicken

Biscuit Dough

1 cup all-purpose flour
¼ teaspoon salt
¾ teaspoon baking powder
2 tablespoons butter or margarine
½ cup milk

Gravy

2 tablespoons all-purpose flour
1 egg yolk
1/3 cup milk
1/2 teaspoon salt
1 1/2 cups chicken broth

Grease a 2-quart casserole dish, and in it put the melted butter, salt, parsley, potato, water, and chicken. Mix well and top with a biscuit dough that has been prepared by sifting together the flour, salt, and baking powder, cutting in the butter, and stirring in the milk. Bake uncovered at 350 degrees, for 45 to 60 minutes, or until the biscuit dough is brown.

Meanwhile, prepare the gravy by combining the flour, egg yolk, milk, and salt, stirring the mixture into the chicken broth, and cooking until thickened and smooth. When the biscuit dough is browned, cut it in strips and pour over the gravy. Let the casserole sit for 5 minutes before serving.

Serves: 4 to 6

Fanny Lehman
Fredericksburg, Ohio

CHICKEN AND DUMPLINGS

Eaten often with relatives and visitors alike during the week.

1 stewing chicken
1 cup chopped celery
4 to 6 potatoes, peeled and diced
6 carrots, peeled and sliced
6 medium onions, coarsely chopped
1 tablespoon salt

Dumplings

1 1/2 cup flour
2 teaspoons baking powder
3/4 teaspoon salt
3 tablespoons shortening
3/4 cup milk

Cook the chicken in water to cover until tender (from 1 1/2 to 2 hours), then remove the meat from bones. Set aside. Cook the celery, potatoes, carrots, and onions in the broth. Add salt when almost tender (in about 30 minutes), add the meat, and bring to a boil.

Meanwhile, make the dumplings. Sift together the flour, baking powder, and salt. Cut in the shortening, then stir in the milk and mix just until blended. Drop the batter into the hot broth by spoonfuls, then cook, covered, for 20 minutes.

Serves: 6 to 8 *Mrs. Jake Leslein*

SUNDAY CHICKEN CASSEROLE

"This is a very hearty, good-tasting dish."

1 two-and-one-half-pound chicken, cut up
4 tablespoons butter or margarine
1 cup raw long-grain rice
1 ten-and-one-half-ounce can condensed cream of celery soup
1 ten-and-one-half-ounce can condensed cream of chicken soup
1 cup water
Salt, pepper, and paprika to taste

In a large skillet, brown the chicken pieces on all sides in the butter. Set aside. Combine the rice, celery soup, cream of chicken soup, and water and place in a greased 2-quart casserole. Place the browned chicken pieces on top, then sprinkle with the desired amounts of salt, pepper, and paprika. Cover and bake for 1 hour and 15 minutes at 400 degrees.

Serves: 4 to 6 *Mrs. L. D. Kaufman*
Montgomery, Georgia

CHICKEN CASSEROLE

The thick gravy on this makes it a great "sopping" dish.

Diced, cooked meat from 1 chicken
1 cup diced celery
2 teaspoons salt
Pinch of pepper
1 medium-sized bag potato chips
2½ cups chicken broth
¼ cup all-purpose flour

In a 2-quart greased casserole, layer the chicken, celery, salt, pepper, and chips, repeating until all the ingredients are used up and ending with a layer of chips for a topping. Stir the flour into the broth and cook until smooth and thickened, then pour over the casserole and bake, uncovered, at 350 degrees for 15 to 25 minutes.

Serves: 4 to 6

Mrs. Melvin L. Kuhns
Ligonier, Indiana

SCALLOPED TUNA

"This has a cheesy flavor."

16 ounces noodles
Salt
3 tablespoons butter
1/3 cup all-purpose flour
2 cups milk
1 cup grated Cheddar cheese
1/2 teaspoon salt
1 seven-ounce can tuna
2 sliced hard boiled eggs

Cook the noodles in salted water according to package directions, then drain and set aside. Melt the butter in a skillet and add the flour. Mix well; don't allow it to burn. Add the milk and stir to thicken—it should be the consistency of a thin gravy—and bring to a boil. Add the cheese and 1/2 teaspoon salt to the milk mixture.

In a 9 x 9-inch baking dish, arrange a layer of noodles, a layer of tuna, and a layer of sliced egg. Repeat the layers until all the ingredients are used up, ending with a layer of noodles, then pour the cheese sauce over, being sure it goes to the bottom of the casserole. Bake, uncovered, at 350 degrees for 30 to 35 minutes.

Serves: 6 to 8

Mrs. Paul M. Landis
Crockett, Kentucky

NOODLE-TUNA CASSEROLE

Serve a tossed green salad with this and it will add up to a satisfying meal.

4 ounces noodles
1 eight-ounce can tomato sauce
2 eggs
1 cup milk
1/2 teaspoon salt
1/8 teaspoon pepper
1 onion, minced
1 seven-ounce can (drained) tuna
1 cup shredded Cheddar cheese

Cook the noodles according to package directions, then drain and toss with the tomato sauce. Arrange in the bottom of a greased 8 x 10-inch baking dish. Beat the eggs, then add the milk, salt, pepper, onion, and tuna. Pour over the noodle layer, sprinkle with cheese, and bake, uncovered, at 350 degrees for 40 minutes, or until brown and bubbly.

Serves: 4

Katie E. Byler
Fredericksburg, Ohio

TUNA CASSEROLE

"A kind of unusual tuna, spaghetti, and cheese dish."

8 ounces spaghetti
1 ten-and-one-half-ounce can cream of mushroom soup
1 seven-ounce can tuna, drained
1 cup diced Cheddar cheese
Salt and pepper
1 cup milk

Cook the spaghetti according to package directions, then drain and combine with the soup, tuna, and cheese. Season to taste and place in a greased 2-quart casserole. Pour the milk over and bake, uncovered, for 30 minutes at 400 degrees.

Serves: 4 to 6

Mrs. Enos Lapp

NOODLE-SALMON CASSEROLE

"If you make this casserole ahead and refrigerate it for a while, the flavors blend better."

8 ounces noodles
2 tablespoons butter or margarine
$1^1/_2$ tablespoons all-purpose flour
Salt and pepper
1 cup milk
1 cup canned peas, drained
1 seven-ounce can salmon
$^1/_4$ cup cracker crumbs

Cook the noodles according to package directions, then drain and set aside. Melt the butter in heavy saucepan or in the top of a double boiler. Add the flour, salt, and pepper and stir with a whisk until well blended. Slowly add the milk, stirring constantly until a smooth paste is formed.

Combine the noodles, peas, and salmon and place in a greased 2-quart casserole. Pour the white sauce over the noodle mixture and top with the cracker crumbs. Bake, uncovered, at 350 degrees for 25 minutes.

Serves: 6 to 8

Mrs. Elmer J. Zook
Oakland, Maryland

SALMON PUFF

This takes only ten minutes to make, and it has a fine, light flavor.

4 eggs, slightly beaten
1/2 cup milk
1 ten-and-one-half-ounce can condensed mushroom soup
1 sixteen-ounce can salmon
1 tablespoon minced fresh parsley
2 cups soft bread crumbs
2 tablespoons melted butter

Combine the eggs, milk, and soup, then blend in the remaining ingredients and place in a buttered 1 1/2-quart casserole. Bake, uncovered, for 45 to 50 minutes in a 350-degree oven.

Serves: 6

Mrs. William Kushno
Wilmot, Ohio

MACARONI WITH EGGS

This is a really simple and economical dish.

4 ounces elbow macaroni
3 hard-boiled eggs, sliced
2 tablespoons plus 1 1/2 teaspoons butter
1 tablespoon all-purpose flour
1 1/2 cups milk
1 teaspoon salt
3 tablespoons soft bread crumbs

Cook the macaroni in boiling salted water until tender (about 10 minutes), then drain and arrange in alternate layers with the hard-boiled egg slices in a baking dish. Melt the 1 1/2 teaspoons butter, then stir in the flour to make a paste. Add the milk, stirring constantly until thickened. Add the salt and pour the mixture over the macaroni. Dot with the 2 tablespoons butter, sprinkle with the bread crumbs, and bake, uncovered, at 350 degrees for 30 minutes.

Serves: 4

Nancy Schmidt
Linwood, Ontario

MACARONI AND CHEESE CASSEROLE

An unusual macaroni casserole with a creamy cheese flavor, topped with a tasty crumb crust.

4 ounces elbow macaroni
4 tablespoons butter or margarine
3 tablespoons all-purpose flour
2 cups milk
1/2 to 1 cup grated Cheddar cheese
1 cup buttered bread crumbs

Cook the macaroni according to package directions, then drain and set aside. Melt the butter in a saucepan, add the flour, and cook until the mixture bubbles. Add the milk and cook, stirring, until thickened. Then add the cheese. Mix in the macaroni, pour into a greased 2-quart casserole and top with the bread crumbs. Bake at 350 degrees until bubbly (about 20 minutes).

Serves: 4

Mrs. Dan D. Hostetler, Jr.
Middlefield, Ohio

MACARONI CASSEROLE

A simple and very appetizing dish.

4 ounces elbow macaroni
2 cups cooked peas
4 sliced hard boiled eggs
1 1/2 cups grated Cheddar cheese
1 ten-and-one-half-ounce can condensed cream of mushroom soup

Cook the macaroni according to package directions, then drain. Place alternating layers of macaroni, peas, sliced hard-boiled eggs, and grated cheese in a greased, 1 1/2-quart casserole. Pour the mushroom soup over and bake, uncovered, in a 400-degree oven until bubbly (about 20 minutes).

Serves: 6 to 8

Alta C. Schlabach
Berlin, Ohio

SCALLOPED CABBAGE, SPAGHETTI, AND CHEESE

As unique a flavor as the Amish have ever produced.

1/2 cup cooked spaghetti
1 cup cooked cabbage
2 tablespoons butter
2 tablespoons all-purpose flour
1 cup milk
1/4 cup grated Cheddar cheese
1/2 teaspoon salt
Pinch of pepper
6 tablespoons soft bread crumbs

Combine spaghetti and cabbage. Melt the butter in a sauce pan and stir in the flour, then add the milk and cook, stirring, until thickened and smooth. Add the cheese, salt, and pepper, then combine with the spaghetti and cabbage. Place the mixture in a greased 1 1/2-quart casserole and sprinkle with the bread crumbs. Bake in a 350-degree oven for 20 minutes.

Serves: 4

Miss Rachel Yoder
Oakland, Maryland

DUTCH NOODLE RING WITH CHEESE SAUCE

Noodles in cream and a zesty cheese sauce.

4 ounces egg noodles
Salt
3 tablespoons butter
3 tablespoons all-purpose flour
1½ cups milk
1/2 teaspoon paprika
1 1/2 cups grated Swiss cheese
2 eggs, well beaten

Boil the noodles in salted water for 10 minutes, then drain and put in a well-greased ring mold. Melt the butter, add the flour, and blend with a whisk. Stir in the milk and continue to cook until the mixture thickens, stirring constantly. Add 1/2 teaspoon salt, the paprika, and the cheese and cook until the cheese melts. Reserve half of the sauce for later use.

To the remaining sauce, add the well-beaten eggs, mix thoroughly, and pour over the noodles. Set the mold in a pan containing hot water and bake at 300 degrees for 45 minutes. Unmold on a large platter, pour over the remaining hot cheese sauce, and fill the center with any desired vegetables or meat.

Serves: 6

Mrs. Louis Mast
Middlefield, Ohio

Company Fare

These special recipes comprise a broad variety of main dishes that include beef, pork, chicken, and even small game. Although they are "special" in that they are not usually found in run-of-the-week meals, they reflect the frugality and good flavor that are musts for Amish cooks. Still, they are easy to prepare and easy on the pocketbook.

STUFFED CABBAGE ROLLS

"This will be a family favorite."

12 large cabbage leaves
1¼ pounds ground beef
1 cup cooked rice
1 small onion, chopped
1 egg
2 tablespoons salad oil
2 eight-ounce cans tomato sauce
¼ cup water
1 tablespoon brown sugar
1 tablespoon lemon juice or vinegar

Pour boiling water over the cabbage leaves and let sit until limp. Combine the ground beef, rice, onion, and egg. Divide into twelve equal portions, place a portion on each leaf, and roll up. Fasten each roll with a toothpick and brown in the salad oil.

Meanwhile, combine the tomato sauce, water, brown sugar, and lemon juice. Pour over the rolls and simmer for 1 hour.

Serves: 4 to 6

Mrs. Levi Miller
Millersburg, Ohio

MEAT BALLS WITH MUSHROOM SAUCE

Add a 1- to 3-ounce can of mushrooms to this if you like.

1 1/2 pounds ground beef
2 eggs, beaten
8 soda crackers, crumbled
1 1/4 cups milk
1/4 cup chopped onion
1/4 cup chopped celery
1 teaspoon salt
1/4 teaspoon pepper
All-purpose flour
3 to 4 tablespoons butter
1 ten-and-one-half-ounce can condensed cream of mushroom soup
1 pimento, chopped

Combine the ground beef, eggs, and cracker crumbs; moisten with 1/4 cup of the milk. Add the chopped onion, celery, salt, and pepper and form into balls about 1 inch in diameter. Roll in flour and brown on all sides in the butter, then place in a greased 1 1/2-quart casserole dish.

Combine the mushroom soup, remaining milk, and chopped pimento. Heat and stir until blended, then pour over the meat balls. Bake in a 350-degree oven for 30 minutes.

Serves: 8 *Mrs. Moses Raber*

GRANNY'S MEAT BALLS

"Good to serve with spaghetti. Very spicy."

1 ten-and-one-half-ounce can condensed tomato soup
2 cups water
1 teaspoon chili powder
4 teaspoons salt
2 onions, chopped
1/2 green pepper, chopped fine
1 pound ground pork
1 pound ground beef
2 eggs
1 medium onion
2 1/2 cups soft bread crumbs, soaked in milk or water and squeezed dry

In a saucepan, combine the tomato soup, water, half the chili powder, 1 teaspoon of the salt, half the chopped onion, and the chopped green pepper. Bring to a boil, then simmer while you make the meat balls. Mix the ground pork, ground beef, eggs, remaining chopped onion, remaining salt, remaining chili powder, and bread crumbs together. Form into balls "about the size of a small egg" and drop in the simmering sauce. Cover and bake 1 hour in a 350-degree oven.

Serves: 8 to 10 *Mrs. Alex Winkelman*

PORCUPINE MEAT BALLS

A satisfying dish that will stay with you.

4 slices bread
1 cup milk
1 egg
1 pound ground beef
2 onions, chopped fine
1/2 cup chopped celery
1/4 cup raw rice
1 teaspoon salt
1/4 teaspoon pepper
2 cups tomato juice

Crumble the bread and soak it in the milk, then add the egg. Combine the soaked bread with the ground beef, onion, celery, and rice. Season with salt and pepper, then shape into small balls. Place the balls in a buttered casserole, pour the tomato juice over, and bake for 1 1/2 hours in a 350-degree oven.

Serves: 4 *Mrs. Simon Yoder*
Salisburg, Pennsylvania

CROWN OF GOLD MEAT LOAF

This attractive meat loaf is frosted with egg white and mustard.

1 1/2 pounds ground beef
4 egg yolks
1 tablespoon prepared mustard
2 tablespoons minced onion
1 1/2 cups soft bread crumbs
1 1/2 teaspoons salt
3 tablespoons diced green pepper
1/3 cup catsup

Topping

4 egg whites
1/4 teaspoon cream of tartar
1 1/2 tablespoons prepared mustard

Combine the ground beef, egg yolks, mustard, onion, bread crumbs, salt, green pepper, and catsup. Pack the ingredients into a 9-inch casserole and bake at 350 degrees for 30 minutes.

Meanwhile, prepare the topping. Beat the egg whites till foamy. Add the cream of tartar and beat until stiff, then fold in the mustard. Swirl on top of the hot meat, then return to the oven and bake an additional 20 minutes, or until the topping is tipped with brown.

Serves: 4

Mrs. Melvin P. Maurer
Millersville, Pennsylvania

POTATO MEAT LOAF

This less traditional meat loaf is made with potatoes and seasoned with bacon.

3 eggs, beaten
2 pounds lean ground beef
2 1/2 teaspoons salt
1/4 teaspoon pepper
2 1/2 cups ground raw potatoes
1 small onion, chopped
4 slices bacon, ground

Combine the eggs with the ground beef. Mix well and season with salt and pepper. Combine the potatoes, onion, and bacon, then add to the egg-beef mixture. Pack into a greased 9 x 5 x 2-inch loaf pan and bake at 350 degrees for 1 hour 15 minutes.

Serves: 6 to 8

Lucy Yoder
Greenwich, Ohio

PLAIN MEAT LOAF

An oatmeal meat loaf with a subtle taste.

1 1/2 cups ground beef
3/4 cup oatmeal
2 eggs
1/4 cup minced onion
2 teaspoons salt
1/4 teaspoon pepper
1 cup tomato juice

Mix all the ingredients thoroughly and bake for 1 hour at 350 degrees. Let sit 5 minutes before cutting.

Serves: 4 to 6

Mrs. Eli Detweiler

FRANKFURTER LOAF

This tastes like a corned-beef casserole, even though it is made with frankfurters.

1 1/2 pounds frankfurters
3/4 cup milk
2 tablespoons chopped onion
1 cup fine, dry bread crumbs
2 eggs, well beaten
1 teaspoon dried sage

Grind the frankfurters, then combine them with the milk, onion, bread crumbs, eggs, and sage. Mix thoroughly, place in a greased 2-quart casserole, and bake for 45 minutes at 350 degrees.

Serves: 4 to 6

Mrs. Ray Weaver
Madisonburg, Pennsylvania

BARBECUED HAMBURGERS

"Even fussy eaters will say this hamburg recipe is excellent."

1 pound ground beef
1 cup soft bread crumbs
1/2 cup milk
1 teaspoon salt
1/8 teaspoon pepper
2 to 3 tablespoons butter

Sauce

2 tablespoons brown sugar
2 tablespoons Worcestershire sauce
2 tablespoons vinegar
1 cup catsup

Combine the beef with the bread crumbs, milk, salt, and pepper. Form into patties and brown on both sides, in the butter, in a skillet. Meanwhile, combine all the ingredients for the sauce.

When the patties are browned, place in a baking dish and cover with the sauce. Bake in a 350-degree oven for 30 minutes.

Serves: 4

Mrs. LeRoy Yoder

POTATO MEAT CAKES

"Like beef hash, only much tastier."

1 cup ground beef
1 medium onion, chopped
Pinch of pepper
1 egg, beaten
$1/4$ teaspoon salt
1 cup mashed potatoes
$1/4$ cup all-purpose flour
1 teaspoon baking powder
3 to 4 tablespoons butter or margarine

Combine all the ingredients except the butter and form into patties. Fry these in the butter until browned on both sides, and serve at once while they are still nice and hot.

Serves: 4

Nancy Schmidt
Linwood, Ontario

POOR MAN'S STEAK

A delicious economy meal—and excellent for sandwiches the next day, too.

1 pound ground beef
1 cup cracker crumbs
1 cup milk
1 teaspoon salt
$1/4$ teaspoon pepper
1 small onion, chopped fine
3 to 4 tablespoons butter
1 ten-and-one-half-ounce can condensed cream of mushroom soup, more if necessary

Combine all the ingredients except the butter and soup thoroughly and shape into a narrow loaf. Let sit, refrigerated, for at least 8 hours, or overnight, then slice into pieces and fry in the butter till brown.

Put the slices, in layers, in a roaster and spread mushroom soup on each, using at least one can of soup. Bake for at least 1 hour at 325 degrees.

Serves: 4

Mrs. Eli B. Miller
Wooster, Ohio

HOMEMADE SCRAPPLE

The classic Amish meat extender.

1 medium onion, chopped
4 to 6 tablespoons bacon fat or butter
1/2 pound beef or pork, chopped
1 1/4 teaspoons salt
1/8 teaspoon pepper
4 1/2 cups water
1 cup yellow corn meal

In a large saucepan, brown the onion in some of the fat, then add the meat, seasonings, and water. Cook slowly for 20 minutes, then add the corn meal and boil for 1 hour. Turn into a mold. Cool, then cut in slices and fry in the remaining fat until brown. Serve with gravy or tomato sauce.

Serves: 4 to 5 *Mrs. Elmer Lembright*

SKILLET STROGANOFF

Ground beef replaces the traditional steak here.

1 pound ground beef
1/2 cup soft bread crumbs
1/2 cup milk
2 tablespoons chopped fresh parsley
1 teaspoon salt
Pinch of pepper
3 to 4 tablespoons butter
1 package onion gravy mix
2 1/2 cups water
1 1/3 cups raw rice
1/2 cup sour cream

Combine the ground beef, soft bread crumbs, milk, parsley, salt, and pepper. Form the mixture into 16 meatballs and brown on all sides, in the butter, in a skillet. Add the gravy mix to the water and add to the skillet. Bring to a boil, add the rice, and stir. Cover, reduce the heat, and simmer for 10 minutes. Stir in the sour cream and serve.

Serves: 4 *Anna Mae Miller*

AMISH PIZZA

The Amish love pizza and country music. This is an example of their first love.

Dough

1 package active dry yeast
3/4 cup warm water
2 1/2 cups packaged biscuit mix

Sauce

1 six-ounce can tomato paste
1 teaspoon dried oregano
1/8 teaspoon black pepper
1/4 teaspoon ground cloves
1 one-pound can tomatoes, chopped
1 teaspoon garlic salt
1 small onion, chopped
1 cup Cheddar cheese, grated
1/2 pound ground beef, browned

Dissolve the yeast in the warm water, then add to the biscuit mix. Let sit for 10 to 15 minutes after mixing, then divide in half and pat out on two cookie sheets.

Combine the tomato paste, oregano, pepper, cloves, chopped tomatoes, garlic salt, and onion. Spread half of this mixture on each half of the pizza dough, then sprinkle on the browned beef, top with the cheese, and bake for 15 minutes at 450 degrees.

Serves: 8 *Mrs. Eli Yoder*

CORNED BEEF AND CABBAGE

A canned corn beef dish that is really flavored and seasoned well.

8 cups shredded cabbage (1 medium head)
2 cups shredded carrots (4 medium)
1/4 cup dry onion soup
2 tablespoons butter
1 twelve-ounce can corned beef, cut in 4 slices

Toss together the cabbage, carrots, and soup mix. Divide into 4 portions and center each portion on a twelve-inch square of heavy foil. Dot with butter, then top each with a slice of corned beef. Close the foil and seal well, allowing for steam. Grill over medium heat for about 10 minutes, turning the foil packages once.

Serves: 4 *Sue Miller*

BEEF AND VEGETABLE PIE

Beef and vegetables in gravy with either a crust or a biscuit topping.

1½ pound canned beef, cut in 1 inch cubes, or ground beef
2 tablespoons butter
4 medium carrots, sliced
1 medium onion, sliced
4 medium potatoes, peeled and diced
3 tablespoons flour
¼ cup cold water
Salt and pepper
Pastry for a one-crust pie or 1 can baking powder biscuits

Brown the meat slowly in hot butter. Add enough boiling water to cover the meat and simmer for 15 minutes. Add the vegetables and more water, if necessary, just to cover, and simmer until all are tender (20 to 30 minutes). Thicken the gravy by making a paste of 3 tablespoons of flour and ¼ cup cold water. Stir this into the hot gravy, and let cool for 2 to 3 minutes, then add salt and pepper to taste. Bring to a boil and pour into a 2-quart casserole.

If using pie pastry, roll it out thin, cover the pie, and crimp the edges, cut slashes in it to allow steam to escape. Or cover with the baking powder biscuits. Bake in a 425-degree oven until the crust is golden brown (about 15 minutes).

Serves: 6 to 8 *Mrs. Jim Hammond*
Fresno, Ohio

PICKLED TONGUE

Standard recipe—easy to make, even easier to eat.

1 three-pound fresh beef tongue
Salt
½ cup vinegar
1¼ cups water
⅓ cup granulated sugar

Place the beef tongue in boiling water to cover and boil for about 10 minutes. Pull off the skin, then cook in fresh, salted water to cover until tender (about 3 hours). Let cool in the broth.

When the tongue has cooled, drain, slice, and pour the vinegar, water, and sugar over. Let the tongue stand until the vinegar has penetrated (at least 30 minutes).

Serves: 6 to 8 *Sue Miller*

BAKED SLOPPY JOES

A good luncheon dish.

1 pound ground beef
1 cup milk
1 cup fine, dry bread crumbs
1 egg, beaten
1 cup tomato juice
2 medium onions, chopped
1/2 cup chopped celery
1 teaspoon salt
1/8 teaspoon pepper

Combine all the ingredients in a 3-quart ovenproof bowl. Bake in the same bowl for 2 hours at 300 degrees. Serve on rolls.

Serves: 6 to 8 *Mrs. Hank Miller*

SUPPER SANDWICH BAKE

A beef, hot dog, and cheese sandwich combination.

6 slices bread
Butter or margarine
1 pound lean ground beef
1/4 cup catsup
1 teaspoon salt
6 frankfurters, cut almost in half lengthwise
2 medium onions, sliced
6 ounces Cheddar cheese, sliced
2 eggs beaten
1 cup milk

Spread the bread with butter, arrange in the bottom of a greased 13 x 9 x 2-inch pan, and toast in a moderate oven at 350 degrees for about 15 minutes. Combine the beef, catsup, and salt and spread over the toast (1/3 cup per slice). Top each with a frankfurter, opened out, and onion and cheese slices. Combine the eggs and milk; pour over the bread. Bake, uncovered, in a moderate oven for about 50 minutes.

Serves: 6 *Mrs. William Hochstetler*

A WARM SANDWICH

Fine for quick energy, snack style. Or try it on a cold evening for dinner.

1 pound large-sized bologna
1 medium onion
1/4 pound Cheddar cheese
2 tablespoons granulated sugar
1/2 cup salad dressing of your choice
2 tablespoons evaporated milk
6 hamburger buns

Grind together the bologna, onion, and cheese. Mix in the sugar, salad dressing, and the evaporated milk. Spread the mixture onto the buns, wrap individually, and heat in a 300-degree oven for about 20 minutes.

Serves: 6 *Mrs. Glenn Immel*

CHIP CHOP HAM FOR SANDWICHES

"Good tasting."

2 pounds chip chopped ham
4 tablespoons butter
All-purpose flour
3 tablespoons brown sugar
1 cup catsup
1/4 cup vinegar
1 cup water
1 tablespoon Worcestershire sauce

Cut the meat into bite-sized pieces. Fry briefly in butter, then sprinkle with a little flour and add the rest of the ingredients. Bake, covered, for 1 hour at 250 degrees, and use as a spread for sandwiches.

Makes: 15 to 21 sandwiches *Lauretha Hershberger*
Cindy Schrock

SMOKED SAUSAGES AND POTATOES

"One of my absolute favorite dishes. Children enjoy it, too."

2 1/2 pounds smoked sausages, cut into 1/2-inch slices
8 medium potatoes, peeled and sliced thick
Pinch of pepper

Cover the sausage and potato slices with water, add a pinch of pepper, and boil until potatoes are done (about 45 minutes).

Serves: 6

Mrs. A. Dale Fasnecht
Massillon, Ohio

SAUSAGE LOAF

Meat loaf made with sausage and topped with tomato.

1 pound sausages
1 cup cracker crumbs
1 tablespoon minced onion
1 1/2 teaspoons catsup
4 teaspoons chopped fresh parsley
1/2 teaspoon prepared mustard
1/2 teaspoon salt
1 egg, lightly beaten
1/2 cup milk
2 cups chopped canned tomatoes

Combine the sausages, cracker crumbs, onion, catsup, parsley, mustard, and salt. Moisten with the egg and milk, then shape into a loaf, place in a pan, and top with the tomatoes. Bake 1 to 1 1/2 hours at 350 degrees.

Serves: 4 to 6

Mrs. Andy Lehman

HAM LOAF

"The flavor of this is more like city chicken than ham."

1 pound lean cured ham
2 pounds fresh pork
1 egg
2 cups soft bread crumbs
1 cup milk
Pepper

Grind the meats together, then combine with the egg, bread crumbs, milk, and pepper (no salt). Put in a 9 x 5 x 3-inch loaf pan and bake for 2 hours at 400°, covered for the first hour.

Serves: 8

Mrs. Enos Bontrager
Jamesport, Missouri

HAM BAKED IN MILK

"This makes the ham very smooth, with the texture not grainy or stringy. It is very easy to cut and chew."

1 large, round slice ham, 1 to 1½ inch thick
Prepared mustard
5 whole cloves
1 cup milk

Spread the slice of ham with mustard. Insert whole cloves in the ham, put in a flat baking dish, cover with milk, and bake at 350 degrees for 1 hour.

Serves: 4 to 6 — *Mrs. Walter Jacobs*

POTATOES AND CABBAGE

A well-known midweek family and visitors' dish.

1½ pounds ham or beef
Salt
5 peppercorns
4 medium potatoes, peeled and chunked
½ large head cabbage, cut into wedges

Cut the meat into bite-sized pieces. Cook, covered, in salted water to cover, to which has been added 5 peppercorns, until tender (about 2 hours). Cook the potatoes in salted water until tender and add to the meat broth. Cook the cabbage in 1 inch salted boiling water for 15 minutes, then drain and add to the meat and broth. Let simmer gently for 10 minutes to blend the flavors.

Serves: 6 to 8 — *Mrs. Eli Schlabach*
Fredericksburg, Ohio

CHOPS AND RICE

"A really nice one-dish meal."

6 pork chops
⅔ cup raw rice
1 cup water
2 teaspoons salt
½ cup chopped onion
1 one-pound can chopped tomatoes
1 cup whole-kernel corn
¼ teaspoon pepper

Trim some fat from the chops and heat in a large skillet. Add the chops and brown very slowly on both sides, then lift out and pour off excess fat. Spread the rice over the bottom of the skillet, add water, and sprinkle with 1 teaspoon salt. Arrange the chops over the rice, sprinkle with another teaspoon of salt, then add the onion and tomatoes. Spoon on the corn and pepper, bring to a boil, cover and simmer 25 to 35 minutes, or until the rice is done. Add a small amount of water, if necessary.

Serves: 6 *Katie Miller*

PORK SPARERIBS AND "POT PIE"

A nontypical boiled dinner with dumplings.

3 to 4 pounds pork spareribs
Salt and pepper
2 to 3 medium potatoes, peeled and sliced
1½ cups all-purpose flour

Cover the spareribs with water seasoned with salt and pepper and cook for 2 hours, then add the sliced potatoes and cook until partially done before adding the "pot pie."

Combine the flour with ½ cup of broth; the dough should be of rolling consistency. Roll very thin and cut into 2-inch squares, then add to the boiling broth, a square at a time to prevent sticking together, and stirring often. Cook until tender.

Serves: 4 to 5 *Mrs. Carroll E. Swarty*
Harrisonburg, Virginia

PORK AND APPLE PIE

Two standard Amish foods combined in an unusual pie.

1½ pounds pork, cooked and cubed
¼ cup brown sugar
1 cup pork gravy
2 tart apples, sliced
½ teaspoon cinnamon
1 nine-inch pie shell

Combine the pork, sugar, gravy, apples, and cinnamon. Put in the pie shell and bake at 350 degrees for 45 minutes.

Serves: 4 to 6 *Mrs. Elizabeth Troyer*
Medford, Wisconsin

CREAMED CHICKEN

Amish-style creamed chicken with carrots.

2½ cups chopped, cooked chicken
1 twelve-ounce can peas, undrained
1 cup cooked carrots
Salt and pepper
1 tablespoon all-purpose flour
1 tablespoon butter

Put the chicken into a casserole. Add the peas, carrots, salt and pepper to taste. Thicken the broth with flour, add a little butter, then add to the rest. Bake, uncovered, in a 350-degree oven for 30 minutes, or until brown.

Serves: 4 to 6

Nancy Schmidt
Linwood, Ontario

CHICKEN–POTATO CHIP LOAF

"A husband-pleasing recipe."

1 pound cut-up, cooked chicken
1 onion, chopped
½ cup cracker crumbs
1 eight-ounce can tomato juice
2 eggs, beaten
1 cup crushed potato chips

Combine the chicken, onion, tomato juice, crackers, eggs, and ½ cup of the potato chips. Pour into a buttered baking dish and put the other ½ cup chips on top. Bake, uncovered, 375° for 20 minutes, or until browned.

Serves: 4 to 6

Mrs. S. A. Hershberger
Holmes County, Ohio

CHICKEN LOAF

A layered noodle-chicken loaf with mushroom gravy.

1 chicken
¼ cup chopped onion
¼ cup chopped celery
Salt and pepper
8 ounces noodles
2 tablespoons all-purpose flour
1 ten-and-one-half-ounce can condensed cream of mushroom soup
1½ cups buttered bread crumbs

Cover the chicken with water, add the onions, celery, salt, and pepper to taste, and bring to a boil. Reduce the heat and simmer until tender (about 1½ hours). Remove meat from the bones and set both meat and broth aside. Cook the noodles in salt water until tender (about 10 minutes), then drain and set aside.

Blend the flour with 1½ cups of the chicken broth and cook, stirring, until thickened. Add the mushroom soup.

Grease a 2- to 3-quart casserole and in it arrange alternate layers of chicken, bread crumbs, noodle and gravy mixture. Repeat until all the ingredients are used up, ending with a top layer of bread crumbs. Bake for 1 hour at 350 degrees.

Serves: 4 to 6

Mrs. Joel D. Miller
Archbold, Ohio

OVEN-CRISP CHICKEN

The Amish call this the "very best" chicken.

1 cup packaged biscuit mix
2 teaspoons salt
¼ teaspoon pepper
2 teaspoons paprika
½ cup shortening
1 frying chicken, cut up

Combine the biscuit mix with the salt, pepper, and paprika and place in a bag. Melt the shortening in a 13 x 9 x 2-inch baking pan. Shake the pieces of chicken in the bag, a few at a time, and coat thoroughly, then lay, skin side down, in single layer in the hot shortening. Bake in a preheated 425-degree oven for 45 minutes, turning the pieces over for last 15 minutes.

Serves: 4

Marilyn Troyer
Millersburg, Ohio

CHEESY BAKED CHICKEN

A standard dinner dish of oven-fried chicken with a cheesy crust.

5 slices dry bread
¼ pound sharp Cheddar cheese, grated
1 teaspoon chopped fresh parsley
⅛ teaspoon pepper
½ teaspoon garlic salt
2 teaspoons salt
1 teaspoon monosodium glutamate
¾ cup melted butter
1 two-and-one-half to three-pound chicken, cut up

Grind the bread, then combine with the cheese, parsley, pepper, garlic salt, salt, and monosodium glutamate. Dip the chicken pieces in the butter, then in the crumb mixture, coating thoroughly. Arrange in an uncrowded layer in a shallow baking pan and bake, uncovered, in a preheated 350-degree oven for about 1 hour, or until tender.

Serves: 4

Mrs. Raymond N. Troyer
Sugarcreek, Ohio

CHICKEN PIE

. . . in a creamy sauce with a biscuit crust.

1½ cups peeled, diced potato
½ cup diced carrots
¼ cup minced onion
½ cup chopped celery
1 cup peas, fresh or canned
2½ cups fresh or canned chicken broth
3 cups cold water
1 cup all-purpose flour
Diced, cooked meat from 1 chicken

Biscuit Dough

2 teaspoons baking powder
¼ teaspoon cream of tartar
½ teaspoon salt
1 tablespoon granulated sugar
¼ cup shortening
⅓ cup milk
1 small egg, beaten

Cook the potato, carrots, onion, celery, and peas (if the peas are canned, add after the other vegetables are tender) in the broth. Make a gravy of the flour and water. Add to the vegetables when they are tender, then add the chicken. Place in a baking dish or deep pie plate and set aside while you make the biscuit dough.

Sift the dry ingredients into a bowl, then add the shortening and mix well until crumbly. Add the milk to beaten egg, then to the crumbs. Mix, then pat out on a floured surface and use to cover the chicken pie. Bake at 350 degrees for 30 to 45 minutes.

Serves: 6 to 8

Mrs. Alvin Miller
Shreve, Ohio

SALMON PATTIES

"The flavor hangs in the roof of your mouth."

1 one-pound can salmon
2 tablespoons chopped celery leaves
1 teaspoon chopped onion
2 eggs
1 tablespoon chopped fresh parsley
Salt and pepper to taste
Soda crackers
Fat for deep frying

Place all the ingredients except the crackers and fat in a large bowl. Mix thoroughly and use broken crackers to soak up excess liquid. Shape into cakes and fry in deep fat until browned.

Serves: 4

Andrew E. Slabach
East Canton, Ohio

MUSHROOM SCRAMBLED EGGS

A very different and exciting little dish. For a summer special, serve with sliced fresh tomatoes.

8 eggs
1 ten-and-one-half-ounce can condensed cream of mushroom soup
1/4 cup milk
1/8 teaspoon pepper
2 tablespoons butter
1/2 cup shredded Swiss cheese
Chopped fresh parsley

Beat the eggs lightly, then blend in the soup, milk, and pepper. Melt the butter in a skillet, pour in the egg mixture, and cook slowly until the eggs are set, stirring or turning occasionally. Sprinkle with the cheese and parsley just before serving.

Serves: 6

Emma E. Hershberger

RABBIT, GERMAN STYLE

Every Amish family has this occasionally, after early hunting trips by youngsters.

1 rabbit, skinned and cut up
1/2 cup all-purpose flour
1 teaspoon salt
1/4 teaspoon pepper
2 cups water
1 cup sour cream

Roll the rabbit pieces in the flour and brown in a 350-degree oven. Add the salt and pepper, then place in a pan with the water and let simmer until almost done (about 1 hour). Add the sour cream and let simmer (do not boil) for 30 minutes longer.

Serves: 4

Lovina Miller
Navarre, Ohio

Vegetables

Vegetables are a basic part of all Amish meals. They are especially important as side dishes at dinner and supper offerings but are frequently served on their own as main luncheon dishes. Vegetable casseroles, favored by Amish families, are very tasty dishes.

ASPARAGUS CASSEROLE

This is nice served over toast or with a roll.

18 fresh or frozen asparagus spears
1/4 pound butter
1/4 cup all-purpose flour
1/2 teaspoon salt
1 1/2 cups milk
1 three-ounce ounce package cream cheese, softened
1/2 cup cracker crumbs
2 hard-boiled eggs

If the asparagus is fresh, cook it in boiling salted water for 10 to 12 minutes, or until tender. Drain. In a saucepan melt half the butter and stir in the flour and salt. Blend in enough milk to make a smooth paste, then stir in the remaining milk and cook until the white sauce is thick, stirring constantly. Stir in the cream cheese.

Place the asparagus in a 1 1/2-quart casserole, pour the white sauce over, and top with the cracker crumbs. Melt the remaining butter and pour over, then bake, uncovered, in a 350-degree oven for about 30 minutes, or until the mixture bubbles. Place under a broiler for about 2 minutes to brown top, then arrange the sliced eggs on top of the casserole and serve.

Serves: 5 to 6 *Mrs. Forest Kornhaus*

BARBECUED BEANS

"If you want, add a little garlic or garlic salt to the mixture."

2 tablespoons butter
1 pound ground beef
1/2 cup chopped onion
1 one-pound can pork and beans
2 tablespoons dark molasses
1/2 cup catsup
1 tablespoon Worcestershire sauce
1 tablespoon vinegar
Salt to taste

Heat the butter in a flameproof 1 1/2-quart casserole and fry the ground beef and onion until nice and brown. Add the rest of the ingredients and bake, uncovered, for 30 minutes at 350 degrees.

Serves: 5 to 6 *Mrs. L. D. Kaufman*
Montgomery, Georgia

BAKED BEANS

"If you have never made home baked beans before, try these. You're sure to make them again."

1/2 pound navy beans
3 cups water
1/8 teaspoon baking soda (optional)
1/4 pound bacon ends, diced into 1-inch squares
1 small onion, quartered
2 tablespoons brown sugar
3 tablespoons molasses
1 teaspoon dry mustard
1 teaspoon salt
1/8 teaspoon pepper
1 tablespoon vinegar
1 cup hot water, more if necessary

Soak the beans overnight in the 3 cups water; add 1/8 teaspoon baking soda if the water is hard. The next day, parboil beans for 20 minutes. (As a short cut, parboil the beans for 2 minutes in the water with the baking soda. Allow to soak for one hour, then parboil again for 10 minutes.) Drain the beans after parboiling; rinse with cold water.

Place half the diced bacon in the bottom of a 1-quart bean pot or casserole along with the quartered onion, then add the beans. Mix the brown sugar, molasses, dry mustard, salt, pepper, and vinegar with the hot water and pour over the top of the beans. Top with the remaining bacon, cover, and bake in a 300-degree oven for 7 hours, adding hot water as needed to keep the beans moist.

Serves: 4

Mrs. Wilma Lambright
Wolcottville, Indiana

BEAN CASSEROLE

"This is a fun side dish when you're tired of plain vegetables."

1 ten-ounce package frozen cut green beans
1 ten-and-one-half-ounce can condensed cream of mushroom soup
1 tablespoon Worcestershire sauce
2 small onions, sliced
2 tablespoons grated Parmesan cheese

Cook the beans till almost tender (about 8 minutes), then put half of them into a 1-quart casserole. Add half the soup, with the Worcestershire sauce mixed in, then add half the sliced onions. Repeat the layers, top with the grated Parmesan cheese, and bake at 350 degrees until bubbly (about 20 minutes).

Serves: 4

Lovina Yoder

GREEN BEAN CASSEROLE

The onion rings give an interesting texture and flavor to the beans.

1/2 pound fresh green beans, ends trimmed off
1/2 ten-and-one-half-ounce can cream of chicken or cream of mushroom soup
1 cup French-fried onion rings or 1/2 cup cracker crumbs

Cook the beans until almost tender (about 8 minutes), then drain and place in the bottom of a 1-quart casserole. Pour over the soup and bake, covered, in a 350-degree oven for 30 minutes. Uncover, arrange the onion rings on top of the beans, and return the casserole to the oven to bake, uncovered, until the onions are crisp.

Serves: 4

Barbara Ann Schwartz
Monroe, Indiana

GREEN BEAN AND POTATO CASSEROLE

This is a well-known Ohio Amish vegetable dish.

1½ cups cooked green beans
1 cup diced, boiled potatoes
½ cup diced celery
4 slices bacon
2 tablespoons finely chopped onion
1 tablespoon all-purpose flour
1 cup evaporated milk
1¼ cups shredded Cheddar cheese
½ cup cracker crumbs

Place the beans, potatoes, and celery in a 1-quart casserole. Fry the bacon, drain, reserving 1 tablespoon of the drippings, then crumble and set aside. Sauté the onion in the reserved bacon drippings, until crisp. Then slowly stir in the flour and the evaporated milk. Stirring constantly, cook until thickened and smooth. Add 1 cup of the shredded cheese and stir until melted.

Pour the sauce over the vegetables in the casserole and mix well. Sprinkle the remaining ¼ cup cheese, cracker crumbs, and crumbled bacon over the top and bake in a 350-degree oven for 30 minutes.

Serves: 6

Mrs. William Weaver

KIDNEY BEAN CASSEROLE

A lunch or dinner dish—a good meat replacer.

2 cups cooked kidney beans
1 large onion
½ pound Cheddar cheese
2 tablespoons melted butter
3 eggs, beaten
2 cups soft bread crumbs
Salt and pepper

Grind together the beans, onion, and cheese, then add the remaining ingredients. Form into a loaf, place in a greased casserole, and bake at 375 degrees for 40 minutes. Serve with tomato sauce.

Serves: 4

Mary R. Weaver
Madisonburg, Pennsylvania

QUICK BARBECUED LIMA BEANS IN CASSEROLE

This is an inexpensive dish with a quite distinctive taste.

1 cup dried lima beans
3 cups water
1/2 onion, chopped
2 tablespoons butter
1/2 ten-and-one-half-ounce can tomato soup
Pinch of pepper
2 tablespoons granulated sugar
2 slices bacon, chopped

Put the lima beans in the water and boil for 2 minutes, then let stand for 1 hour. Meanwhile, sauté the onions in the butter until tender. Add the soup, pepper, and sugar, and simmer for 5 minutes.

Put the beans, reserving the soaking liquid, in a 1-quart casserole; add the bacon. Pour the soup and three-quarters of the bean liquid over the beans; then bake, uncovered, for 3 hours at 300 degrees.

Serves: 4

Mrs. Jonas D. Troyer
Baltic, Ohio

SWEET-AND-SOUR CABBAGE

A standard, quite tangy recipe.

1 head cabbage
1 egg
1/4 cup vinegar
1/4 cup granulated sugar
Salt and pepper to taste

Shred the cabbage and cook in boiling water until tender (about 10 minutes), then drain. Beat the egg and add the vinegar and sugar. Add the sauce to the cabbage, toss, and season with salt and pepper. Serve hot.

Serves: 4 to 6

Mrs. A. M. Wenger
Leola, Pennsylvania

CARROTS AU GRATIN

You can also use cream of mushroom or chicken in this recipe.

1½ cups diced carrots
½ ten-and-one-half-ounce can condensed cream of celery soup
1 cup shredded Cheddar cheese
1 tablespoon melted butter
¼ cup fine, dry bread crumbs

Combine the carrots, soup, and cheese and place in a 1-quart casserole. Melt the butter in a small pan, then stir in the bread crumbs. Sprinkle on the casserole and bake at 350 degrees for 20 to 25 minutes, until heated through and the crumbs are brown.

Serves: 4

Mrs. Jonas Yoder
Millersburg, Ohio

BAKED CARROTS

Carrots in a very different form and with a very different taste.

1¼ cups cooked, mashed carrots
Salt and pepper to taste
1½ teaspoons finely chopped onion
2 medium-sized eggs, beaten
½ cup fine, dry bread crumbs
1½ tablespoon melted butter
1 cup milk

Combine all the ingredients, and pour into a 1-quart casserole, and bake at 375 degrees for 1 hour.

Serves: 4

Mrs. Aaron Hoover
Leola, Pennsylvania

BAKED CORN

"Slightly heavier flavor than regular corn dishes."

1 cup fresh, whole-kernel corn
3 cups milk
1 teaspoon granulated sugar
2 eggs, beaten
1 teaspoon salt
1 tablespoon butter

Grind the corn in a food chopper, then place in a bowl. Heat 2 cups of the milk and pour over the corn and let stand for an hour in order to soak it well. Stir in the sugar, eggs, salt, and remaining milk, then pour into a greased baking dish and dot with the butter. Bake 30 minutes (no longer) at 350 degrees.

Serves: 4

Mrs. Melvin Mauren
Millersville, Pennsylvania

CORN PUDDING

Distinctive tasting, easily made.

3 eggs, slightly beaten
2 cups milk
2 tablespoons granulated sugar
1 teaspoon salt
2 tablespoons butter
1/2 cup chopped celery
1 tablespoon minced onion
2 cups fresh, whole-kernel corn

Combine all the ingredients, turn into a buttered casserole, and bake at 350 degrees for 1 hour.

Serves: 6

Mrs. Joe L. Raber

CORN FRITTERS

A puffy, light bread substitute—tasty and filling.

2 cups crushed fresh corn
2 eggs
1 cup flour or cracker dust
Salt and pepper to taste
2 tablespoons granulated sugar
2 teaspoons baking powder
Milk, enough just to moisten
Fat for deep frying

Combine all the ingredients except the fat. Heat the fat in a deep-fryer and drop in the batter, a few spoonfuls at a time. Fry until brown, then drain on paper towels.

Serves: 4

Rebecca Flaud
Sarasota, Florida

SCALLOPED CORN

Corn in a cream sauce topped with bread crumbs—a "new-look" corn side dish.

2 medium eggs
½ cup milk
¼ cup cream
1½ teaspoons melted butter
Salt
1½ teaspoons granulated sugar
1 cup fresh or canned whole-kernel corn
Cracker crumbs

Beat the eggs and add the milk, cream, butter, salt, and sugar. Add the corn to the mixture and stir, then turn into a greased baking dish. Top with cracker crumbs and bake at 350 degrees for 1 hour.

Serves: 3 to 4

Mrs. Jacob Miller
Apple Creek, Ohio

EGGPLANT PATTIES

Mashed eggplant formed into patties and fried; a good substitute for potatoes or rice.

2 cups cooked and mashed eggplant
1 teaspoon salt
2 eggs
½ cup milk
1 cup cracker crumbs
3 to 4 tablespoons shortening

Combine all the ingredients except the shortening and form into patties. Melt the shortening in a skillet and fry the patties until brown on both sides.

Serves: 4

Annie Erb

SCALLOPED ONIONS

"Even if your family is not very fond of onions, you will enjoy this recipe. Try making it for your next pot luck."

6 medium-sized onions, quartered
1 tablespoon all-purpose flour
¼ teaspoon salt
¼ pound Cheddar cheese
1 cup buttered bread crumbs

Boil the onions until tender (about 20 minutes), then drain, retaining ½ cup of the liquid. Thicken the liquid with the flour, add the salt, and cut in the cheese. Cook, stirring constantly until the cheese has melted. Place the onions in a 1-quart baking dish, pour the cheese mixture over, and cover with buttered bread crumbs. Cover and bake in a 350-degree oven for 30 minutes.

Serves: 6 to 8

Susie Peachy
Allensville, Ohio

SKILLET HASHED BROWNS

Everybody likes this kind of potato along with meat.

3 cups cooked, diced potatoes
3 tablespoons all-purpose flour
1 tablespoon finely chopped onion
1/4 cup light cream
1 teaspoon salt
1/8 teaspoon pepper
3 tablespoons shortening

Combine the cooked, diced potatoes with the flour, onion, cream, salt and pepper and toss lightly to coat. Heat the shortening in a skillet, tipping the skillet so the entire bottom is covered. Add the potatoes and press down with a spatula. Cook till brown on the first side (about 15 minutes), then turn and let brown on the second side for an additional 5 to 10 minutes.

Serves: 4

Susan Schrock

POTATO PUFFS

"This is a good way to use leftover mashed potatoes."

1 cup mashed potatoes
1 egg
1/2 teaspoon salt
All-purpose flour
Lard or cooking oil for deep frying

Combine the potatoes, egg, salt, and 1/4 cup flour and mix well. Form into balls about the size of a walnut, dust with flour, and fry in lard or oil at least 1 inch deep. Turn once with a slotted spoon and fry until brown on both sides. Drain on paper towels and serve at once.

Serves: 3 to 4

Mrs. Gideon Weaver
Fredericksburg, Ohio

POTATO LOAF

A light, soufflé-like dish that is baked covered.

3 medium potatoes
1 medium onion
5 soda crackers
1 1/2 tablespoons milk
1/4 cup grated Cheddar cheese
2 eggs, separated
1/2 teaspoon salt
1/4 teaspoon pepper

Peel and grate the potatoes and onions, then combine. Crumble the crackers and soak in the milk for a few minutes, then add, along with the cheese, to the potatoes and onions. Beat the egg yolks slightly and add to the potato mixture, along with the seasonings. Beat the egg whites until stiff but not dry and fold into the potato mixture. Pour into a greased, 1-quart casserole, cover, and bake at 350 degrees for 1 hour, or until the potatoes are tender.

Serves: 6

Mrs. Elmer Stolzfies
Atglen, Pennsylvania

PAPRIKA-POTATO CASSEROLE

Imagine a paprika butter taste; this has it.

8 small potatoes, peeled
2 tablespoons paprika
5 tablespoons melted butter

Boil the potatoes until just tender (20 to 30 minutes). Put them in a plastic bag with paprika and shake to coat well. Put in a 1-quart casserole, pour the melted butter over the top, and cover. Bake at 350 degrees for 1 hour.

Serves: 4

Katie Ruth Schmucker
Fredericksburg, Ohio

EGG AND POTATO CASSEROLE

Make this for the children's breakfast.

4 tablespoons butter
3 to 4 medium-sized potatoes, peeled and sliced
1 teaspoon salt
4 eggs
1/4 cup water or milk

Melt the butter in a frying pan. Fry potatoes until tender and brown, then add the salt. Beat the eggs, add the milk or water, then pour the mixture over the potatoes. Cook until the eggs are done.

Serves: 4

Mrs. David Troyer
Dundee, Ohio

SUPER SCALLOPED POTATOES

Potatoes layered in a sauce—rich and tasty.

1 ten-and-one-half-ounce can condensed cream of mushroom soup
1/2 to 3/4 cup milk
Pinch of pepper
4 cups peeled, thinly sliced potatoes
1 small onion, sliced
Paprika
1 tablespoon butter

Blend the mushroom soup with milk and pepper to make a sauce. In a buttered 1 1/2-quart casserole, arrange alternate layers of potato, onion, and sauce. Sprinkle with paprika and dot the top with butter. Cover and bake for 1 hour at 375 degrees, then uncover and bake 15 minutes more.

Serves: 4 to 6

Mrs. Alvin R. Mullet
Topeka, Indiana

Salads

Gelatin is the constant in most Amish salads, and again the Amish manage an ingenious diversity despite the framework of simplicity and standard ingredients within which they work. Here you will find layered, creamy, and clear salads, representative of the distinct types favored by the Amish. Potatoes and beans are frequently used as a base for salads. The three-bean salad, of course, is world famous. The salads are usually served with a traditional dressing, although there are unique, outstanding homemade dressings like Betty Miller's.

CLUB SALAD

"Very tasty. Once you make it, you will surely make it again."

1 three-ounce package lime gelatin
1 three-ounce package lemon gelatin
15 miniature marshmallows
1 cup whipped cream
1 eight-ounce can crushed pineapple
1/2 cup granulated sugar
1 three-ounce package cream cheese
1 three-ounce package cherry gelatin

Dissolve lime gelatin as directed on the package. Pour into a 9-inch-square pan, refrigerate, and let set until firm. Dissolve the lemon gelatin in boiling water. Mix in the marshmallows before adding cold water. Add the cold water, then cool and add the whipped cream, drained pineapple, sugar, and cream cheese. Pour over the lime gelatin and let set, refrigerated, until firm. Mix the cherry gelatin as directed on the package, let cool, and pour over the first mixtures. Let set until firm, refrigerated, then unmold and serve.

Serves: 8

Mandy Ann Shetler
Kalona, Iowa

BLUEBERRY SALAD

"It's really great with fresh blueberries."

- **1 three-ounce package lemon gelatin**
- **3 cups boiling water**
- **1 eight-ounce can crushed pineapple**
- **1 eight-ounce package cream cheese**
- **1 teaspoon vanilla extract**
- **3 tablespoons milk, more if necessary**
- **2 tablespoons confectioners' sugar**
- **1 three-ounce package black cherry gelatin**
- **1 eight-ounce can blueberries or 1 cup fresh blueberries**

Dissolve the lemon gelatin in 1½ cups of the boiling water, add the pineapple, and pour into a 9-inch-square pan. Refrigerate and let stand until firm. Combine the cream cheese, vanilla, milk, and sugar, adding more milk if the mixture is not thin enough to spread. Spread the cream cheese mixture over lemon gelatin and return to the refrigerator. Dissolve the black cherry gelatin in the remaining boiling water, add the blueberries, and pour over the gelatin-cheese mixture. Refrigerate until firm, then unmold and serve.

Serves: 9

Iva I. Miller
Sugarcreek, Ohio

FROSTED SALAD

This is an excellent dessert-type salad.

- **1 six-ounce package lemon gelatin**
- **2 cups boiling water**
- **2 cups club or orange soda**
- **1 sixteen-ounce can crushed pineapple**
- **1 cup miniature marshmallows**
- **2 large bananas, sliced**

Topping

1/2 cup granulated sugar
2 tablespoons all-purpose flour
1 cup pineapple juice
1 egg, lightly beaten
2 tablespoons butter
1 cup whipped cream

Dissolve the gelatin in the boiling water. Stir in the club or orange soda and chill until partly set. Drain the pineapple, saving the juice for the topping. Fold the marshmallows, pineapple, and bananas into the gelatin, then pour into a 13 x 9 x 2-inch dish. Chill until firm.

Meanwhile, make the topping. Combine the sugar and flour in a saucepan. Stir in the pineapple juice and beaten egg, then cook over low heat until thick. Remove from the heat, add the butter, stir, and chill. Fold in the whipped cream.

Spread the topping on the chilled and set gelatin mixture and chill overnight. Unmold, slice in squares, and serve on lettuce leaves.

Serves: 8

Mrs. Elmer Hershberger
New Paris, Indiana

PEACH SALAD

Teen-agers will like this—it's good tasting and attractive.

1 sixteen-ounce can peaches
10 maraschino cherries
1 1/2 cups boiling water
2 three-ounce packages lemon gelatin
1 cup evaporated milk
2 tablespoons lemon juice
1 three-ounce package cream cheese
1/2 cup mayonnaise
1/2 cup chopped nuts
1/2 cup chopped celery

Drain the peaches, reserving the juice. Arrange 6 or 8 peach slices and the maraschino cherries in the bottom of a 1 1/2-quart dish. Add 1 package of gelatin and 1/2 cup reserved peach juice to the boiling water. Cool and pour over the peaches. Chill until set.

Bring 1 cup peach juice to boil and add the remaining package of gelatin. Cool, stir in 3/4 cup of the evaporated milk and the lemon juice, and chill until partly set. Meanwhile, blend the remaining 1/4 cup milk with the cream cheese and fold in the mayonnaise. Chop the remaining peaches, celery, and nuts. Add to the partly set gelatin mixture and pour over the chilled and set peach-cherry mixture. Chill until set, then unmold and serve on lettuce leaves.

Serves: 8 *Mrs. Jonas Hershberger*

LEMON SALAD

"This is a good 'special occasion' salad."

1 three-ounce package lemon gelatin
1 cup boiling water
1 twenty-ounce can pineapple tidbits or chunks, drained
1/2 cup creamy cottage cheese
1/2 cup chopped nuts
1/2 cup maraschino cherries
1 cup whipped cream

Mix the gelatin with the boiling water and chill until syrupy. Add the pineapple, cottage cheese, nuts, and cherries and chill until the mixture just begins to set. Fold in the whipped cream, pour into a mold, and chill until firm. Unmold to serve.

Serves: 6 to 8 *Mrs. Miller*
Millersburg, Ohio

CREAM CHEESE SALAD

An economical version of a creamy gelatin salad.

2 three-ounce packages any flavor gelatin
1 three-ounce package cream cheese
6 large marshmallows, cut up
4 cups boiling water
2 four-ounce packages whipped topping mix
1 eight-ounce can fruit cocktail, well drained
1 eight-ounce can orange sections, well drained
1/4 cup chopped nuts

Cream together the gelatin and cream cheese. Add a small amount of boiling water to the mixture to dissolve, then add the remaining water and the marshmallows. Stir until all dissolved and chill until partly set.

Prepare the whipped topping according to the directions on the package, then add well-drained fruit. Fold in the gelatin mixture, put into a large pan or dish, and sprinkle with the chopped nuts. Return to the refrigerator to set.

Serves: 8 to 12

Amanda Coblentz
Holmesville, Ohio

CARROT SALAD

Contrasts the smoothness of gelatin with the crunchy textures of vegetables.

1 six-ounce package orange-pineapple gelatin
1 cup pineapple juice
1½ cups crushed pineapple
1 orange, cut up fine
1 cup diced carrots
1 stalk celery, chopped fine

Mix the gelatin according to package directions. Substituting 1 cup pineapple juice for 1 cup cold water. Chill until partially set. Meanwhile, combine the pineapple, orange, carrots, and celery. Fold into the partially set gelatin, then pour into a mold and chill until set. To serve, unmold and serve on lettuce leaves.

Serves: 10

Mrs. Roman H. Miller
Millersburg, Ohio

CRANBERRY SALAD

An orange-cranberry mold accented with the flavors of apples, nuts, and pineapples.

½ pound cranberries
3 apples
2 oranges or ½ cup crushed pineapple
¼ cup chopped nuts
1½ cups granulated sugar
1 six-ounce package cherry or strawberry gelatin
1 cup hot water
1 cup cold water

Wash the cranberries, then grind them through a food chopper. Pare and core the apples; chop very fine. Add the peeled and chopped oranges, or the pineapple, along with the nuts and sugar.

Dissolve the gelatin in the hot water, then add the cold water. When partially set, fold in the salad mixture. Chill until completely set, then unmold on lettuce.

Serves: 10 to 12

Mrs. J. J. Pitts
Blountstown, Florida

AMBROSIA SALAD

This is a good, easy-to-make salad, fine for a pot-luck dinner.

1 twelve-ounce can fruit cocktail
1 eight-ounce can mandarin oranges
1 twelve-ounce can pineapple chunks
2 cups miniature marshmallows
1 cup grated coconut
1/2 cup granulated sugar
1/2 pint sour cream
1 teaspoon vanilla extract

Drain the canned fruits well, then combine with all the other ingredients, folding to blend well. Refrigerate and chill at least 30 minutes, then serve on lettuce leaves.

Serves: 10

Amanda Coblentz
Holmesville, Ohio

AMISH FRUIT SALAD

A make-ahead sweet salad with a different flavor.

2 tablespoons granulated sugar
3 egg yolks
Pinch of salt
2 tablespoons pineapple juice
2 tablespoons vinegar
1 tablespoon butter
2 cups fresh green or red grapes
2 cups pineapple bits
2 cups sliced oranges, soaked in 1/2 cup sugar
24 miniature marshmallows
1 cup whipped cream

Combine the sugar, egg yolks, salt, pineapple juice, vinegar, and butter and cook until thick. Cool, then add the drained fruits and chill 24 hours. When ready to serve, fold in the whipped cream.

Serves: 10 to 12

Mrs. William Burkholder
Spartanburg, Pennsylvania

APPLE SALAD

A crunchy salad with a different, tangy taste.

4 apples, peeled, cored, and cut into chunks
1/2 cup chopped celery
1/2 cup chopped nuts

Dressing

1 cup granulated sugar
1 egg, beaten
1 tablespoon flour
3/4 cup vinegar
1 cup water

Combine the apples, celery, and nuts, then set aside while you make the dressing.

Combine the sugar, egg, flour, and vinegar in a saucepan. Add a small amount of the water and stir. Add the remaining water and bring to a boil, stirring constantly until thickened. (You must watch it closely, as it will burn easily.) Cool and pour over the salad.

Serves: 4

Mrs. Joe M. Yoder
Sugarcreek, Ohio

BEAN SALAD

A colorful, sweet-sour salad.

2 cups cooked beans of your choice
4 hard-boiled eggs, sliced
1 onion, diced
1 stalk celery, diced
Lettuce (optional)

Dressing

1 cup granulated sugar
1/2 cup vinegar
1/4 cup vegetable oil
Salt to taste

Combine the beans, eggs, onion, and celery in a bowl. Make a dressing by beating together the sugar, vinegar, oil, and salt, then combine with the ingredients in the bowl. Serve on lettuce leaves, if desired.

Serves: 4

Mary Stutzman
Blountstown, Florida

THREE-BEAN SALAD

The most famous Amish salad.

1 sixteen-ounce can cut green beans
1 sixteen-ounce can yellow wax beans
1 sixteen-ounce can red kidney beans
1 green pepper, chopped fine
1 small onion, chopped fine

Dressing

1/2 cup vinegar
1/2 cup salad oil
3/4 cup granulated sugar
1 teaspoon salt
1/2 teaspoon pepper

Drain all the beans thoroughly and place in a bowl. Add the green pepper and onion. Combine the dressing ingredients and toss with the bean mixture. Refrigerate several hours or overnight, then drain and serve.

Serves: 6 to 8

Laura Miller
Baltic, Ohio

KIDNEY BEAN SALAD

A brightly colored, sweet-sour-tasting salad.

2 hard-boiled eggs
1/4 cup chopped celery
1 medium-sized onion, minced
2 1/2 cups cooked, drained kidney beans

Dressing

2 tablespoons vinegar
6 tablespoons granulated sugar
2 tablespoons cream

Chop the eggs and combine with the celery and onion. Add the beans, mix well, and chill. When ready to serve, combine the vinegar and sugar and stir in the cream. Blend well with the mixed vegetables and serve.

Serves: 4

Ruth Stutzman
Blountstown, Florida

ANDY'S MIXED VEGETABLE SALAD

Mixed vegetables in an oil-and-vinegar dressing.

1 ten-ounce package frozen mixed vegetables
1 twelve-ounce can red kidney beans, drained
1 small green pepper, chopped
1 small onion, chopped
1 cup chopped celery

Dressing

1/4 cup water
1/4 cup vinegar
1 tablespoon prepared mustard
1/2 cup granulated sugar
1 tablespoon all-purpose flour

Cook the mixed vegetables. Drain and cool, then add the kidney beans, pepper, onion, and celery. In a separate pan, combine the water, vinegar, mustard, sugar, and flour. Bring to a boil, then cool and pour over the vegetables.

Serves: 4 to 6 *Mrs. Andy Mast*

DANDELION OR ENDIVE SALAD

A good idea for making salad eaters out of people who rarely eat salad.

4 cups dandelion greens or endive
3 hard-boiled eggs, chopped
2 tablespoons minced onion

Dressing

3 slices bacon
2 tablespoons all-purpose flour
3/4 cup water
3/4 cup milk
1 teaspoon salt
2 tablespoons vinegar

Wash and drain the greens, then chop. Add the chopped eggs and onion and set aside while you make the dressing.

Fry the bacon until crisp, then remove from the skillet, crumble, and set inside. Stir the flour into the bacon fat, make a smooth paste.

Add the water very slowly, then the milk. Add the salt and vinegar and cook, stirring, until smooth and thickened. Cool slightly, add the crumbled bacon, and pour over the reserved greens.

Serves: 4 to 6 *Mrs. E. Schlabach*

MATTIE'S TOSSED SALAD

A perennial favorite perked up with a super dressing.

1 head iceberg lettuce, torn up
4 tomatoes, sliced
3 small cucumbers, sliced
6 radishes, sliced
1 large onion, chopped
1 cup chopped celery
1 cup sliced carrots

Dressing

1/2 cup salad oil
1/2 cup granulated sugar
1/2 cup vinegar
2 tablespoons water
1/4 teaspoon paprika
1/4 teaspoon salt
1 medium-sized onion, chopped

Combine the vegetables in a large bowl. Combine the dressing ingredients, and when well mixed, pour over the vegetables. Serve immediately.

Serves: 4 to 6 *Mattie Schlabach*

PEPPER CABBAGE

Really a hot cole slaw.

4 cups shredded cabbage
1 green pepper, chopped fine
1 teaspoon salt

Dressing

1/4 cup granulated sugar
1/4 cup vinegar
1 tablespoon vegetable oil

Combine the cabbage, green pepper, and salt and let stand for an hour or so. Drain. Combine the sugar, vinegar, and oil in a saucepan, heat, and pour over the cabbage. Serve at once.

Serves: 4

Rebecca Periman
Columbus, Ohio

EVERLASTING COLE SLAW

Use a blender to cut the vegetables. "Fine taste."

1 medium-sized head cabbage
2 small onions
1 carrot
1 green pepper
3 stalks celery

Dressing

½ cup vinegar
1½ cups sugar
1 teaspoon mustard seed
1 teaspoon celery seed

Cut all the vegetables up very fine, combine, and set aside. Heat the vinegar and sugar and stir until the sugar is dissolved. Let stand until cool, then pour over the slaw. Add the mustard seed and celery seed and mix well.

Store in a covered container in the refrigerator and use as needed. "The recipe makes about 2 quarts of slaw and will keep for 2 to 4 weeks."

Serves: 8 to 10

Mrs. Elmer Hershberger
New Paris, Indiana

SAUERKRAUT SALAD

A make-ahead salad with a strong flavor.

1 twenty-ounce can sauerkraut, washed in cold water and drained
1 cup diced celery
1 medium onion, diced
1 cup diced green pepper
1 carrot, shredded

Dressing

1 cup granulated sugar
1 cup vinegar
1/4 cup vegetable oil
Salt to taste

Combine the vegetables, then combine all the ingredients for the dressing. Pour the dressing over the vegetables and mix well, then let sit for from 4 to 24 hours before serving.

Serves: 8 to 10

Mary Stutzman
Blountstown, Florida

CUCUMBER SALAD

"You can use a nondairy creamer in this."

4 large cucumbers, peeled and sliced
1 medium onion, sliced
1 teaspoon salt

Dressing

1 cup cream
2 tablespoons vinegar
1/4 cup granulated sugar

Place the cucumbers in a bowl with the onion and sprinkle with the salt. Let stand an hour, then drain. Prepare the dressing by mixing the cream, vinegar, and sugar and add to the cucumbers when ready to serve.

Serves: 6 to 8

Deborah Troyer
Millersburg, Ohio

HOT GERMAN POTATO SALAD

"Very delicious! Plan on serving this dish to your family and guests often."

6 medium potatoes
6 slices bacon
3/4 cup chopped onion

Dressing

2 tablespoons all-purpose flour
1 1/2 tablespoons sugar
1 1/2 teaspoons salt
1/2 teaspoon celery seed
Pinch of pepper
3/4 cup water
1/3 cup vinegar

Boil potatoes in their jackets, then peel and dice or slice. Fry the bacon in a skillet, drain on paper, and set aside. Sauté the onion in the bacon fat until golden brown. Blend in flour, sugar, salt, and celery seed and a dash of pepper. Cook over low heat, stirring, until smooth and bubbly, then remove from heat and stir in the water and vinegar. Return to the heat and bring to a boil, stirring constantly. Boil for 1 minute, then carefully stir in the potatoes and crumbled bits of bacon. Remove from the heat, cover, and let stand until ready to serve.

Serves: 6 to 8

Martha Wengert
Brookville, Ohio

AMISH POTATO SALAD

A combination potato-macaroni salad, brightly colored and tossed in a traditional Amish dressing.

1/4 cup cooked macaroni
2 hard-boiled eggs, chopped
1/4 cup chopped celery
2 cups diced potatoes, cooked in salted water and drained
1 1/2 tablespoons chopped onion
2 teaspoons finely chopped green pepper
1 teaspoon finely chopped pimento

Dressing

1 egg yolk
1 tablespoon all-purpose flour
1/2 teaspoon salt
1/4 cup granulated sugar
1/2 cup water
1 tablespoon vinegar
1/2 teaspoon dry mustard

Place the macaroni, chopped hard-boiled eggs, celery, potatoes, onion, green pepper, and pimento in a large bowl. In a saucepan, combine the egg yolk, flour, salt, sugar, and water and cook, until smooth and thickened, then cool and add the vinegar and mustard. Mix well, pour over the potato-macaroni mixture, and serve.

Serves: 4

Lydia Ann Miller
Fredericksburg, Ohio

WORLD'S BEST POTATO SALAD

A simple, tasty potato salad.

6 medium potatoes
2 hard-boiled eggs
1 medium-sized onion, finely chopped
1 tablespoon salt
1/2 cup bottled French dressing
1/2 cup sour cream
1/2 cup mayonnaise
Paprika

Cook the potatoes until just tender enough to remove the skins (15 to 20 minutes), then cut into 1/2-inch cubes while still warm. Force the eggs through a sieve with a spoon. Combine the potatoes, onion, eggs, salt, and French dressing in a shallow pan. Refrigerate and allow to marinate for 3 to 4 hours.

Just before serving, combine the sour cream and mayonnaise. Gently mix with the potatoes, garnish with paprika, and serve.

Serves: 4

Mrs. John Mast

DRESSINGS

CASCADE DRESSING

A mayonnaise-type dressing with zing.

1/4 cup granulated sugar
1 teaspoon celery seed
1 tablespoon salt
1 teaspoon dry mustard
1/4 teaspoon garlic salt
1/4 cup catsup
1/4 cup vinegar
1 cup vegetable oil

Combine the sugar, celery seed, salt, mustard, garlic salt, and catsup, then add the vinegar and mix until thoroughly blended. Slowly add the oil, beating constantly with an electric beater. Chill before serving.

Makes: About 2 cups

Mrs. Elmer Hershberger
New Paris, Indiana

SWEET FRENCH DRESSING

Red in color and zippy tasting on salads—particularly tossed or potato.

1 cup granulated sugar
1 cup salad oil
1/2 cup vinegar
1/4 cup fresh lemon juice
3/4 cup catsup
1 tablespoon salt
1 teaspoon paprika
3 tablespoons grated onion
1 teaspoon celery seed

Combine all the ingredients, mix well, and store in the refrigerator (where the dressing will keep well) until needed.

Makes: About 4 cups

Mrs. Ervin Schrock

OIL AND VINEGAR DRESSING

A basic dressing for all kinds of salads.

1/3 cup vinegar
1/2 cup granulated sugar
1 teaspoon salt
1 teaspoon dry mustard
Pinch of celery seed
Pinch of celery salt
1 cup salad oil
1 onion, chopped

Combine all the ingredients and mix well.

Makes: About 1 1/2 cups *Mrs. Mose Kaufman*

BETTY'S SALAD DRESSING

One of the finest recipes of one of Ohio's most famous Amish cooks. Try it on spinach or fruit salads.

1 cup sweet cream
1/2 cup brown sugar
1/4 cup vinegar
1/2 cup granulated sugar
Salt to taste

Beat the cream until slightly thickened, then add the remaining ingredients and mix well. Refrigerate overnight to thicken.

Makes: About 2 cups *Betty Miller*
Millersburg, Ohio

Breads and Dumplings

Amish bread products are truly the staff of life. There are many different Amish breads, including quick and yeast breads, dumplings, pancakes, cereals, doughnuts, and pretzels. Breakfast is a major meal for farm people. A morning meal of Amish-made grapenuts and other fiber cereals, in combination with crisp toast and butter, is a great way to start the day.

QUICK BREADS

BISCUIT MIX

"Excellent to have on hand. Quick and easy to make. I would advise keeping it in the refrigerator."

8 cups all-purpose flour
2 2/3 tablespoons granulated sugar
6 tablespoons baking powder
2 teaspoons salt
1 3/4 cup lard

Sift together, three times, the flour, sugar, baking powder, and salt. Add the lard by cutting it in until the mixture resembles fine crumbs. Pack loosely in an airtight container.

To reconstitute, combine 1 cup mix and 1/3 cup milk into a soft dough. Roll or pat out on a floured board, cut into rounds, and bake at 450 degrees for 10 to 12 minutes.

1 cup mix makes: 8 large muffins

Mrs. E. D. Stutzman
Apple Creek, Ohio

BAKING POWDER BISCUITS

You can use whole milk, and instead of baking in an oven put in a large skillet with butter; cook over medium heat, stirring once. Serve with molasses, syrup, honey, or jelly; years ago the Amish used to take these to school for lunch.

2 cups all-purpose flour
4 teaspoons baking powder
1/2 teaspoon salt
2 tablespoons granulated sugar
1/2 teaspoon cream of tartar
1/2 cup shortening
2/3 cup milk
1 egg

Sift together the flour, baking powder, salt, sugar, and cream of tartar into a bowl, then add the shortening and cut it in until the mixture has the consistency of corn meal. Pour the milk in slowly, add the egg, and stir to a stiff dough. Knead briefly. Roll to a 1/2-inch thickness, cut with a round 1 1/2-inch cutter, and bake on an ungreased aluminum cookie sheet for 10 to 15 minutes at 450 degrees.

Makes: 15 biscuits

Mary Helen Miller
Baltic, Ohio

PUMPKIN MUFFINS

Light and tasty—easy to make.

3 cups all-purpose flour
3 teaspoons baking powder
1 1/2 teaspoons grated nutmeg
1 1/2 teaspoons ground cinnamon
3/4 teaspoon salt
3/4 cup butter
1 1/2 cups plus 3 tablespoons granulated sugar
3 eggs
1 1/2 cups milk
1 1/2 cups canned pumpkin
1 1/2 cups raisins

Sift the dry ingredients together. In a separate bowl, cream the butter and 1 1/2 cups sugar well, then add the eggs, milk, and pumpkin.

Stir in the dry ingredients briefly (only 10 to 20 seconds); do not worry about lumps. Fold in the raisins.

Place the batter in greased muffin tins and bake at 375 degrees for about 25 minutes, sprinkling the 3 tablespoons of sugar on the muffins before baking.

Makes: 4 dozen small muffins

Mrs. Laura Swartzentruber
Virginia Beach, Virginia

CORNMEAL MUFFINS

These have a flavor of corn and bacon—nice.

1 cup cornmeal
1 cup sifted all-purpose flour
1 cup granulated sugar
1/2 cup shortening
1 teaspoon salt
1 teaspoon baking soda
1/2 teaspoon baking powder
1 egg, beaten
1 cup sour milk
2 strips of bacon, fried, drained, and crumbled

Combine the cornmeal and flour; cut in the shortening. Add the salt, soda, and baking powder, then the egg, sour milk, and crumbled bacon. Put the batter in muffin pans or an 8 x 12-inch pan. Bake at 350 degrees for 30 minutes.

Makes: 8 muffins

Mrs. Doris Rohrer
Wilmot, Ohio

CORN BREAD

"Real old-fashioned texture and taste."

1/4 cup lard
1/3 cup granulated sugar
1 egg
1/2 cup milk
1 cup all-purpose flour
1/4 cup cornmeal
1 tablespoon baking powder

Combine the lard and sugar, then add the egg and milk. Blend well. To this mixture add the flour, corn meal, and baking powder. Place in a greased 8-inch-square pan and bake at 250 degrees for 20 minutes, or until it is nice and brown.

Serves: 4

Mrs. J. Stutzman
Blountstown, Florida

SOUR-CREAM CORN BREAD (AN OLD RECIPE)

"Adding the sour cream gives it a great taste, plus the moisture that fine corn bread needs."

1 cup all-purpose flour
3/4 cup cornmeal
1 teaspoon baking soda
1 teaspoon cream of tartar
1 teaspoon salt
2 1/2 tablespoons granulated sugar
1 egg, well beaten
2 tablespoons melted butter
1 cup thick sour cream
1/4 cup milk

Sift together the flour and corn meal; add the soda, cream of tartar, salt, and sugar and sift again. Add the beaten egg, butter, sour cream, and milk and beat thoroughly. Pour into a greased 9-inch-square pan and bake at 425 degrees for 20 minutes.

Makes: 20 small servings

Mrs. Andy Yoder
Apple Creek, Ohio

BANANA NUT BREAD

A sweeter, more breadlike banana bread.

1 1/2 sticks butter
1 1/2 cups granulated sugar
2 eggs, beaten
3 cups all-purpose flour
2 teaspoons baking powder
1/2 teaspoon salt
1/2 teaspoon baking soda
1/4 cup milk
3/4 cup mashed bananas
1 cup chopped nuts

Cream the butter and sugar, then add the eggs. In a separate bowl, sift the flour, baking powder, salt, and soda. Add the milk and flour mixture alternately to the creamed mixture, beginning and ending with the dry ingredients, then fold in the mashed bananas and nuts to the mixture. Divide the batter in half, place in greased loaf pans, and bake at 350 degrees for 40 to 45 minutes.

Makes: 2 loaves

Sarah Jane Yoder
Middlefield, Ohio

DATE NUT LOAF

"A richer quick bread with more fruit than bread in the batter."

1 cup sifted all-purpose flour
2 teaspoons baking powder
1 pound dates, chopped
1 pound nuts, chopped
1 cup granulated sugar
1 teaspoon vanilla extract
4 eggs, separated

Sift together the flour and baking powder, then add the chopped nuts and dates to the mixture. Beat together the sugar and egg yolks, add the flour-date-nut mixture, and stir until well blended, then fold in the egg whites, stiffly beaten, and the vanilla. Pour into a greased 4 x 9 x 4-inch loaf pan and bake at 300 degrees for 1½ hours.

Serves: 10

Mrs. Jacob S. Byler
New Wilmington, Pennsylvania

PUMPKIN BREAD

"This is also good with raisins or dates and some nuts. Very moist." And it freezes well.

½ cup shortening
1½ cups granulated sugar
½ cup water
2 eggs
1 cup canned pumpkin
1⅔ cups all-purpose flour
¾ teaspoon salt
½ teaspoon grated nutmeg
½ teaspoon ground cloves
½ teaspoon baking powder
1 teaspoon baking soda
1½ teaspoons ground cinnamon

Cream the shortening and sugar, then stir in the water, eggs, and pumpkin. Sift together the dry ingredients; add to the pumpkin mixture. Pour into two 8 x 4 x 2-inch loaf pans and bake at 350 degrees for 45 to 60 minutes. When cool, serve with cream cheese or whipped cream.

Makes: 2 loaves

Mrs. M. R. Miller
Virginia Beach, Virginia

BROWN RAISIN BREAD

Full-bodied, similar to banana bread.

2 cups all-purpose flour
2 teaspoons baking soda
1/2 teaspoon salt
2 tablespoons dark molasses
2 cups buttermilk
1 cup granulated sugar
2 cups bran cereal
1 cup raisins

Sift together the flour, soda, and salt. Add the dark molasses and buttermilk and mix well, then add the sugar, bran cereal, and raisins. Pour into one large loaf pan or two small loaf pans and bake at 400 degrees for 30–45 minutes until very brown and the bread starts pulling away from the sides of the pan.

Makes: 1 large or 2 small loaves

Esther Shetter
Middlefield, Ohio

SOUR CREAM COFFEE CAKE

"You can use more nuts and a bit more sugar in the topping if you want. And you can also dribble this with a powdered-sugar glaze."

1/4 pound butter
1 cup granulated sugar
2 eggs
2 cups sifted all-purpose flour
1 teaspoon baking powder
1/2 teaspoon salt
1 teaspoon baking soda
1/2 pint sour cream
1 teaspoon vanilla extract

Topping

1/3 cup chopped nuts
1 teaspoon ground cinnamon
1/3 cup brown sugar

Cream the butter with the sugar, then beat in the eggs. Sift together the dry ingredients, then add, alternately with the sour cream and vanilla, to the creamed mixture. Put half the batter in a greased 10-inch tube pan and sprinkle with half the topping ingredients. Add the remaining batter and sprinkle on the rest of the topping. Bake at 350 degrees for 45 minutes.

Serves: 8 — *Katie E. Byler, Fredericksburg, Ohio*

PLAIN COFFEE CAKE

A simple, easy-to-make, good-tasting breakfast cake.

- **1 cup brown sugar**
- **1/2 cup granulated sugar**
- **1 teaspoon vanilla extract**
- **2 cups sifted all-purpose flour**
- **1/4 pound margarine**
- **1 egg**
- **1 cup buttermilk**
- **2 Heath bars**

Combine the sugars and vanilla with the flour, then cut in the margarine. Setting aside 1/2 cup of the mixture for the topping, combine the remainder with the egg and buttermilk. Crush the Heath bars and mix into the reserved 1/2 cup of crumbs. Pat the batter into a greased 9-inch-square pan. Spread the topping over, and bake at 350 degrees for 30 minutes.

Serves: 6 to 8 — *Anna Stoltzfus*

APPLE CAKES

Small, round, deep-fried doughnuts.

- **4 cups sifted all-purpose flour**
- **1/4 teaspoon salt**
- **2 teaspoons baking powder**
- **3 eggs, beaten**
- **3/4 cup milk**
- **10 to 12 apples, peeled and sliced**
- **Fat for deep frying**

Sift together the flour, salt, and baking powder. Combine with the eggs and milk, then fold in the apples. Drop the batter, which should have the consistency of pancake batter, by small spoonfuls into hot deep fat and fry until golden brown. Serve with maple syrup.

Makes: About 36 cakes — *Mrs. Eli J. D. Miller*

AMISH DOUGHNUTS

These favorites are made with mashed potatoes.

1 cup hot mashed potatoes
1 cup granulated sugar
1 tablespoon butter
2 medium-sized eggs
1/4 teaspoon vanilla extract
1/2 cup milk
3 1/2 cups sifted all-purpose flour
1 tablespoon baking powder
Fat for deep frying
Confectioners' sugar

Combine the hot potatoes with the granulated sugar and butter and then let cool. When cool, add the eggs, vanilla, milk, flour, and baking powder. Divide the dough into four parts and roll out, one part at a time, to a thickness of no thinner than about 1/4 inch. Cut with a doughnut cutter. Fry the doughnuts, four to six at a time, in medium-hot deep fat about 1 minute on each side, turning once, or till light brown. Sprinkle confectioners' sugar on the doughnuts while they are still warm.

Makes: About 30 doughnuts

Mrs. Jacob S. Byler
New Wilmington, Pennsylvania

CEREALS

GRAPENUTS

Made by all Amish families, this is very much in favor with health-food followers. To be eaten as a cereal.

3 cups whole-wheat flour
2 teaspoons baking soda
1 cup brown sugar or syrup
1 teaspoon salt
Sour milk or buttermilk

Combine all the ingredients, using just enough milk to bind the other ingredients together, and put into a cake pan. Bake at 300 degrees until golden brown, then crumble and dry.

Serves: 6 to 8

Mrs. John Yoder

FRIED CORNMEAL MUSH

Standard Depression dish, typical Amish breakfast fare.

1 cup cornmeal
Salt
3 cups boiling water

Moisten the cornmeal with enough cold water to make a paste. Stir the paste into the boiling salted water, beating thoroughly. Stir until thickened, then cook at a low heat for 10 to 15 minutes. Pour into a narrow baking pan and let stand until cold and solid. Cut in thick slices and fry on both sides in a hot, well-buttered skillet until nicely browned.

Serves: 3 to 4

Mrs. David Kline
Fredericksburg, Ohio

CORN PONE

A traditional favorite.

1 cup cornmeal
1½ teaspoons baking powder
½ teaspoon salt
¼ cup all-purpose flour
2 eggs
4 tablespoons granulated sugar
½ cup milk
¼ cup melted shortening

Sift together the dry ingredients. In a separate bowl, beat the eggs and stir in the sugar. Add the milk and stir the mixture into the dry ingredients; add the melted shortening. Bake in a well-greased 9 x 12-inch pan for 25 minutes at 425 degrees.

Serves: 8

Mrs. Jonas Troyer

PANCAKES

RAISED BUCKWHEAT CAKES

The batter for these unusual-flavored buckwheat cakes can be used for several days.

1 package active dry yeast
2 cups warm water
1 teaspoon granulated sugar
1 teaspoon salt
4 cups buckwheat flour

Dissolve the yeast in the warm water, along with the sugar and salt, allowing it to stand for 5 minutes. Combine the buckwheat flour with the yeast mixture; the batter should be as thick as cake batter. If the batter is made at night for use in the morning, keep it in a warm place overnight. The batter may thicken by standing and may require a little water; if it's too thin, add more flour. To keep over, stand in a cool place and add more flour and water. After the second day add a pinch of soda to the batter.

To bake the cakes, drop by spoonfuls onto a hot griddle and cook until brown on both sides.

Makes: 8 servings

Mrs. Dan Schwasty
Geneva, Indiana

POTATO PANCAKES

There is a little different texture and flavor to these pancakes.

1 cup packaged pancake mix
1 teaspoon salt
1 cup milk
2 eggs, beaten
2 cups grated raw potatoes
1 teaspoon grated onion
2 tablespoons melted butter

Combine the pancake mix with the salt, then add the milk and beaten eggs. Stir lightly and fold in the remaining ingredients. Pour 1/4 cup of batter for each pancake onto a hot, lightly greased griddle. Bake to a golden brown, turning only once. Serve with hot applesauce.

Serves: 4

Mrs. Albert Schie
Millersburg, Ohio

HELEN'S BLUEBERRY PANCAKES

"Rich, but quite light and excellent tasting."

2 eggs, separated
1/4 cup melted margarine
1 cup buttermilk
3/4 cup sifted all-purpose flour
1/2 teaspoon salt
1/2 teaspoon baking soda
1/2 cup fresh blueberries

Beat the egg yolks, then add the margarine, buttermilk, flour, salt, and soda. Mix well. Fold in the egg whites, stiffly beaten, and the blueberries. Drop by spoonfuls onto a lightly greased griddle and cook until brown on both sides.

Makes: 14 to 16 pancakes *Helen Phillips*

MELTAWAY PANCAKES

"These are very light, and do not leave you with a heavy feeling when eaten."

3 eggs, separated
1/2 cup sour cream
1/4 cup sifted all-purpose flour
1/4 teaspoon salt
1 tablespoon granulated sugar

Beat the egg yolks well and combine with the sour cream. Sift the dry ingredients together, then stir into the egg-yolk mixture. Beat the egg whites until stiff and fold in. Drop the batter by large spoonfuls onto a hot griddle until the top is bubbly, then turn and brown on the other side.

Makes: 10 pancakes *Mrs. W. L. Row*

LIGHT PANCAKES

Light and tender, with a good flavor, and just a little different from regular pancakes.

1 cup sifted all-purpose flour
1 teaspoon baking soda
3 tablespoons granulated sugar
3/4 teaspoon salt
1 egg
2 tablespoons vinegar
1 cup milk
2 tablespoons melted shortening

Sift together the dry ingredients. In a separate bowl, combine the egg, vinegar, and milk. Mix well and add to the dry ingredients. Add the melted shortening and beat until smooth, then drop by spoonfuls on a hot griddle and cook till both sides are brown. Serve with maple syrup.

Makes: 10 pancakes

Mrs. David Kline
Fredericksburg, Ohio

YEAST BREADS

WHOLE-WHEAT BREAD

A natural yeast bread with a distinctive flavor.

2 packages active dry yeast
1 teaspoon granulated sugar
2 cups lukewarm water
2 cups milk, scalded and cooled to lukewarm
1 2/3 tablespoons salt
1/4 cup honey
2 tablespoons corn oil
2 1/2 cups whole-wheat flour
7 cups all-purpose flour, approximately

Dissolve the yeast with the sugar in 1 cup of the lukewarm water and let stand for 5 or 10 minutes. Pour the milk and remaining water over the salt, honey, and oil. Add the softened yeast, the whole-wheat flour, and enough white flour to make a soft dough. Let the dough rest for 10 minutes, then add the remaining flour. Knead on a floured board until smooth and satiny (about 10 minutes), then place in a greased bowl, cover, and let rise for 1 hour in a warm place.

Punch the dough down and form into three loaves. Place in three 9 x 5 x 3 loaf pans and let rise, covered, in a warm place till doubled in bulk. Bake at 350 degrees for 35 to 40 minutes, brushing with butter both before and after baking; this makes for a more tender crust.

Makes: 3 loaves

Mrs. Amos Yoder
Mount Hope, Ohio

CREOLE CASSEROLE BREAD

An unusual-shaped loaf with a molasses flavor.

1 cup milk
1 tablespoon brown sugar
2 tablespoons dark molasses
1 teaspoon salt
2 tablespoons butter
2 packages active dry yeast
1 cup lukewarm water
1 teaspoon ground cinnamon
1/2 teaspoon grated nutmeg
4 1/2 cups all-purpose flour

Scald the milk, stir in the sugar, molasses, salt, and butter and cool to lukewarm. Dissolve the yeast in the lukewarm water and add to the milk mixture. Add the cinnamon and nutmeg to 1 cup of the flour and sift into the milk mixture. Add the rest of the flour and beat well until a soft, smooth dough is formed. Cover and let rise in a warm place until more then doubled in bulk (about 1 hour).

Stir the batter down and beat vigorously for about 30 seconds, then turn into a well-greased 2-quart casserole and put in the oven at once; do not let it rise again. Bake at 375 degrees for about 1 hour. Grease the top of the loaf after you take it out of the casserole, and be sure it has cooled completely before slicing.

Makes: 1 loaf

Mrs. John Burkholder
Greencastle, Pennsylvania

RICH DINNER ROLLS

"A very easy recipe to make, also very quick."

1/2 cup milk
2 tablespoons granulated sugar
1 teaspoon salt
2 tablespoons vegetable oil
1/4 cup warm water (105 to 115 degrees)
1 package active dry yeast
1 egg
2 3/4 cups flour

Scald the milk, then stir in the sugar, salt, and oil and cool to lukewarm. Measure the warm water into a large bowl and sprinkle in the yeast; stir until dissolved. Add the lukewarm milk mixture, egg, and 1 cup of the flour and beat until smooth.

Stir in the remaining flour to make a soft dough, then turn out onto a lightly floured board and knead until smooth and elastic (about 8 to 10 minutes). Place in a greased bowl, turning to grease the top. Cover and let rise in a warm, draft-free place until doubled in bulk (about 30 minutes). Punch down, form into rolls, place on greased cookie sheets or in greased muffin tins, and let rise again till doubled in bulk. Bake in a 350-degree oven for about 15 to 20 minutes.

Makes: 18 rolls

Mrs. S. Gingerich
Mount Penny, Ohio

POTATO ROLLS

"A good and simple recipe. You can use it often."

2 packages active dry yeast
1/2 cup lukewarm water
1 cup milk
1/4 pound plus 2 2/3 tablespoons butter
1/2 cup granulated sugar
1 1/2 teaspoons salt
2 large potatoes, boiled and mashed
5 1/2 cups sifted all-purpose flour
2 eggs beaten
Melted butter

Dissolve the yeast in the lukewarm water. Scald the milk and add the butter, sugar, and salt. Stir until sugar is dissolved, then add the mashed potatoes and mix well. Cool to lukewarm. Add the yeast mixture and half of the flour and mix well. Beat in the eggs, add the remaining flour, and mix thoroughly. Knead the dough on a lightly floured board for 10 minutes, or until smooth and elastic. Place in a greased bowl turning to grease the surface. Cover with a damp cloth and let rise till doubled in bulk.

Punch the dough down and divide into 60 pieces. Form into rolls, place in greased muffin pans, and let rise in a warm place for 30 minutes. Brush the rolls with melted butter and bake in a 375-degree oven for 20 minutes.

Makes: 60 rolls

Mrs. V. Burkholder
Greencastle, Pennsylvania

MRS. MILLER'S SWEET ROLLS

"Put a simple powdered sugar and milk frosting on for added sweetness. Delicious."

1 package active dry yeast
1/2 cup lukewarm water
1 cup mashed potatoes
2/3 cup shortening
7 cups all-purpose flour
1/2 cup granulated sugar
2 eggs
1 teaspoon salt
1 cup warm milk

Filling

2 tablespoons melted butter
2 tablespoons brown sugar
1 1/2 teaspoons cinnamon

Dissolve the yeast in the lukewarm water, then add the mashed potatoes, shortening, and flour. Add the sugar, eggs, salt, and warm milk and knead till well blended. Place in a greased bowl and let rise till doubled in bulk (about 1 1/2 hours). Roll out till 1/2 inch thick, then brush with the butter and sprinkle with the brown sugar and cinnamon. Roll up like a jelly roll and cut into 1/2-inch slices. Place the slices, cut sides down, on greased baking sheets and let rise until doubled in bulk, then bake in a 400-degree oven for 15 minutes.

Yields: 5 dozen *Mrs. Roman H. Miller*

PLUCKETS

"You can underbake a second pan and freeze for future use. The crustiness as well as the flavor makes these a favorite." These are also called "pull buns."

1/3 cup sugar
1/3 cup melted butter
1/2 teaspoon salt
1 cup milk, scalded
1 package active dry yeast dissolved in 1/4 cup lukewarm water
3 eggs, well beaten
3 3/4 cups all-purpose flour
Melted butter
1 1/2 cups granulated sugar
1 cup ground nuts
4 to 5 teaspoons ground cinnamon

Add the sugar, butter, and salt to the scalded milk and let cool to lukewarm, then add the yeast, eggs, and just enough flour to make a stiff dough. Cover and let rise until the mixture doubles in bulk, then punch down and let rise again until doubled in bulk. Roll the dough into small balls about the size of walnuts and dip in melted butter, then roll each ball in the granulated sugar, ground nuts, and cinnamon. Pile the balls loosely in an ungreased angel cake pan and let rise again for about 30 minutes.

Bake at 400 degrees for 10 minutes, then lower the heat to 350 degrees and continue baking for another 30 minutes, or until the buns are browned. Turn the pan upside down, remove the buns immediately, and serve warm. "The buns will be stuck together, and that's the way you serve them. Everyone plucks or pulls his bun right from the central supply."

Makes: 24 buns

Mrs. Amanda Hershberger
Apple Creek, Ohio

DOUBLE BUTTERSCOTCH CRESCENTS

Sweet rolls with a coconut-sugar filling, slightly "butterscotchy."

1 small package butterscotch pudding
1½ cups milk
¼ pound butter
2 packages active dry yeast
½ cup warm water
2 eggs
2 teaspoons salt
5 to 5½ cups all-purpose flour
1 tablespoon melted butter
⅔ cup brown sugar
⅔ cup shredded coconut
⅓ chopped nuts

Prepare the pudding according to package directions, using the milk. When finished cooking, remove the pudding from the heat and stir in the butter. Cool to lukewarm, stirring once or twice.

Dissolve the yeast in the warm water, then stir into the cooled pudding. Beat in the eggs and salt and gradually add just enough flour to make a moderately soft dough. Turn out onto a floured surface and knead for 5 to 10 minutes, until the dough is soft and elastic. Place in a greased bowl and let rise for 10 minutes. Meanwhile, stir together the butter, brown sugar, coconut, and nuts.

Divide the dough into four parts and roll each piece out separately. Spread each with one-quarter of the brown-sugar mixture and cut into twelve triangles. Form crescents by rolling at the outside edge to the center. Curve in the ends and place, point down, on greased baking sheets. Let rise until almost doubled in bulk (about

45 minutes), then bake in a 375-degree oven for 12 to 15 minutes. Cool on a wire rack.

Makes: 4 dozen rolls *Mrs. Elmer Lehman*

RAISED DOUGHNUTS

These are very similar—but far superior—to commercial glazed doughnuts.

2 packages active dry yeast
1 cup lukewarm water
1 cup milk
2/3 cup granulated sugar
1 1/2 teaspoons salt
1/4 pound butter
2 eggs, well-beaten
1/8 teaspoon grated nutmeg
4 1/2 to 5 cups all-purpose flour
Fat for deep frying

Glaze

1 three-ounce package unflavored gelatin
1/4 cup cold water
1 1/2 pounds confectioners' sugar
1 tablespoon melted butter
1 teaspoon vanilla extract
1/2 cup boiling water

Dissolve the yeast in the lukewarm water, stir, and let stand for 5 minutes. Scald the milk and cool until lukewarm. Cream together the sugar, salt, and butter, then add the eggs and nutmeg. Add the lukewarm milk to the softened yeast, then blend this liquid with 3 cups of the flour and beat until smooth. Add the butter mixture and enough flour to make a medium-soft dough. Knead until smooth, but keep as soft as possible without sticking.

Place the dough in a greased bowl, cover, and let rise in a warm place until doubled in bulk. Punch down and roll out into a sheet 3/4 inch thick. Cut with a doughnut cutter, place on a board, and let rise until doubled in bulk. Fry the doughnuts in deep fat at about 375 degrees until brown on both sides.

To make the glaze, soften the gelatin in the cold water, then combine with the sugar, butter, and vanilla. Dissolve the mixture in the boiling water and dip the doughnuts in the glaze immediately, while still hot.

Makes: About 4 dozen *Mrs. Leroy R. Troyer*

PRETZELS

A delicious and unconventional pretzel.

1 package active dry yeast
1/2 cup lukewarm water
1 cup milk
1/4 pound butter
1 1/2 teaspoons sugar
1/2 teaspoon salt
1 egg, separated
3 3/4 cups all-purpose flour
Coarse salt

Dissolve the yeast in the lukewarm water. Scald the milk, then add the butter, sugar, and salt and cool to lukewarm. Stir in the yeast and the egg white, beaten. Stir in the flour gradually, adding enough to make a soft dough. Knead the dough on a floured board for 3 to 4 minutes, then cover and let rise in a warm place until doubled in bulk.

Punch the dough down and roll out on a floured board to a thickness of about 1/2 inch. Cut into strips, shape into pretzels, and let stand on the board until they begin to rise.

Fill in a shallow pan half full of water. Heat the pan, and when the water is very hot but not boiling, drop the pretzels in, one at a time. Cook them, under the boiling point, on one side, then turn and cook on the other side. Drain, brush with beaten egg yolk, and sprinkle with coarse salt. Bake on a buttered baking sheet in a 400-degree oven for 15 minutes.

Makes: About 36 pretzels *Naomi Brenneman*

DUMPLINGS

APPLE DUMPLINGS

A typical Amish recipe, simplified but tasty.

6 apples

Dough

2 cups sifted all-purpose flour
1/2 teaspoon salt
2 1/2 teaspoons baking powder
2/3 cup shortening
1/2 cup milk

Syrup

2 cups brown sugar
4 tablespoons butter
2 cups water
1/2 teaspoon ground cinnamon

Peel and halve the apples and set aside. Sift together the flour, salt, and baking powder and cut in the shortening. Mix in the milk, then divide the dough in half. Roll each half out and cut it into squares. Place one apple half on each square, wet the edge of the dough, and press into a ball around the apple. Set the apples in a baking pan.

Prepare the syrup by combining the sugar, butter, water, and cinnamon. Pour over the apples and bake at 375 degrees for about 35 minutes.

Serves: 12

Mrs. Moses E. Miller
Conewango Valley, New York

RASPBERRY DUMPLINGS

A fine dessert dumpling.

2 cups whole raspberries or juice
2 cups water
1 cup plus 1 tablespoon granulated sugar
1/2 cup sifted all-purpose flour
1 2/3 tablespoons baking powder
Pinch of salt
2/3 cup milk
3 tablespoons cornstarch

Combine the raspberries, water, and sugar in a saucepan and bring to a boil. Meanwhile, combine the flour, baking powder, sugar, salt, and milk into a smooth dough. Mix the cornstarch with enough water to make a smooth paste and stir into the hot raspberry mixture; return to a boil. Drop the dough by spoonfuls into the boiling raspberry mixture, cover with a tight lid, and let cook slowly for 20 minutes. Do not uncover during the boiling period. Serve hot, with milk.

Serves: 4

Mrs. Lewis Knepp
Montgomery, Indiana

BROWN SUGAR DUMPLINGS

Dessert dumplings with nuts and raisins cooked in a thick syrup.

1/4 pound plus 2 tablespoons butter
1 cup granulated sugar
2/3 cup milk
2 teaspoons baking powder
2 cups sifted all-purpose flour
1 cup chopped nuts
1 cup raisins
2 cups brown sugar
2 cups boiling water

Cream the 2 tablespoons butter and the granulated sugar. Add the milk, baking powder, and flour, then stir in the chopped nuts and raisins. In a saucepan, combine the brown sugar, 1/4 pound butter, and boiling water and bring to a boil. Drop the dumplings in the boiling syrup, then place in a greased baking dish and bake at 350 degrees for 20 minutes.

Serves: 5 to 6

Eli Burkholder
Saint James, Missouri

CARAMEL DUMPLINGS

"For even more flavor when it is served, the ingredients for the sauce should be increased by one half."

Syrup

2 tablespoons shortening
1½ cups brown sugar
1½ cups boiling water
¼ teaspoon salt

Dough

1¼ cup sifted all-purpose flour
1½ teaspoons baking powder
⅓ cup granulated sugar
¼ teaspoon salt
2 tablespoons shortening
⅓ cup milk
½ teaspoon vanilla extract

Place the ingredients for the syrup in a saucepan and cook for 5 minutes while mixing the dough.

Sift the dry ingredients together, then cut in the shortening. Add the milk and vanilla. Divide the dough into 25 pieces, roll into balls, and drop in the syrup. Cover tightly and simmer over low heat for 20 minutes without removing the lid. Serve plain or with whipped cream.

Makes: 25 dumplings

L. Miller
Baltic, Ohio

DAMPH KNEPP

The famous Amish yeast dumpling, often served—as here—in a caramel sauce.

1 package active dry yeast
1 cup warm water
1 egg
3 tablespoons granulated sugar
1 tablespoon salt
2 cups sifted all-purpose flour
1 tablespoon melted shortening

Syrup

2 cups brown sugar
3 cups water
1 tablespoon granulated sugar

Dissolve the yeast in the warm water. Beat the egg and add the sugar and salt, then combine with the yeast mixture. Add flour and melted shortening and work into a smooth dough. Turn out on a floured board and knead for several minutes, then place in a greased bowl, cover, and let rise until doubled in bulk. Divide the dough into six round, smooth balls, cover, and let rise until light.

To make the syrup, cook the brown sugar, water, and butter together for 5 minutes. Place the dough balls in syrup and cook slowly on top of the stove for 30 minutes, making sure the pot is covered. Serve with milk.

Serves: 6 *Mrs. Yost N. Hochstetler*

"CAN'T FAIL" DUMPLINGS

"These dumplings can't be stored; they must be used immediately."

1 cup sifted all-purpose flour
1/2 teaspoon salt
2 teaspoons baking powder
3/4 cup milk, approximately

Sift the dry ingredients into a bowl, then add enough milk to make a soft dough. Drop by spoonfuls into hot stew and steam, covered, for 10 minutes.

Makes: 12 dumplings *Mrs. John Summy*

Sweet Things

Amish women are gifted bakers and frequently bake cakes and pies for family and friends. Several sweet things are a must for most Amish meals and special occasions bring forth a tremendous selection of rich and good-looking desserts. In this collection are most of the standard Amish goodies, from fruit-filled pastries to crumbly cookies and homemade candies. The Amish standard for sweetness is unique, best exemplified by the super rich shoofly pie.

CAKES

APPLESAUCE CAKE

"Has a nice spicy taste."

2½ cups sifted all-purpose flour
2 cups granulated sugar
½ teaspoon baking powder
1½ teaspoons baking soda
1½ cups applesauce
1½ teaspoons salt
½ cup nuts or raisins
¾ teaspoon ground cinnamon
½ teaspoon ground cloves
½ teaspoon ground allspice
½ cup shortening
2 eggs
½ cup water

Icing

½ cup plus 1 tablespoon brown sugar
2 tablespoons butter
6 tablespoons cream
1 cup confectioners' sugar

Preheat the oven to 350 degrees; grease and flour a 13 x 9 x 2-inch pan. Measure all the ingredients for the cake into a large mixing bowl and blend for 30 seconds at low speed, scraping the bowl occasionally. Then beat for 3 minutes at high speed, scraping the sides. Pour into the prepared pan and bake for 50 to 55 minutes at 350 degrees. Let cool while you prepare the icing.

Boil the brown sugar, butter, and cream for one minute. Stir until cool, then add the confectioners' sugar to thicken. Spread on the cooled cake.

Serves: 12 to 16

Mrs. Amos Knepp
Washington, Indiana

SELF-ICED APPLE CAKE

The apple flavor of this nut- and cinnamon-topped cake really comes through.

1½ cups sifted all-purpose flour
¼ teaspoon baking powder
1 cup granulated sugar
¼ teaspoon salt
1 teaspoon baking soda
1 egg
¼ cup shortening, softened
¼ cup milk
3 cups peeled, diced apples

Topping

3 tablespoons melted butter
2 teaspoons cinnamon
1 cup chopped nuts or coconut
1 cup brown sugar
1 tablespoon all-purpose flour

Sift together the flour, baking powder, sugar, salt, and soda. Combine the egg, shortening, and milk and add to the dry ingredients, then fold in the apples. Pour into a greased and floured 9-inch-square cake pan. Combine the melted butter, cinnamon, nuts, brown sugar, and flour and spread over the cake batter. Bake at 350 degrees for 30 minutes.

Serves: 8

Mrs. Wayne J. Miller
Dundee, Ohio

BANANA CAKE

The frosting accents this cake nicely.

1/2 cup shortening
2 cups brown sugar
2 eggs
3 cups sifted all-purpose flour
1 1/2 teaspoons baking soda
1 1/2 teaspoons baking powder
1 cup buttermilk or sour milk
1 banana, mashed

Icing

2 1/2 cups confectioners' sugar
2 tablespoons cold water
1/3 cup granulated sugar
1 egg white, beaten
1/2 cup vegetable shortening, softened
1 teaspoon vanilla or banana extract

Cream together the shortening and brown sugar, then beat in the eggs. Sift together the flour, soda, and baking powder and add alternately with the milk to the creamed mixture. Fold in the banana. Pour the batter into two greased and floured 8-inch-square cake tins and bake in a 350-degree oven for 35 minutes.

Meanwhile, prepare the icing. Sift the confectioners' sugar into a bowl. Combine the cold water and the granulated sugar in a saucepan and boil for 2 minutes. Stir the beaten egg white into the confectioners' sugar, then add the syrup and mix well. Stir in the vegetable shortening and flavoring.

When the cakes have cooled, on racks, spread them with the icing.

Serves: 16

Mrs. Aden A. Troyer
Orrville, Ohio

BUTTERSCOTCH BANANA CAKE

This is a delightful combination of flavors—and so easy to make.

1 three-and-three-quarter-ounce package butterscotch pudding or pie filling
1 twenty-ounce package banana cake mix
Whipped cream and nuts for garnish

Prepare the butterscotch pudding as directed on the package. Pour into a well-greased 13 x 9 x 2-inch baking dish and refrigerate until cold.

Meanwhile, prepare the banana cake mix according to package directions. When the pudding is cold, pour the banana cake mix over and bake at 350 degrees for 35 to 40 minutes, or until a cake tester comes out clean. Refrigerate until cold.

To serve, loosen all edges with a spatula and invert the cake on a plate. Garnish with whipped cream and nuts.

Serves: 12 to 16

Mrs. Roman S. Hershberger
Millersburg, Ohio

TOASTED BUTTER PECAN CAKE

The toasted pecans are what make this cake special.

2 cups chopped pecans
1½ pounds plus 4 tablespoons butter
3 cups sifted all-purpose flour
2 teaspoons baking powder
1 teaspoon salt
2 cups granulated sugar
4 eggs
1 cup milk
2 teaspoons vanilla extract

Frosting

4 tablespoons butter
4 cups confectioners' sugar
1 teaspoon vanilla extract
1⅔ tablespoons evaporated milk
⅔ cup reserved toasted pecans

Toast the pecans in the 4 tablespoons butter in a 350-degree oven for 20 to 25 minutes, stirring frequently. Meanwhile, sift together the flour, baking powder, and salt. Cream the 1/2 pound butter and gradually add the sugar, creaming well. Blend in the eggs, one at a time, beating well after each. Add the dry ingredients alternately with the milk, beginning and ending with the dry ingredients. Blend well after each addition. Stir in the vanilla and 1 1/3 cups of pecans, reserving the remainder for the icing, then pour the batter into three greased and floured 8- or 9-inch round layer pans. Bake at 350 degrees for 25 to 30 minutes, then let cool while you prepare the frosting.

Cream the butter, then blend in the confectioners' sugar, vanilla, and evaporated milk until the frosting is of spreading consistency. Stir in the reserved pecans. Spread over the tops and sides of the three cooled layers.

Serves: 12 to 16

Mrs. Laura Swartz
Virginia

CARROT CAKE

"A good company cake."

1 1/2 cups salad oil
2 cups granulated sugar
4 eggs
2 cups sifted all-purpose flour
1 teaspoon baking soda
1 teaspoon baking powder
1/4 teaspoon salt
2 teaspoons ground cinnamon
2 cups grated raw carrots
Brown sugar (optional)

Combine the salad oil and sugar and beat for 15 minutes, or until the sugar is dissolved. Add the eggs, one at a time, while continuing to beat at high speed. Sift together the flour, soda, baking powder, salt, and cinnamon and then fold in the carrots. Place in three greased and floured layer pans or one greased and floured 13 x 9 x 2-inch pan and bake in a 350-degree oven for 35 to 40 minutes.

For a quick icing, sprinkle brown sugar on top of the cake (or the layers) before the cake is done.

Serves: 12 to 16

Mrs. Aden Miller
Millersburg, Ohio

BLACK MIDNIGHT CAKE

"Has a nice cocoa flavor."

2/3 cup shortening
1 2/3 cups granulated sugar
3 eggs
2 1/4 cups sifted all-purpose flour
2/3 cup cocoa
1/4 teaspoon baking powder
1/4 teaspoon baking soda
1 teaspoon salt
1 1/3 cups water
1 teaspoon vanilla extract

Cream the shortening then add the sugar and cream well. Add the eggs, one at a time, and beat well until fluffy. Sift together the flour, cocoa, baking powder, soda, and salt. Add, alternately with the water and vanilla, to the creamed mixture. Pour the batter into a greased and floured 13 x 9 x 2-inch pan and bake in moderate oven at 375 degrees for 35 minutes.

Serves: 12 to 16

Mrs. Eli D. Stutzman
Apple Creek, Ohio

LOVELIGHT YELLOW CHIFFON CAKE

A very light and airy family cake.

3 eggs, separated
1 1/2 cups granulated sugar
2 1/4 cups sifted all-purpose flour
3 teaspoons baking powder
1 teaspoon salt
1/3 cup vegetable oil
1 cup water or milk
1 1/2 teaspoons vanilla extract
1/2 cup chopped nuts

Beat the egg whites until foamy, then gradually beat in 1/2 cup of the sugar until stiff and glossy. In another bowl, sift together the remaining sugar, flour, baking powder, and salt. Add the oil, water or milk, egg yolks, and vanilla and beat for 2 minutes with a mixer or 150 strokes by hand. Add the nuts, if desired, then fold in the meringue, and pour into a greased and floured 13 x 9 x 2-inch pan. Bake at 350 for 35 minutes.

Serves: 12 to 16

Mrs. Jonas Hershberger

GERMAN CHOCOLATE CAKE

If you use the traditional German frosting—thick and creamy, very rich—this cake will be a sensation.

1 four-ounce package sweet chocolate
1/2 cup boiling water
1/2 pound butter or shortening
2 cups granulated sugar
4 eggs, separated
1 teaspoon vanilla extract
1/4 teaspoon salt
1/2 teaspoon baking soda
2 1/2 cups sifted all-purpose flour
1 cup buttermilk

Melt the chocolate in the boiling water, then let cool. Cream the butter and sugar until light and fluffy, then add the egg yolks, one at a time, beating after each. Add the melted cooled chocolate and the vanilla and mix well. Sift together the salt, soda, and flour, then add, alternately with the buttermilk, to the creamed mixture and beat until smooth. Beat egg whites until stiff peaks form and fold into the batter. Place in three greased and floured 9-inch cake pans. Bake at 350 degrees for 30 to 40 minutes, then cool and frost as desired.

Serves: 12 to 16

Mrs. Emanuel Miller
Monroe, Indiana

NEVER-FAIL CHOCOLATE CAKE

"Quick and easy—a good dessert for carried lunches."

1 cup granulated sugar
1/2 cup cocoa
1/4 pound butter or shortening
1 egg
1/2 cup sour milk or buttermilk
Pinch of salt
1 teaspoon vanilla extract
1 teaspoon baking soda
1/2 cup hot water
1 1/2 cups sifted all-purpose flour

Put all the ingredients in a mixing bowl. Do not mix until they are all added. Then beat thoroughly. Pour into a greased 9 x 5 x 3-inch loaf pan and bake at 350 degrees for 55 to 60 minutes.

Serves: 8 to 10

Lovina J. Raber

REAL OLD-FASHIONED COCONUT CAKE

A quick-mix coconut cake with a custard filling and fluffy frosting.

Cake

2 twenty-ounce packages white cake mix
1/2 cup grated coconut
1/2 teaspoon almond extract

Filling

4 tablespoons butter
1 cup granulated sugar
2 eggs, beaten
Juice of 1 1/2 lemons
1 grated lemon rind

Frosting

2/3 cup granulated sugar
3 tablespoons light corn syrup
2 egg whites
1 teaspoon vanilla extract
Shredded coconut

Prepare the cake mix according to package directions, adding the coconut and almond extract. Bake in four greased and floured 9-inch layer pans.

To prepare the filling, melt the butter in a double boiler and mix in the sugar. Stir in the eggs, lemon juice, and rind and cook, stirring constantly, until thick (20 or 30 minutes). Chill for several hours, then use to fill the layers of the cake. Prepare the frosting by combining the sugar, syrup, and water in a saucepan. Bring to a boil and continue cooking to 244 degrees on a candy thermometer, or until the syrup spins a 6- to 8-inch thread. Beat the egg whites until stiff, then pour the syrup in a thin stream into them, beating continuously until the mixture is stiff and glossy. Add the vanilla, spread on the cake, and sprinkle the cake with shredded coconut.

Serves: 12 to 16

Mrs. Elmer Hershberger
New Paris, Indiana

CRUMB CAKE

This could be made on a Sunday morning for breakfast, topped with nuts or apples.

2 cups sifted all-purpose flour
$1^1/_2$ cups granulated sugar
$^3/_4$ cup shortening
2 teaspoons ground cinnamon
$^3/_4$ teaspoon ground cloves
$^1/_4$ teaspoon salt
1 egg, beaten
1 teaspoon baking powder
1 teaspoon baking soda
1 cup sour milk

Sift the 2 cups flour with the sugar, then blend in the shortening with the tips of your fingers to make fine crumbs. Reserve 1 cup for the top of the cake and to the remainder add the spices, salt, beaten egg, baking powder, and soda. Stir in the sour milk, mixing well. Pour into a greased, waxed-paper-lined 13 x 9 x 2-inch pan, cover with the reserved crumbs, and bake in a 350-degree oven for 45 minutes.

Serves: 12 to 16

Mrs. Joseph Binder
Catlett, Virginia

APPLE CAKE PUDDING

A typical Amish dessert cake.

1 cup granulated sugar
$^1/_3$ cup shortening
$1^1/_2$ cups sifted all-purpose flour
$^1/_4$ teaspoon baking powder
1 teaspoon ground cinnamon
1 teaspoon salt
1 cup milk
1 egg
5 apples, peeled and sliced

Topping

2 tablespoons all-purpose flour
1 cup brown sugar
1 tablespoon butter

Cream the sugar and shortening, then add the flour, baking powder, cinnamon, salt, milk, and egg. Stir well and fold in the apples. Pour the batter into a greased and floured 13 x 9 x 2-inch pan.

Combine the topping ingredients, crumble, and sprinkle on top of the cake. Bake at 350 degrees for 45 minutes. Serve warm, with milk.

Serves: 12 to 16

Mrs. Robert Detweiler

GRANDMA'S BUTTERMILK CAKE

For a treat, try fresh fruit and milk with this.

4 cups sifted all-purpose flour
2 cups granulated sugar
1/4 teaspoon salt
3/4 cup shortening
1 1/2 cups buttermilk
1 teaspoon baking soda
1 teaspoon ground cinnamon

Combine the flour, sugar, and salt in a bowl and blend in the shortening with your fingertips until the mixture resembles crumbs. Set aside 1 cup for the topping. To the rest of the crumbs add the buttermilk, soda, and cinnamon and mix well. Pour the batter into a greased and floured 13 x 9 x 2-inch pan and sprinkle the reserved cup of crumbs on top. Bake at 350 degrees for 30 minutes, or until a toothpick inserted into the cake comes out clean.

Serves: 12 to 16

Mrs. Ora Gruber
Mossley, Ontario

DATE MAYONNAISE CAKE

Total preparation time is only 20 minutes. You can frost the cake before baking. To dress it up for a very special affair, lightly sift powdered sugar through a doily over the top.

1 1/2 teaspoons baking soda
1 cup boiling water
1 cup cut-up dates
1 cup granulated sugar
2 cups sifted all-purpose flour
1/2 cup chopped nuts, more if desired
1 cup mayonnaise
1/2 cup brown sugar, packed
2 tablespoons evaporated milk

Add the soda to the boiling water and pour over the dates. Set aside. Combine the granulated sugar, flour, nuts, and mayonnaise, then add the date mixture and mix thoroughly. Place in a greased and floured 13 x 9 x 2-inch pan and cover the top with a layer of brown sugar moistened with evaporated milk. (Put nuts on top of the cake also, if desired.) Bake at 350 degrees for about 30 minutes. (If you want a darker cake, bake for 30 minutes, then turn off the heat and leave in the oven for 5 minutes more.)

Serves: 12 to 16

Mrs. Ervin Slabach

DATE-NUT CAKE

Dates and nuts are everyday delicacies for the Amish; this is a standard family cake.

1 cup hot water
$1^1/_4$ cup finely cut dates
4 tablespoons butter or vegetable shortening
1 cup granulated sugar
1 egg
1 teaspoon vanilla extract
$1^3/_4$ cup sifted all-purpose flour
1 teaspoon baking soda
$^1/_2$ teaspoon salt
$^1/_2$ cup chopped nuts

Pour the hot water over the dates; cool. Combine the butter, sugar, egg, and vanilla in a mixing bowl and beat for 5 minutes. Sift together the flour, soda, and salt, then add, alternately with the dates, in four additions, to the butter-egg mixture. Blend just until smooth, then fold in the nuts. Bake at 350 degrees in a greased and floured 13 x 9 x 2-inch pan for 30 to 35 minutes.

Serves: 12 to 16

Mrs. Levi S. Erb
Baltic, Ohio

CHOCOLATE-DATE CAKE

This frosts itself, with chocolate and nuts, while baking.

1 cup chopped dates
1 cup boiling water
$^2/_3$ cup shortening
1 cup granulated sugar
1 tablespoon vanilla extract
2 eggs
$1^3/_4$ cups sifted all-purpose flour
2 tablespoons cocoa
1 teaspoon baking soda
$^1/_2$ teaspoon salt
1 twelve-ounce package chocolate bits
1 cup chopped nuts

Chop the dates and combine with the boiling water, then cool to room temperature. Cream the shortening, then add the sugar and cream until fluffy. Blend in the vanilla and add the eggs, one at a time, beating well after each addition. Sift together the flour, cocoa, soda, and salt, then add to the creamed mixture alternately with the date mixture, beating after each addition. Spread the mixture in a greased and floured 13 x 9 x 2-inch pan and sprinkle with the chocolate bits and nuts. Bake in a moderate oven at 350 degrees for 40 to 45 minutes, or until a cake tester inserted in the cake comes out clean.

Serves: 12 *Mrs. Jacob Schlabach, Jr.*

BANANA–GRAHAM-CRACKER CAKE

Try this with a banana butter cream frosting.

1/4 cup cake flour
2 teaspoons baking powder
1/4 cup granulated sugar
1/2 teaspoon salt
2 cups graham-cracker crumbs
1/4 cup milk
1 teaspoon vanilla extract
2 eggs
3 bananas, sliced

Sift together the flour, baking powder, sugar, and salt. Add the crumbs, milk, and vanilla and stir to blend. Beat 2 minutes, then add the eggs and beat well. Pour into an 8-inch-square, waxed-paper-lined pan and bake at 350 degrees for about 40 minutes. Cool the cake in pan for 5 minutes, then cut into squares and top with the sliced bananas. Serve with whipped cream.

Serves: 9 *Mrs. John Hochstetler*

GRAHAM-CRACKER-NUT CAKE

Very easy to prepare, this cake has a nice buttercream and nut frosting.

3 eggs, separated
2 cups granulated sugar
1/4 pound butter or margarine
5 cups finely rolled graham-cracker crumbs
3 teaspoons baking powder
1 cup chopped nuts
2 cups milk
1 teaspoon vanilla extract

Icing

1 cup milk
5 tablespoons sifted all-purpose flour
1/2 pound butter
1 cup confectioners' sugar
1 teaspoon vanilla extract

Cream together the egg yolks, sugar, and butter. Combine the graham-cracker crumbs, baking powder, and chopped nuts and add, alternately with the milk and vanilla, to the creamed mixture. Beat the egg whites until stiff and fold in. Pour the batter into a greased and floured 13 x 9 x 2-inch pan and bake at 350 degrees for 30 to 40 minutes.

Meanwhile, prepare the icing. Combine the milk and flour in a saucepan. Stir until smooth, then cook over low heat until the mixture thickens, stirring constantly. Let the mixture cool completely. Cream together the butter, sugar, and vanilla, add the cooled mixture, and beat at high speed until the frosting is like whipped cream in texture.

When the cake has cooled, spread on the icing.

Serves: 12 to 16

Mrs. Kenneth McClintock
Galion, Ohio

AMISH CAKE

A yellow butter cake with an unusual icing.

1/4 pound butter or margarine
2 2/3 cups brown sugar
3 cups sifted all-purpose flour
2 teaspoons baking soda
2 cups sour milk or buttermilk
2 teaspoons vanilla extract

Topping

6 tablespoons butter or margarine
1 cup brown sugar
4 tablespoons milk
1/2 cup nuts or canned coconut

Cream together the butter and brown sugar. Sift together the flour and soda and add, alternately with the buttermilk and vanilla, to the creamed mixture. Pour the batter into a greased and floured 13 x 9 x 2-inch cake pan and bake in a 375-degree oven for 30 to 40 minutes.

Meanwhile, prepare the topping. Cream together the butter and sugar, then stir in the milk and the nuts. Spread on the cake and put the cake under the broiler until the topping bubbles.

Serves: 12 to 16

Mrs. Harlan Immel
Sugarcreek, Ohio

OATMEAL PICNIC CAKE

"One of those 'can't wait till it comes out of the oven' cakes. You'll cut it while it's still warm."

1 cup quick-cooking oats
1 1/4 cups boiling water
1/2 cup shortening
1 cup granulated sugar
1 cup brown sugar
1 teaspoon vanilla extract
2 eggs
1 1/2 cups sifted all-purpose flour
1 teaspoon cinnamon
1 teaspoon nutmeg
1 teaspoon soda
1/2 teaspoon salt

Topping

6 tablespoons butter
2/3 cup brown sugar
1 cup grated coconut
1/4 cup evaporated milk
1 teaspoon vanilla extract
1 cup chopped nuts

Gradually stir the oats into the boiling water; let stand for 20 minutes. Cream the shortening, then gradually add the sugars, creaming until light. Add the vanilla and beat in the eggs, one at a time. Sift together the dry ingredients, then add, alternately with the oatmeal, to the creamed mixture, beating after each addition. Pour into a greased 13 x 9 x 2-inch pan and bake at 350 degrees for 1 hour.

Meanwhile combine all the topping ingredients. Spread on the hot cake and place it under the broiler until slightly browned.

Serves: 14 to 18

Mrs. Silvana Yoder
Hadley, Pennsylvania

COFFEE OATMEAL CAKE

A really coffee-flavored cake topped off with a coffee buttercream icing.

2 tablespoons instant coffee
1 1/3 cups boiling water
1 cup quick-cooking oatmeal
1/4 pound butter
1 cup granulated sugar
1 cup brown sugar
2 eggs
1 1/2 cups sifted all-purpose flour
1 teaspoon baking soda
1 teaspoon salt
1/2 cup chopped nuts

Frosting

3 tablespoons butter
2 cups sifted confectioners' sugar
Pinch of salt
1 teaspoon vanilla extract
2 teaspoons reserved coffee

Combine the coffee and water. Reserving 2 teaspoons for the frosting, pour the remaining coffee over the oatmeal and stir. Cover and let stand for 20 minutes. Meanwhile, cream the butter until fluffy. Add the sugars and cream until well blended, then add the eggs and the oatmeal mixture and blend well. Sift together the flour, soda, and salt and add to the creamed mixture. Add the nuts to the batter, then pour into a greased 13 x 9 x 2-inch pan. Bake at 350 degrees for 50 to 55 minutes.

Meanwhile, prepare the frosting. Beat the butter until creamy, then add the remaining ingredients and beat until smooth and of a spreading consistency.

Cool the cake, then cover with the frosting.

Serves: 12 to 16 *Mrs. Ben A. Byler*

PINEAPPLE CAKE

A white butter cake flavored with pineapple.

1/4 pound butter
1 1/2 cups granulated sugar
2 1/2 cups sifted cake flour
1 tablespoon baking powder
Pinch of salt
1/4 cup water
1 teaspoon vanilla
1 cup crushed pineapple
3 egg whites, stiffly beaten

Cream the butter and sugar. Sift together the flour, baking powder, and salt and add, alternately with the water and vanilla, to the creamed mixture. Add the pineapple and mix well, fold in the egg whites. Pour the batter into a greased and floured 13 x 9 x 2-inch cake pan and bake at 350 degrees for 35 minutes.

Serves: 12 to 16 *Mrs. Vernon J. Miller*

PUMPKIN CAKE

This cake is quite moist, with a subtle pumpkin flavor.

1/2 cup shortening
1 cup granulated sugar
1 cup brown sugar
2 eggs, beaten
1 cup canned or cooked, mashed fresh pumpkin or winter squash
3 cups sifted cake flour
4 teaspoons baking powder
1/4 teaspoon baking soda
1/2 cup milk
1 cup chopped walnuts
1 teaspoon maple flavoring

Cream the shortening, then gradually add the sugars, eggs, and pumpkin. Sift together the flour, baking powder, and soda and add, alternately with the milk, to the pumpkin mixture. Fold in the walnuts and maple flavoring. Pour the batter into a greased and floured 13 x 9 x 2-inch cake pan and bake at 350 degrees for 45 minutes. Cool and frost with your favorite frosting.

Serves: 12 to 16 *Mrs. Bernard Mazelin*

LIGHT-AS-A-FEATHER GINGERBREAD

A spicy bread, but really very light in both taste and texture.

1/2 cup boiling water
1/2 cup shortening
1/2 cup brown sugar
1/2 cup light molasses
1 egg, beaten
1 1/2 cups sifted all-purpose flour
1/2 teaspoon salt
1/2 teaspoon baking powder
1/2 teaspoon baking soda
3/4 teaspoon ground ginger
3/4 teaspoon ground cinnamon

Pour the water over the shortening. Add the sugar, molasses, and egg and beat well. Sift together the dry ingredients and beat until smooth. Pour into a greased and floured 8-inch-square pan and bake at 350 degrees for 35 minutes. Cool before serving.

Serves: 8 *Mrs. Aden Miller*
Sugarcreek, Ohio

BUTTERSCOTCH RHUBARB UPSIDE-DOWN CAKE

The rhubarb flavor, while not pronounced, is what makes this cake so distinctive.

1 cup shortening
1 cup granulated sugar
3 eggs, separated
2 cups sifted cake flour
3 teaspoons baking powder
1/2 teaspoon salt
2/3 cup milk
1/2 teaspoon vanilla extract
1 1/2 cups brown sugar
4 cups diced rhubarb

Cream the shortening and sugar, then add the egg yolks and mix well. Sift together the dry ingredients and add, alternately with the milk and vanilla, to the creamed mixture. Mix well, then fold in the egg whites, stiffly beaten.

Grease the bottom of a 13 x 9 x 2-inch pan and sprinkle it with the brown sugar. Spread it with the rhubarb, then cover the rhubarb with the batter. Bake at 350 degrees for 45 minutes, then let stand a few minutes and invert on a large platter. Serve with whipped cream.

Serves: 12 to 16

Mrs. Tobe Yoder
Stuarts Draft, Virginia

SPICE CAKE

Use a vanilla-flavored frosting as a topping for this spicy cake.

2 cups brown sugar
1/2 cup shortening
2 eggs
2 cups sifted all-purpose flour
1 teaspoon baking soda
1 teaspoon baking powder
1/2 teaspoon salt
1/2 teaspoon ground allspice
1/4 teaspoon ground ginger
1 teaspoon ground cinnamon
1 cup buttermilk or sour milk
1 teaspoon vanilla extract

Cream together the sugar and the shortening, then add the eggs and mix well. Sift together the dry ingredients and add alternately with the buttermilk, to the creamed mixture. Mix well, then stir in the vanilla. Pour the batter into a greased and floured 9-inch-square pan and bake in a 350-degree oven for 35 minutes.

Serves: 8

Leah Lapp

BROWN SUGAR–SPICE CAKE WITH BAKED ICING

This cake has a brown-sugar meringue nut icing that's baked right on.

1 cup shortening
2 cups brown sugar
4 eggs
$2^2/_3$ cups sifted cake flour
1 teaspoon baking soda
1 teaspoon baking powder
$^1/_2$ teaspoon salt
1 teaspoon ground cloves
1 teaspoon ground cinnamon
1 cup sour milk

Topping

2 reserved egg whites
1 cup brown sugar
$^1/_2$ cup broken nutmeats

Cream the shortening, then add the sugar gradually and cream thoroughly. Separate two of the eggs and set the whites aside for the topping. Combine the yolks with the whole eggs and beat well, then beat into the creamed mixture. Sift together the dry ingredients and add, alternately with sour milk, to the creamed mixture. Pour the batter into a greased and floured 13 x 9 x 2-inch pan.

Beat the reserved egg whites until they hold a peak. Beat in the brown sugar, then spread the mixture on top of the cake batter. Sprinkle with the nuts, then bake at 325 degrees for 50 minutes.

Serves: 12 to 16

Mrs. David Schwartz
Geneva, Indiana

APPLESAUCE FRUITCAKE

A very special all-holiday fruitcake with a very different flavor. The cakes are best if left to mellow for 2 weeks.

3 cups thick applesauce
1 cup shortening
2 cups granulated sugar
1 pound dark raisins
1 pound dates, pitted and chopped
$^1/_4$ pound candied cherries, quartered
1 pound nuts, coarsely chopped
$^1/_4$ pound candied pineapple, chopped
$4^1/_2$ cups sifted all-purpose flour
1 teaspoon salt
4 teaspoons baking soda
1 teaspoon grated nutmeg
$2^1/_2$ teaspoons ground cinnamon
$^1/_2$ teaspoon ground cloves

Glaze

1/2 cup light corn syrup
1/4 cup water
Candied fruit and/or nuts

Boil the applesauce, shortening, and sugar together for 5 minutes, stirring occasionally. Let stand until cool. Meanwhile, line four or five 1-pound coffee cans (or pans close to that size) with waxed paper. (If the cans cannot be lined with waxed paper, they should be well greased and floured.)

Mix the fruit and nuts together in a big bowl. Sift the flour, salt, soda, and spices over the fruit and nuts, mixing until each piece is coated. Stir in the cooled applesauce mixture and turn into the lined or greased cans, filling each one about three-fourths full. Bake at 250 degrees for about 2 hours, or until a toothpick comes out clean. Remove from the cans and cool on racks, then wrap and store in a cold place or freeze.

Before serving, bring the water and corn syrup to a boil. Let cool to lukewarm, then pour over the cooled cakes for a shiny glaze. Decorate immediately with candied fruit and/or nuts.

Serves: 40 to 50

Lizzie R. Troyer
Fredericksburg, Ohio

STRAWBERRY SHORTCAKE

A simple, biscuitlike cake that is topped with strawberries and whipped cream.

1 cup granulated sugar
2 eggs
1 cup sour cream
2 cups sifted all-purpose flour
1 teaspoon cream of tartar
1 teaspoon baking soda
1 to 2 pints strawberries, washed and hulled
Whipped cream

Combine the ingredients in the order given and place in a greased and floured 9-inch-square pan. Bake at 350 degrees for 25 minutes, serve topped with the strawberries (or any desired fruit) and whipped cream.

Serves: 8 to 10

Mrs. Moses A. Coblentz
Sarasota, Florida

FRUIT-FILLED CAKE ROLL

The smooth berry filling makes this a very tasty cake indeed.

3/4 cup sifted cake flour
3/4 teaspoon baking powder
1/4 teaspoon salt
4 eggs, at room temperature
3/4 cup granulated sugar
1 teaspoon vanilla extract
1/3 cup grated coconut
Confectioners' sugar

Filling

1 package raspberry gelatin
1 cup boiling water
1 ten-ounce package frozen red raspberries

Topping

Confectioners' sugar or whipped cream

Sift together the flour, baking powder, and salt. In a separate bowl, beat the eggs, then gradually add the sugar, beating until thick and light colored. Gradually fold in the flour mixture, then add the vanilla.

Line a greased 15 1/2 x 10 1/2 jelly-roll pan with waxed paper, then grease again and sprinkle with flour. Pour in the batter and sprinkle with the coconut. Bake in a 400-degree oven for about 13 minutes, then turn the cake out on a cloth that has been sprinkled with confectioners' sugar. Remove the waxed paper and trim off the edges. Roll the cake up, cloth and all, and cool thoroughly on a cake rack.

Meanwhile, dissolve the gelatin in the boiling water. Add the frozen fruit and stir until the berries separate, then let stand until thickened, stirring occasionally. Unroll the cake, spread with the filling, and roll up again, this time without the cloth. Sprinkle with confectioners' sugar or top with whipped cream. Chill in the refrigerator until ready to serve.

Serves: 8 to 10

Mrs. Alvin Mullett
Topeka, Indiana

FROSTINGS

BROWN SUGAR FROSTING

Thin this and use it to drizzle on kuchens. If you don't have cream on hand, take a small piece of butter and a little water, just enough to melt butter, then mix in as cream.

1 cup brown sugar
1/2 cup all-purpose flour
1 tablespoon heavy cream, approximately
1 teaspoon vanilla extract or maple flavoring, or to taste

Combine the brown sugar and flour, then add enough cream to make the frosting the right consistency to spread. Mix well. Add the vanilla or maple flavoring to taste.

Makes: Enough to frost 1 cake *Lovina J. Raber*

FROSTING FOR SPICE CAKE

A frosting with a very special taste that will accent any spice cake.

1 cup brown sugar
2 tablespoons butter
3 tablespoons water
2 tablespoons corn syrup
1 cup confectioners' sugar
1/2 teaspoon maple flavoring
Shredded coconut (optional)

Combine the brown sugar, butter, water, and corn syrup in a saucepan and cook for 4 minutes. Cool slightly, then add enough confectioners' sugar to make the mixture creamy and easy to spread. Mix well, then add the maple flavoring and coconut, if desired. Spread immediately.

Makes: Enough to frost 1 sheet cake *Esther Miller*
Fredericksburg, Ohio

3–6–9 GLAZE FROSTING

The name comes from the proportions (in tablespoons) of butter, cream, and brown sugar used.

3 tablespoons butter or margarine
6 tablespoons heavy cream
9 tablespoons (1/2 cup plus 1 tablespoon) brown sugar
1 teaspoon vanilla extract
1 1/2 cups confectioners' sugar

Combine the butter, cream, brown sugar, and vanilla in a saucepan and boil for 2 minutes. Cool, then add the confectioners' sugar and spread.

Makes: Enough to frost 1 cake

Mrs. Noah Miller
Sugarcreek, Ohio

WHITE WONDER ICING

A light, fluffy icing.

2 egg whites (about 1/4 cup)
1/2 cup granulated sugar
2 teaspoons white corn syrup
Pinch of cream of tartar
1/2 teaspoon flavoring of your choice

In the top of a double boiler, combine the egg whites, sugar, corn syrup, and cream of tartar. Place the mixture over boiling water and stir with your finger until you can no longer keep the finger in it. Remove the mixture from heat and beat until it holds a shape, then add the flavoring and spread.

Makes: Enough to frost 1 small cake

Barbara Borntrager

PIES

OPEN-FACED APPLE PIE

Try this warm, with milk or ice cream.

1 whole apple
1 unbaked 9-inch pie shell
6 cups peeled, quartered apples
$1^1/_3$ cups granulated sugar
3 tablespoons all-purpose flour
$^3/_4$ teaspoon salt
$^1/_3$ cup light cream
$^1/_4$ teaspoon ground cinnamon

Peel the apple, then slice it thin and lay the slices across the bottom of the pie shell. Arrange the quartered apples, rounded side up, to fill the pie shell, overlapping the pieces. Combine the sugar, flour, salt, and cream and mix well. Cover the apples with the mixture and sprinkle with cinnamon. Bake at 375 degrees for $1^1/_2$ to 2 hours, or until the apples are soft, covering the top with foil during the first hour to prevent overbrowning of the crust.

Serves: 6 to 8 *Ruby Yoder*

ROYAL APPLE PIE

A pie with a cooked-to-thicken apple filling.

1 cup brown sugar
$^1/_4$ cup all-purpose flour
1 teaspoon salt
$^1/_4$ cup water
1 tablespoon vinegar
2 tablespoons butter
1 teaspoon vanilla extract
6 or 7 cups peeled, sliced apples
Pastry for a 2-crust pie

Combine the sugar, flour, salt, water, and vinegar in a saucepan and cook until thick, stirring constantly. Remove from the flame, add the butter and vanilla, and cool. Pour the syrup over the apples.

Roll out half of the pastry and fit into a 9-inch pie pan. Pour in the filling. Roll out the remaining pastry and use it to cover the pie. Crimp the edges and cut vents on top, then bake the pie at 425 degrees for 50 to 60 minutes.

Serves: 8

Mrs. Jonas Borntrager
Sugarcreek, Ohio

DRIED "SNITZ" PIE

The standard Amish dried-apple pie.

2 cups dried tart apples
1½ cups warm water
⅔ cup granulated sugar
½ teaspoon ground cinnamon
Pastry for a 2-crust pie

Soak the apples in the warm water, then cook them in the soaking water until soft. Put the apples through a sieve and add the sugar and cinnamon.

Roll out half the pastry and fit it into a 9-inch pie pan. Put the apple mixture in the shell, roll out the remaining pastry, and cover the pie. Crimp the edges and cut vents on top. Bake at 425 degrees for 15 minutes, then at 375 degrees for 35 minutes longer, or until nicely browned.

Serves: 8

Mrs. Eli Schlabach

HALF-MOON PIES ("HURRY UP")

The Amish classic, shaped so it can be eaten by hand.

1 gallon dried apples (snitz)
6 cups water
6 cups granulated sugar
1 tablespoon ground allspice
1½ teaspoon ground cinnamon
Pie pastry of your choice

Wash the snitz, add the water, cover, and cook until soft and the water is all taken up. Add the sugar and spices and cook for 10 minutes longer, then remove from the heat. Stir until smooth, put through a ricer, and set aside to cool.

Divide the pie pastry into balls about the size of large walnuts. Roll out each piece into a circle. Put the filling on one half of the circle and fold the other half over, shaping the pastry like a half moon. Press the edges together and cut vents on top. Continue until all the pastry and filling are used, then bake in a 400-degree oven until done (about 20 minutes).

Makes: 4 to 5 dozen pastries

Susie Swarey
Reedsville, Pennsylvania

PEACH CREAM PIE

Fresh peaches in a creamy filling with a crumb crust.

3/4 cup granulated sugar
2 tablespoons all-purpose flour
1/4 teaspoon salt
1 cup sour cream
1 egg, beaten
1/2 teaspoon vanilla extract
2 cups sliced fresh peaches
1 unbaked 9-inch pie shell

Crumb Topping

1/3 cup brown sugar
3/4 cup all-purpose flour
1 teaspoon ground cinnamon
4 tablespoons butter

Combine the sugar, flour, and salt. Add the sour cream and blend well, then add the beaten egg and vanilla and beat until smooth. Fold in the peaches and pour into the unbaked pie shell.

Combine the dry ingredients for the topping, then cut in the butter until well blended. Spread on top of peach mixture. Bake the pie at 400 degrees for 15 minutes, then reduce the heat to 350 degrees and bake for approximately 30 minutes more.

Serves: 6 to 8

Mrs. Ben Miller
Fredericksburg, Ohio

STRAWBERRY PIE DELUXE

Fresh strawberry pie in a sweet glaze, garnished with whipped cream.

4 cups sliced fresh strawberries
1/2 cup confectioners' sugar
1 tablespoon butter
1 cup plus 2 tablespoons water
1/2 teaspoon salt
3/4 cup granulated sugar
2 tablespoons cornstarch
2 tablespoons water
Red food coloring
1 baked 9-inch pie shell
Whipped cream

Combine 3 cups of the berries with the confectioners' sugar. Mix well and let stand for 1 hour. Meanwhile, combine the remaining berries, the butter, the 1 cup water, and the salt in a saucepan. Bring to a boil, then remove from the heat and put through a sieve. Combine the granulated sugar, cornstarch, and the 2 tablespoons water into a thin paste. Stir into the mixture in the saucepan, add a few drops red food coloring, bring to a boil, and let cool. Mix with the berries and pour into the pie shell. Top with whipped cream and serve.

Serves: 6 to 8

Mrs. Mose Yoder
Baltic, Ohio

STRAWBERRY-RHUBARB PIE

Baked strawberries and rhubarb in a lattice-topped pie shell.

3 cups diced rhubarb
1 pint strawberries
1 1/4 cups granulated sugar
1/4 cup all-purpose flour
1/4 teaspoon nutmeg
1 tablespoon butter or margarine
Pastry for a 2-crust pie

Combine the fruit, sugar, flour, and nutmeg. Roll out half the pastry and fit it into a 9-inch pie pan. Add the filling and dot with the butter. Roll out the remaining pastry, cut it into strips, and make a lattice topping on the pie. Bake in a preheated 400-degree oven for 40 to 50 minutes.

Serves: 6 to 8

Mrs. Tobe J. Yoder
Stuarts Draft, Virginia

FLUFFY PUMPKIN PIE

A very light, almost frothy spice-flavored pie.

2 eggs, separated
1 cup canned or cooked, mashed fresh pumpkin
1 cup milk
1/2 cup granulated sugar
1 teaspoon ground cinnamon
1/2 teaspoon grated nutmeg
1/4 teaspoon ground ginger
1/4 teaspoon ground cloves
1/4 teaspoon salt
1 unbaked 9-inch pie shell

Beat the egg yolks, then combine with the pumpkin. Add the milk and mix well, then add the dry ingredients and mix well. Beat the egg whites until stiff, then fold gently into the pumpkin mixture. Pour into the unbaked pie shell and bake at 425 degrees for 40 minutes, or until done.

Serves: 6 to 8 — *Mary Bontrager*

PUMPKIN PECAN PIE

Creamy pumpkin pie with the added crunch of pecans.

3 packages vanilla pudding mix
1/2 teaspoon ground ginger
1/2 teaspoon grated nutmeg
2 teaspoons ground cinnamon
1/4 teaspoon ground cloves
1 teaspoon salt
1/2 cup brown sugar
2 1/2 cups milk
3 1/2 cups canned or cooked, mashed fresh pumpkin
1 cup chopped pecans
2 baked 9-inch pie shells

Combine the pudding mix, spices, salt, sugar, and milk and beat until smooth. Add the pumpkin and blend well, then pour the mixture into a saucepan and cook until thick, stirring constantly. Add the chopped pecans and pour into the baked pie shells. Bake at 350 degrees for approximately 40 minutes.

Serves: 12 to 16 — *Mrs. Daniel Schlabach*
Millersburg, Ohio

SOUTHERN PECAN PIE

A traditional pecan pie with the pecans rising to the top.

3 eggs, well beaten
1/2 cup granulated sugar
1 cup dark corn syrup
1/4 teaspoon salt
1 teaspoon vanilla extract
1/4 cup melted butter or margarine
1 cup pecan meats
1 unbaked 9-inch pie shell

Combine eggs, sugar, corn syrup, salt, vanilla, and butter. Mix well. Spread the pecans on the bottom of the unbaked pie shell. Pour over the filling, then bake in a 350-degree oven for 50 to 60 minutes, or until a knife inserted in the center comes out clean. Serve with whipped cream, if desired.

Serves: 8

Mrs. Dan Hostetler
Middlefield, Ohio

PECAN–CREAM CHEESE PIE

This pie has a layer of sweetened cream cheese and a layer of syrup topped with pecans.

2 three-ounce packages cream cheese
6 tablespoons granulated sugar
4 eggs
2 teaspoons vanilla extract
1/4 teaspoon salt
3/4 cup corn syrup
1 unbaked 9-inch pie shell
1 1/4 cups chopped pecans

In a small bowl, beat together the cream cheese, 1/4 cup of the sugar, 1 egg, 1 teaspoon vanilla, and the salt until thick, creamy, and smooth. Set aside. In another bowl, beat the remaining eggs until the yolks and whites are combined. Add the corn syrup, remaining sugar, and remaining vanilla and beat, gently, only until blended. Spread the cream-cheese mixture in the bottom of the unbaked pie shell. Pour over the syrup mixture, then sprinkle with the pecans. Bake at 375 degrees until the center is firm to the touch (about 35 to 40 minutes).

Serves: 6 to 8

Evelyn Feder

FANCY CRUST RAISIN PIE

This is the famous Amish funeral pie.

1 cup seeded raisins
2 cups water
$1^1/_2$ cups granulated sugar
$^1/_4$ cup all-purpose flour
1 egg, well beaten
Pinch of salt
2 teaspoons grated lemon rind
Juice of 1 lemon
Pastry for a 2-crust pie

Put the raisins in the top of a double boiler and soak in the water for 3 hours, then mix in the sugar, flour, and egg. Add the salt, lemon rind, and lemon juice and cook over hot water for 15 minutes, stirring constantly. Let cool.

Roll out half of the pastry and fit it into a 9-inch pie plate. Pour in the cooled filling. Roll out the remaining pastry and cut into strips. Top the pie with the strips, crisscrossed like you would a cherry pie, then bake at 375 degrees for about 35 to 40 minutes, or until brown.

Serves: 6 to 8 *Catherine L. Portman*

RAISIN CREAM PIE

Raisins in a creamy pie filling.

1 cup raisins
$1^1/_2$ cups water
$^2/_3$ cup granulated sugar
1 teaspoon lemon juice
2 tablespoons cornstarch
$^1/_2$ cup heavy cream
2 eggs, separated
1 baked 9-inch pie shell

Combine the raisins, water, sugar, and lemon juice in a saucepan, then cover and simmer for about 15 minutes, stirring often to prevent scorching. Dissolve the cornstarch in the cream, then add the egg yolks, beaten. Add the cornstarch mixture slowly to the raisins, stirring, and let come to a boil. Cook until thick, then pour into the pastry shell and cool.

Beat the egg whites until stiff, then spread over the pie, making sure the meringue touches the crust on all sides, to prevent shrinking. Brown under the broiler and serve.

Serves: 6 *Mattie Kuhns*

RAISIN CUSTARD PIE

This is quite rich pie—with raisins in a custard filling and a meringue topping.

1 cup seedless raisins
1 cup water
1 cup milk
1/4 cup granulated sugar
Salt
1 tablespoon cornstarch
2 eggs, separated
1 tablespoon butter
1/2 teaspoon vanilla extract
1 baked 9-inch pie shell
1/4 teaspoon cream of tartar

Cook the raisins in the water until tender. (The secret to good flavor is to cook them gently until all the water is cooked off. This means watching carefully, as they will burn.) Remove from the heat.

In a separate saucepan, heat the milk, and add the sugar, 1/4 teaspoon salt, and the cornstarch. Bring to a boil, then cool. Add the egg yolks, well beaten, slowly and bring to a boil again. Remove from the heat, add the butter and vanilla, and cool. Pour into the baked crust.

Have egg whites at room temperature. Beat, with a pinch of salt and the cream of tartar, until light and frothy. Add the sugar, a little at a time, beating well after each addition. Do not underbeat; beat until stiff peaks form. Pile the meringue on top of the pie, being careful to spread to meet the edges of the pie, to avoid shrinking. Bake in a 350 degree oven for 12 to 15 minutes, or until the meringue peaks are browned.

Serves: 6 to 8 *Mrs. Lester Erbs*

OLD FAVORITE CUSTARD PIE

A church supper recipe.

1 1/2 tablespoons all-purpose flour
1/2 cup granulated sugar
2 tablespoons brown sugar
Pinch of salt
1 1/2 cups milk
2 eggs, separated
1 teaspoon vanilla extract
1 unbaked 8–9-inch pie shell

Combine the dry ingredients with a little of the milk and stir until smooth. Beat the egg yolks and combine with the remaining milk. Add the dry-ingredient mixture to the yolk-milk mixture and stir until smooth. Add the vanilla.

Beat the egg whites until peaks form. Slowly pour the custard mixture into the whites, folding in until blended. Pour into the unbaked pie shell and bake at 425 degrees for 10 minutes, then reduce the heat to 375 degrees and bake for 30 minutes longer, or until done.

Serves: 6 to 8

Mrs. Roy Keim
Millersburg, Ohio

COCONUT CUSTARD PIE

A really sweet dessert, great for family gatherings.

3 eggs
1 cup granulated sugar
1 scant tablespoon all-purpose flour
Pinch of salt
1 cup milk
1 teaspoon vanilla extract
Dash of grated nutmeg
1 cup shredded coconut
1 unbaked 9- or 10-inch pie shell

Separate one of the eggs reserving the egg white. Beat the egg yolk, along with the remaining eggs, then beat in the sugar and flour, mixed, and gradually add the milk. Add the salt, vanilla, and nutmeg, then stir in the coconut. Fold in the egg white, stiffly beaten, and pour into the unbaked pie shell and bake in a 350-degree oven for 30 to 40 minutes, or until set.

Serves: 8

Mrs. William Hochstetler
Middlefield, Ohio

MAPLE CUSTARD PIE

Maple flavoring is a standard Amish item; here it is introduced into a custard filling.

1 2/3 cups brown sugar
2 tablespoons all-purpose flour
1 teaspoon ground cinnamon
1/2 teaspoon cream of tartar
2 tablespoons butter, softened
3 eggs
3 cups milk
2 unbaked 9-inch pie shells

Combine dry ingredients, then cream with the butter. Beat the eggs and gradually add to the creamed mixture, beating until smooth. Add the milk and beat well until well blended. Pour the filling into the unbaked pie shells and bake at 450 degrees for 10 minutes, then reduce the heat to 350 degrees and bake for another 30 minutes, or until done.

Serves: 12 to 16

Mrs. Roman Troyer
Fredericksburg, Ohio

"BOB ANDY" PIE

"Serve with strawberries, fresh."

1/4 pound butter
3 eggs, separated
1 1/2 cups brown sugar
3 tablespoons all-purpose flour
3 cups milk
1/2 teaspoon ground cinnamon
1/2 teaspoon ground cloves
2 unbaked 9-inch pie shells

Cream the butter and the egg yolks, then add the sugar and flour and blend well. Stir in the milk and spices. Pour the mixture into a saucepan. Bring to a boil, then cook for a few minutes, stirring. Let cool.

Beat the egg whites until stiff but not dry and fold into cooled mixture. Pour the filling into the unbaked pie shells and bake at 375 degrees for about 45 minutes, or until the custard sets.

Serves: 12 to 16

Mrs. John B. Kurtz

BETTY'S LEMON MERINGUE PIE

Betty Miller's most famous recipe.

3 tablespoons cornstarch
1 1/2 cups plus 2 tablespoons granulated sugar
1/4 cup lemon juice
1 tablespoon grated lemon rind
3 eggs, separated
1 1/2 cups boiling water
6 tablespoons sugar
1 baked 9-inch pie shell

In a saucepan, combine the cornstarch, 1 1/4 cups of the sugar, lemon juice, and lemon rind. Beat the egg yolks and add to the cornstarch mixture. Slowly add the boiling water, then heat until boiling over direct heat, stirring constantly. Simmer, still stirring, for 3 minutes.

Let cool, then pour into the baked pie shell. Beat egg whites with the remaining 6 tablespoons sugar until stiff. Spread the meringue on the cooled pie, making sure it touches the edge of the crust on all sides, and brown in a 425-degree oven. Let cool and serve.

Serves: 6 to 8

Betty Miller
Millersburg, Ohio

OLD-FASHIONED LEMON PIE

This lemon pie has a double-decker effect.

Juice of 2 lemons
1 cup white corn syrup
2 1/2 cups plus 3 tablespoons all-purpose flour
3 cups water
3 1/2 cups granulated sugar
3 eggs
3 unbaked 9-inch pie shells
1/2 pound butter
2 teaspoons baking powder
1 cup milk

In a saucepan, combine the lemon juice, corn syrup, 3 tablespoons flour, water, 1 1/2 cups of the sugar, and 1 egg. Boil until thick, then cool and divide into the unbaked pie shells. Cream the butter with the remaining sugar, then add the remaining eggs. Sift together the 2 1/2 cups flour and baking powder and add, alternately with the milk, to the creamed mixture. Spoon about 6 dabs on top of the lemon filling in each of the pie shells. Bake in a 450-degree oven for 10 minutes, then reduce the heat to 350 degrees and bake until a knife inserted into the center comes out clean (about 35 minutes).

Serves: 18 to 24

Mrs. Lewis Knepp
Montgomery, Indiana

COCONUT CREAM PIE

Creamy coconut filling with a meringue topping.

5 tablespoons sifted cake flour
1/2 cup plus 2 tablespoons granulated sugar
1/4 teaspoon salt
2 cups milk
3 eggs, separated
1 1/2 cups grated coconut
2 teaspoons vanilla extract
1 baked 9-inch pie shell

In the top of a double boiler, combine the flour, 6 tablespoons of the sugar, and salt with 1/2 cup of the milk. Scald the remaining milk, then add gradually to the flour mixture. Cook over simmering water until thickened, stirring constantly. Beat the egg yolks. Pour a small quantity of the hot sauce over the yolks. Mix, then return all to the double boiler. Add 1 cup of the coconut, heat briefly, then remove from the heat and stir in the vanilla. Cool, then pour into the baked shell.

Beat the egg whites until stiff, then slowly beat in the remaining 1/4 cup sugar until smooth and glossy. Spread on the pie, making sure it touches the edges of the pastry on all sides, and sprinkle with the remaining coconut. Brown in a 425-degree oven.

Serves: 6 to 8 — *Mrs. Stephen Stoltzfus*

BUTTERSCOTCH PIE

This pie also tastes quite good with a meringue topping.

1 cup brown sugar
1 1/4 cups milk
2 tablespoons butter
2 eggs, well beaten
1/2 cup granulated sugar
1 tablespoon all-purpose flour
1/4 teaspoon salt
1 teaspoon vanilla extract
1 baked 9-inch pie shell

Combine all the ingredients (except the pie shell) in a blender and blend well, then cook over low heat in a saucepan until thickened. Pour the mixture into the baked pie shell and bake for 8 minutes at 400 degrees, being careful not to brown the top.

Serves: 6 to 8 — *Mrs. John C. Miller*
Apple Creek, Ohio

SPONGE LEMON PIE

A fine-textured, fluffy, really lemony pie. But serve it the same day; the crust tends to get soggy.

1 cup granulated sugar
2 eggs, separated
Grated rind and juice of 1 lemon
2 tablespoons butter
2 tablespoons all-purpose flour
1 1/2 cups milk
1 unbaked 9-inch pie shell

Combine the sugar, egg yolks, lemon rind and juice, butter, and flour, and beat well. Slowly add the milk, blending well. Beat the egg whites stiff and fold into the mixture. Pour into the unbaked pie shell and bake at 325 degrees for 40 to 45 minutes.

Serves: 6 to 8

Mrs. O. E. Sommers
Millersburg, Ohio

PINEAPPLE CHIFFON PIE

A firm, melt-in-your-mouth chiffon pie, flavored with pineapple and topped with meringue.

1 tablespoon unflavored gelatin
1/4 cup cold water
1 cup granulated sugar
4 eggs, separated
1 1/4 cups undrained crushed pineapple
1/4 teaspoon salt
1 baked 9-inch pie shell

Dissolve the gelatin in the cold water and set aside. Combine 1/2 cup of the sugar, the egg yolks, pineapple, and salt in the top of a double boiler. Cook over simmering water until slightly thickened, stirring often, then remove from the heat. Add the gelatin, stir well, and cool.

Beat the egg whites until stiff and fold in the remaining sugar. Fold the cooled custard into egg whites, then pour into the baked pie shell. Cool for several hours and serve.

Serves: 6 to 8

Iva Ramer
Waharuso, Indiana

EGGNOG PIE

A chiffon-type pie with an eggnog flavor, topped with coconut and whipped cream.

1 teaspoon unflavored gelatin
1 teaspoon cold water
1 cup milk
1/2 cup granulated sugar
2 tablespoons cornstarch
1/2 teaspoon salt
3 eggs, separated
1 tablespoon butter
1 pint heavy cream, whipped
1 baked 9-inch pie shell
1/2 cup grated coconut

Soak the gelatin in the cold water and set aside. Scald the milk in the top of a double boiler. Combine the sugar, cornstarch, and salt and mix well, then add the scalded milk and continue cooking for 15 minutes longer.

Beat the egg yolks. Stir a small amount of the sugar-milk mixture into the beaten egg yolks, then return all to the double boiler and cook a few minutes longer. Add the butter and gelatin and stir well, then cool and fold in half the whipped cream. Pour into a baked pie shell and top with the remaining whipped cream and the coconut.

Serves: 6 to 8

Mrs. Amos Yoder
Mount Hope, Ohio

WHITE CHRISTMAS PIE

A chiffon pie with a creamy coconut flavor; great with strawberries on top.

1 tablespoon unflavored gelatin
1/4 cup water
1 cup granulated sugar
1/4 cup all-purpose flour
1/2 teaspoon salt
1 1/2 cups milk
1 1/2 teaspoons vanilla extract
1/2 cup cream, whipped
3 egg whites
1/4 teaspoon cream of tartar
1 cup moist, grated coconut
2 9-inch graham-cracker pie shells

Dissolve the gelatin in the water and set aside. Combine 1/2 cup of the sugar, flour, salt, and milk in a saucepan and cook on low heat until the mixture boils. Stirring constantly, boil for 1 minute, then remove from the heat. Stir in the gelatin and cool. When partly set, beat until smooth, then add the vanilla. Gently fold in the whipped cream.

Beat the egg whites with the cream of tartar and the remaining sugar until stiff, then fold into the other mixture and blend. Fold in the moist coconut. Pour into the graham-cracker crusts, chill, and serve.

Serves: 12

Mrs. Henry Yoder
Millersburg, Ohio

APPLE CHIFFON PIE

An applesauce-flavored chiffon pie.

1 package (1 tablespoon) unflavored gelatin
1/2 cup cold water
2 cups applesauce
1/2 teaspoon cinnamon
1/2 teaspoon lemon juice
2 egg whites
1 9-inch graham-cracker pie shell
Whipped cream

Soften the gelatin in the cold water, then add to the applesauce in a saucepan and bring to a boil. Add the cinnamon and lemon juice and chill.

Beat the egg whites until stiff peaks form. Fold into the chilled apple mixture and pour into the graham-cracker pie shell. Refrigerate to firm, then serve with whipped cream topping.

Serves: 6 to 8

Mrs. O. Detweiler
Inola, Oklahoma

LEMON CHIFFON PIE

The addition of whipped cream would make an even richer pie filling.

1 envelope (1 tablespoon) unflavored gelatin
1/2 cup lemon juice
1/2 cup cold water
1/4 teaspoon salt
3 egg whites
1/2 cup corn syrup
Grated rind of 1 lemon
1 baked 9-inch pie shell

Put the gelatin, lemon juice, and water in a saucepan. Heat and stir until the gelatin is dissolved, then chill until the mixture has the consistency of unbeaten egg white. Add the salt to the egg whites and beat until stiff, not dry. Slowly add the corn syrup, then beat until glossy. Fold into the gelatin mixture along with the lemon rind and chill until thick enough to pile up (about 30 minutes). Pour into the baked 9-inch pie shell, chill again, and serve.

Serves: 8 to 10

Mrs. Ivan S. Miller
Millersburg, Ohio

MOCK MINCE PIE

"You'll enjoy this even if you don't like mince pie."

1 pound raisins, chopped
1/2 cup molasses
1/2 cup water
2 tablespoons soda crackers
3/4 teaspoon ground cinnamon
1/2 cup granulated sugar
1/2 cup vinegar
4 tablespoons cold butter, cut in chunks
1 1/2 teaspoons ground cloves
1 1/2 teaspoons grated nutmeg
1 unbaked 9-inch pie shell

Combine all ingredients in the order given (except for the pie shell), stirring until smooth after each addition. Pour the mixture into the unbaked shell and bake at 450 degrees for 35 minutes, or until the crust looks light brown and crisp.

Serves: 8 to 10

Naomi Brenneman

OATMEAL PIE

An unusual pie—nutty tasting, rich, and delicately spiced—yet easy to make.

4 tablespoons butter
1/2 cup granulated sugar
1/2 teaspoon ground cinnamon
1/2 teaspoon ground cloves
1/4 teaspoon salt
1 cup dark corn syrup
3 eggs
1 cup quick-cooking oats
1 unbaked 9-inch pie shell

Cream together the butter and sugar, then add the spices and salt and stir in the corn syrup. Add the eggs, one at a time, stirring after each addition until well blended. Stir in the oats. Pour into the unbaked pie shell and bake at 350 degrees for about 1 hour, or until a knife inserted in the center comes out clean.

Serves: 6 to 8

Mrs. Wilma Lambright
Wollcottville, Indiana

MOCK PECAN PIE

"Stays fresh for four days."

4 tablespoons butter
1 cup dark corn syrup
1/2 cup grated coconut
1/2 cup granulated sugar
1/4 teaspoon salt
1/2 cup quick-cooking oats
1 unbaked 9-inch pie shell

Combine the butter and corn syrup, then stir in the coconut, sugar, and salt. Stir in the oats and mix well. Pour into the unbaked pie shell and bake at 350 degrees for 50 minutes, or until a knife inserted in the center comes out clean.

Serves: 6 to 8

Mrs. Cornelius Miller
Apple Creek, Ohio

AUNT EMMY'S SHOOFLY PIE

An Amish favorite, this is very, very sweet.

1/4 cup shortening
1 cup brown sugar
1 1/2 cups sifted all-purpose flour
3/4 teaspoon baking soda
1/4 teaspoon salt
3/4 teaspoon molasses or corn syrup
3/4 cup hot water
1/8 teaspoon grated nutmeg
1/4 teaspoon ground cinnamon
1/4 teaspoon ground ginger
1/4 teaspoon ground cloves
1 unbaked 9-inch pie shell

Cream the shortening, brown sugar, and flour until crumbly. In a separate bowl, combine the soda, salt, molasses, water, and spices. Put one-quarter of the crumbs on the bottom of the pie shell, then add the filling. Sprinkle the remaining crumbs on top. Bake for 15 minutes at 450 degrees or 20 minutes at 350 degrees, until firm.

Serves: 6 to 8

Rose Miller
Virginia Beach, Virginia

BROWN SUGAR PIE

A fluffy, sweet, typically Amish dessert pie.

1 cup brown sugar
2 eggs, separated
1 tablespoon all-purpose flour
1 teaspoon vanilla extract
2 cups milk
1 unbaked 9-inch pie shell

Cream the sugar and egg yolks, then add the flour and blend well. Add the vanilla, then slowly add the milk and beat well until smooth. Fold in the egg whites, stiffly beaten, blending very well. Pour into the unbaked pie shell and bake at 425 degrees for 10 minutes, then reduce the heat to 350 degrees and bake for 30 minutes more.

Serves: 6 to 8

C. Mullet
Nappanee, Indiana

UNION PIE

A very unique pie.

1 cup light brown sugar
2 tablespoons all-purpose flour
1 teaspoon baking soda
2 eggs, beaten
1 cup corn syrup
1 cup sour cream
1 cup buttermilk
2 unbaked 9-inch pie shells

Combine the sugar, flour, and soda, then add the beaten eggs and blend well. Slowly add the corn syrup, then the sour cream and buttermilk, blending well after each addition. Pour the filling into the two unbaked pie shells, sprinkle cinnamon on top, and bake at 375 degrees for 35 minutes.

Serves: 12 to 16

Alta C. Schlabach
Berlin, Ohio

TAFFY SPOOF PIE

A crunchy breakfast-cereal pie.

2 eggs
2/3 cups granulated sugar
1/2 cup light corn syrup
1/4 teaspoon salt
3 tablespoons melted butter
1 teaspoon vanilla extract
1 cup Rice Krispies
1 unbaked 9-inch pie shell

Beat the eggs, then add the sugar, corn syrup, salt, melted butter, and vanilla and mix well. Fold in the Rice Krispies and pour the mixture into the unbaked pie shell. Bake at 375 degrees for 35 to 40 minutes.

Serves: 6 to 8

Katie Miller
Middlefield, Ohio

COLLEGE PIE

A two-layered pie, one like cake and the second sugary.

First Layer

1 egg, beaten
1/4 cup lard
1/2 teaspoon baking soda
1 cup granulated sugar
1/2 cup sour cream
1 1/4 cups all-purpose flour
2 unbaked deep 9-inch pie shells

Second Layer

1 egg, beaten
2 cups water
1 teaspoon vanilla extract
1 teaspoon baking soda
1 cup brown sugar
1 tablespoon all-purpose flour
1/2 cup molasses

Combine the ingredients for the first layer as for a cake, then divide the batter into two deep 9-inch pie pans lined with unbaked pie crust.

For the second layer, combine the ingredients in the order given, stirring well after each addition. Pour over the batter in the pie shells and bake at 400 degrees for 15 minutes, then lower the temperature to 325 degrees and bake for 15 minutes longer.

Serves: 12 to 16

Mrs. Chester A. Miller
Goshen, Indiana

VANILLA TARTS

"These tarts get better with age. This recipe has been in my family for forty-five years."

Bottom Layer

1 egg
1 tablespoon all-purpose flour
1 cup light brown sugar
$2^1/_2$ cups water
1 cup dark corn syrup
2 teaspoons vanilla extract
Pinch of salt
3 unbaked 9-inch pie shells

Top Layer

$1^1/_2$ cups granulated sugar
$^1/_2$ cup shortening
1 egg
3 cups sifted all-purpose flour
$^1/_2$ teaspoon salt
1 teaspoon baking powder
1 teaspoon vanilla extract
1 cup sour milk or buttermilk
1 teaspoon baking soda

Combine the first three ingredients for the bottom layer with $^1/_2$ cup of the water and blend until smooth, then add the corn syrup, vanilla, salt, and the rest of the water. Divide the mixture equally into the 3 unbaked pie shells.

For the top layer, cream the sugar and shortening, then add the egg and beat well. Sift together the dry ingredients and add, alternately with the sour milk, to be creamed mixture. Add the vanilla last. Drop by heaping teaspoonfuls on top of the pies. (I put one big spoonful in the center of each pie, plus six around the circle.) Bake for approximately 50 minutes in a 350-degree oven.

Serves: 18 to 24

Mrs. Andrew Miller
Wooster, Ohio

VANILLA CRUMB PIE

A sugary, vanilla-layered pie with a crumb topping.

1½ cups granulated or brown sugar (or half and half)
2 cups light corn syrup
3 heaping tablespoons all-purpose flour
2 pints cold water
2 eggs, well beaten
1 tablespoon vanilla extract
3 unbaked 9-inch pie shells

Crumb Topping

2 cups flour
½ cup granulated sugar
1 teaspoon soda
1 teaspoon cream of tartar
½ cup butter

Combine all the ingredients in a saucepan and boil until smooth. Cool, then pour into the three unbaked pie shells.

Make the topping by sifting together the dry ingredients, then cutting in the butter to make crumbs. Spread on top of the filling and bake at 350 degrees for 30 to 40 minutes, or until brown.

Serves: 18 to 24 — *Mrs. Raymond Miller*

GRAHAM-CRACKER PIE

A vanilla cream pie with both graham-cracker crust and topping.

20 graham crackers, crushed
½ cup melted butter or margarine
1 tablespoon all-purpose flour
¾ cup granulated sugar
3 cups milk
3 eggs, separated
1 teaspoon vanilla extract
2 tablespoons cornstarch
½ teaspoon salt

Combine the cracker crumbs, butter, flour, and ½ cup sugar. Mix well and pack into a 10- or 12-inch pie pan, reserving a small amount for the topping.

Heat the milk to boiling. Beat the egg yolks and combine with 1 tablespoon sugar, the vanilla, cornstarch, and ¼ teaspoon salt. Pour the mixture slowly, while stirring, into the milk and cook until thick, stirring constantly. Cool, then pour into the prepared crust.

Beat the egg whites with ¼ teaspoon salt and remaining 3 tablespoons sugar until stiff. Spread over the pie filling, making sure the meringue touches the pastry on all sides, and sprinkle the reserved cracker crumbs on top. Put in a 425-degree oven for a few minutes to brown.

Serves: 8 to 10

Ervin Schlabach
Millersburg, Ohio

McKINLEY PIE

This pie has the taste of streusel coffee cake, and is good served warm with cream or milk.

1/2 cup molasses
1/2 cup brown sugar
2 eggs, separated
1 1/2 cups water
1 teaspoon baking soda
2 cups plus 1 tablespoon sifted all-purpose flour
1/4 teaspoon grated nutmeg
2 cups granulated sugar
1 cup milk
1/2 cup shortening
2 teaspoons baking powder
1 teaspoon vanilla extract
3 unbaked 9-inch pie shells

Combine the molasses, brown sugar, egg yolks, water, soda, 1 tablespoon flour, and nutmeg and set aside. Beat the egg whites until stiff. Combine the granulated sugar, milk, shortening, baking powder, vanilla, and 2 cups flour and fold into the egg whites. Put molasses–egg yolk mixture into the three pie shells and spoon the sugar–egg white mixture on top. The batter will float; as it bakes a cake will form on top, and sauce on the bottom. Bake for 35 minutes at 375 degrees.

Serves: 18 to 24

Amos Z. Martin
Denver, Pennsylvania

OLD-FASHIONED SWEET POTATO PIE

Sweet potatoes made even sweeter with molasses, and flavored with cloves.

1 cup sifted all-purpose flour
1/2 teaspoon salt
1/3 cup shortening
2 to 3 tablespoons water

Filling

1¾ cups mashed sweet potatoes
3 eggs, beaten
⅔ cup granulated sugar
⅓ cup molasses
1¼ cups milk
¼ teaspoon ground cloves
1 teaspoon vanilla extract

Sift together the flour and salt. Cut or rub in the shortening until the mixture is crumbly, then sprinkle with water, mixing lightly until the dough begins to stick together. Turn out on a floured board or pastry cloth and press the dough together, then roll the dough out into a circle ⅛ inch thick. Fit into a 9-inch pie pan. Trim and flute the edges.

To prepare the filling, make sure the potatoes are mashed to a smooth paste. Add the eggs and mix well, then add the sugar, molasses, and milk and mix thoroughly. Stir in the cloves and vanilla, then pour into an unbaked pie shell. Bake in a 400-degree oven for 15 minutes then reduce the heat to 350 degrees and bake for 35 to 40 minutes longer.

Serves: 6 to 8

Alvin K. Fisher
Gordonville, Pennsylvania

SLICED GREEN TOMATO PIE

An unusual dessert pie made with green tomatoes.

1¼ cups granulated sugar
½ teaspoon ground cinnamon
½ teaspoon grated nutmeg
¼ teaspoon salt
4 to 5 tablespoons all-purpose flour
2 tablespoons lemon juice
4 cups peeled, thinly sliced green tomatoes
Pastry for a 2-crust pie

Combine the sugar, cinnamon, nutmeg, salt, flour, and lemon juice in a bowl. Toss with the green tomatoes.

Roll out half the pastry and fit it into a 9-inch pie pan. Put in the filling. Roll out the remaining dough and cover the filling with it. Flute the edges and cut vents on top. Bake in a 425-degree oven until the tomatoes are soft and the crust is lightly browned (about 50 to 60 minutes).

Serves: 6 to 8

Mrs. Jim Hammond
Fresno, Ohio

COOKIES

CANDY BAR COOKIES

Try these candy-like cookies on your kids.

18 graham crackers, crumbled
3 tablespoons brown sugar or honey
1/2 cup chopped pecans
1 fifteen-ounce can evaporated milk
1 six-ounce package chocolate chips
1/2 cup flaked coconut

Combine all the ingredients and pour into a greased 8-inch-square pan. Bake at 350 degrees for 35 minutes. Cut into squares while still warm and place on waxed paper to cool. (They will firm up when cold.)

Makes: 16 squares

Mrs. Eli A. Yoder
Oakland, Maryland

PUFFED WHEAT SQUARES

Puffed wheat formed into a cookie by a candylike syrup.

2 tablespoons butter
1 cup light molasses
1/3 cup granulated sugar
1 1/2 teaspoons vinegar
1 three-and-one-half-ounce package Puffed Wheat

Melt the butter over low heat, then add molasses and sugar and stir until the sugar is dissolved. Continue to cook, stirring occasionally, until the syrup will form a very hard ball when a teaspoonful is dropped into a cup of cold water (268 degrees on a candy thermometer). Quickly stir in the vinegar and pour over the puffed wheat, then pour into a 13 x 9 x 2-inch pan and pat with a buttered knife until smooth. Cool and cut in squares.

Makes: 24 squares

Mrs. Amos Raber
Baltic, Ohio

DREAM BARS

A layered cookie with a crumbly layer and a firm coconut, nut, and cherry layer.

Bottom Layer

1/4 pound butter or oleo
1 1/2 cups all-purpose flour
1/2 cup brown sugar

Top Layer

2 eggs
1 cup brown sugar
1 teaspoon vanilla extract
1 1/2 cups grated coconut
1 cup chopped nuts
2 tablespoons all-purpose flour
1/2 teaspoon baking powder
1/4 teaspoon salt
1/4 pound candied cherries

Prepare the bottom layer. Combine the butter, flour, and brown sugar until a crumbly mass is formed. Pat into a greased 16 1/2 x 10 1/2 jelly-roll pan and bake at 350 degrees for 10 minutes.

Meanwhile, beat the eggs. Add the sugar and vanilla and blend well. Place the coconut and nuts in a bowl and sift the flour, baking powder, and salt over. Combine with the sugar-egg mixture, add the cherries, and spread over the partially baked crust. Bake for 20 minutes more; do *not* overbake. Cut into squares while still warm.

Makes: About 36 squares

M. Kauffman
Merrell, Michigan

HONEY DOODLES

No-bake cookies with a peanut-butter taste.

1 cup honey
1 cup peanut butter
2 cups nonfat dry milk
2 scant cups quick-cooking oats

Combine the honey and peanut butter, then gradually stir in the dry milk and oats. Roll into a long thin bar and refrigerate. When thoroughly chilled, cut into slices 3/8 inch thick.

Yields: 48 bars

Lina Roth
Farover, Michigan

RAISIN BARS

Crunchy raisin delights.

2 cups granulated sugar
1 cup shortening
3 eggs, beaten
1 pound raisins
1 cup corn syrup or molasses
2 tablespoons baking soda
1/2 teaspoon salt
1 3/4 cups sifted all-purpose flour
1/4 cup boiling water
Beaten egg or egg white (optional)

Cream the sugar and shortening, then add the beaten eggs, raisins, and corn syrup. Mix well. Sift dry ingredients together and add, alternately with the water, to the creamed mixture, mixing very well after every addition. Spread in a greased 15 1/2 x 10 1/2-inch jelly-roll pan and bake at 350 degrees for 18 to 20 minutes, brushing beaten egg or egg whites on top before baking, if desired. Cut into squares when cool.

Makes: 30 squares

Mrs. Eli A. Raber
Millersburg, Ohio

BLONDE BROWNIES

These have a neat vanilla taste—quite different.

2 cups brown sugar
1/4 pound plus 2 2/3 tablespoons butter
2 eggs
2 teaspoons vanilla extract
1/4 teaspoon baking soda
1 teaspoon baking powder
1 teaspoon salt
2 cups sifted all-purpose flour
1 six-ounce package chocolate chips
1 cup chopped nuts

Cream together the sugar and butter until fluffy, then add the eggs and vanilla and beat until smooth. Sift together the dry ingredients, add to the batter, and mix well. Add the chocolate chips and nuts, then put into a greased and floured 13 x 9 x 2-inch pan. Bake in a 350-degree oven for 30 minutes. Slice when cool.

Makes: 24 bars

Mrs. Chester Miller
Goshen, Indiana

BANANA NUGGETS

An oatmeal–chocolate chip cookie with a banana flavor.

1½ cups sifted all-purpose flour
1 cup granulated sugar
½ teaspoon baking soda
1 teaspoon salt
¼ teaspoon grated nutmeg
¾ teaspoon ground cinnamon
1 egg, well beaten
1 cup mashed ripe banana
1¾ cups quick-cooking oats
1 six-ounce package semisweet chocolate chips

Sift together the dry ingredients, then cut in the shortening till the mixture resembles crumbs. Add the egg, banana, and oats and beat until thoroughly blended. Fold in the chocolate chips. Drop by spoonfuls onto ungreased cookie sheets and bake in a 400-degree oven for 15 minutes. Immediately remove from the pan to a rack to cool.

Yields: 36 cookies *Mary Shetler*

DELUXE OATMEAL COOKIES

Very nutritious, with a raisin and cinnamon flavor.

3 cups rolled oats
3 cups sifted all-purpose flour
2 teaspoons baking soda
½ teaspoon ground cloves
2 cups granulated sugar
1 teaspoon ground cinnamon
½ teaspoon salt
1 cup melted shortening
⅔ cup milk
2 eggs, well beaten
1 cup raisins

Combine the oats, with the other dry ingredients. In a separate bowl, combine the shortening, milk, and beaten eggs. Add the dry ingredients, one cup at a time, and stir to blend, then fold in the raisins. Drop the dough on greased cookie sheets, one level teaspoon at a time. Bake at 375 degrees for about 12 minutes. Remove to racks to cool.

Makes: 60 to 72 cookies

Mrs. Cornelius Miller
Apple Creek, Ohio

RANGER COOKIES

The combination of oatmeal, breakfast cereal, and coconut is what makes this an unusual cookie.

2 eggs, beaten
1 cup granulated sugar
1 cup shortening
2 cups rolled oats
1 cup grated coconut
1 teaspoon baking soda
1/2 teaspoon salt
1 cup brown sugar
2 cups sifted all-purpose flour
2 cups Rice Krispies
1/2 teaspoon baking powder

Combine the beaten eggs with the sugar and beat well. Add the shortening and beat again for 2 minutes, then add the remaining ingredients and mix well. Drop by spoonfuls on greased cookie sheets and bake at 400 degrees. Cool on racks.

Makes: 60 to 72 cookies

Mrs. Jonas Borntrager
Sugarcreek, Ohio

"BEST EVER" DROP COOKIES

"These cookies also keep well."

1 1/2 cups granulated sugar
1/4 pound butter
2 eggs, beaten
2 1/2 cups sifted all-purpose flour, more if necessary
1 teaspoon ground cinnamon
1 teaspoon ground cloves
1 teaspoon baking soda dissolved in 1/4 cup sour milk
1 cup raisins

Cream the butter and add the sugar, then add the beaten eggs. Blend well. Sift together the dry ingredients and add, alternately with the soda–sour milk mixture, to the creamed mixture. The dough should be quite stiff; if not, add more flour by tablespoons. Fold in the raisins. Drop by teaspoonfuls onto greased cookie sheets, leaving ample space between each; the cookies do spread out thin. Bake at 350 degrees for 15 minutes, then remove from the sheets with a spatula and cool on racks.

Yield: 48 cookies

Annie Zook
Oakland, Maryland

HONEY GINGER COOKIES

The aroma of these during baking is irresistible!

1/4 pound butter
1/4 cup granulated sugar
1/4 cup brown sugar
1/2 cup honey
1/2 cup buttermilk
1 egg
1 teaspoon baking soda
1/2 teaspoon ground cinnamon
1/2 teaspoon ground ginger
2 cups all-purpose flour
Finely chopped nuts, sugar, and maraschino cherry pieces (optional) for decoration

Cream the butter, then add the sugars and honey and blend well. Add the buttermilk, egg, and dry ingredients, mixing well after each addition. Add the buttermilk, and dry ingredients, mixing well after each addition. Drop by teaspoonfuls on greased cookie sheets. Press some chopped nuts on top of each cookie, along with sugar and maraschino cherry pieces, if desired. Bake at 400 degrees for 8 to 10 minutes. Cool on racks.

Makes: 48 to 60 cookies

Mrs. Amos Yoder
Mount Hope, Ohio

COFFEE COOKIES

"An adult cookie—soft and chewy and not too sweet."

1 1/4 cups granulated sugar
1 cup shortening
1 cup molasses
1 tablespoon baking soda
1 teaspoon ground ginger
1 teaspoon ground cinnamon
Sifted all-purpose flour
1 cup hot, strong coffee

Cream together the sugar and shortening, then add the molasses, beating well. Sift together the dry ingredients, beginning with 1 cup flour and add to the creamed mixture. Blend well. Add the coffee, stirring well, then add enough flour to the dough so that a spoon can stand up in the middle. Refrigerate overnight.

The next day, drop by tablespoonfuls on greased cookie sheets and bake in a 350-degree oven for about 15 minutes. Cool on racks.

Yields: 60 cookies

Alta Schlabach
Millersburg, Ohio

APPLESAUCE COOKIES

"Very good tasting, and light in texture."

1 cup shortening
1 cup brown sugar
2 eggs
4 cups sifted all-purpose flour
2 teaspoons baking soda
1 teaspoon salt
1 teaspoon grated nutmeg
1 teaspoon ground cinnamon
1 teaspoon ground allspice
1 teaspoon ground cloves
2 cups applesauce
1 cup chopped nuts
1 six-ounce package butterscotch chips

Cream together the shortening and sugar, then add the eggs and beat until light. Sift together the dry ingredients and add, alternately with the applesauce, to the creamed mixture, mixing well after each addition. Fold in the nuts and butterscotch chips. Drop by teaspoonfuls, about 1 inch apart, on greased cookie sheets and bake at 350 degrees for about 20 minutes. Cool on racks.

Yields: 90 cookies

Mrs. Ray M. Yoder
Accident, Maryland

OLD-FASHIONED PUMPKIN COOKIES

A spice cookie with a raisin, nut, and pumpkin flavor.

1/4 cup shortening
1/4 cup brown sugar
1/4 cup corn syrup
1 egg, beaten
1/2 cup canned or mashed, cooked fresh pumpkin
3/4 cup sifted all-purpose flour
2 teaspoons baking powder
1/2 teaspoon salt
1 1/4 teaspoon ground cinnamon
1/4 teaspoon ground ginger
1/4 teaspoon grated nutmeg
1/2 cup chopped nuts
1/2 cup raisins

Cream together the shortening, sugar, and corn syrup. Beat until light and fluffy, then add the egg and beat again. Blend in the pumpkin. Sift together the dry ingredients, then add to the pumpkin mixture and blend well. Fold in the nuts and raisins. Drop by teaspoonfuls on greased cookie sheets and bake at 350 degrees for 15 minutes. Cool on racks.

Makes: 48 cookies

Katie M. Hershberger

CHOCOLATE MARSHMALLOW COOKIES

This drop chocolate cookie is topped first with marshmallow, then with frosting, and then with nuts.

½ cup shortening
1 cup brown sugar
1 egg
1 teaspoon vanilla extract
½ cup cocoa
½ teaspoon salt
½ teaspoon baking soda
1¾ cups sifted all-purpose flour
½ cup milk
Miniature marshmallows
½ cup chopped nuts

Frosting

2 cups confectioners' sugar
¼ cup cream
¼ cup cocoa
3 tablespoons butter

Cream together the shortening and sugar, then add the egg and vanilla and mix well. Sift together the dry ingredients and add, alternately with the milk, to the creamed mixture, mixing well after each addition. Drop by teaspoonfuls on greased cookie sheets and bake in a 350-degree oven for 8 minutes. Meanwhile, combine the frosting ingredients and beat until smooth and creamy.

After the 8 minutes are up, top each cookie with a few miniature marshmallows, then return to the oven and bake for 2 minutes longer. Cool on racks, then frost. Top with the chopped nuts.

Makes: 48 to 60 cookies

Mrs. Henry Miller, Jr.
Big Prairie, Ohio

WHOOPIE PIES

A chocolate cakelike cookie with a cream filling.

2 cups granulated sugar
1 cup shortening or lard
2 eggs, well beaten
2 teaspoons vanilla extract
4½ cups sifted all-purpose flour
½ cup cocoa
2 teaspoons salt
1 cup sour milk
2 teaspoons baking soda
1 cup hot water

Filling

1/4 cup milk
1 one-pound box confectioners' sugar
2 teaspoons vanilla extract
1 cup vegetable shortening
4 tablespoons flour
3 egg whites, stiffly beaten

Cream the sugar and shortening, then add the beaten eggs and vanilla and mix well. Sift together the flour, cocoa, and salt, then add, alternately with the sour milk, to the creamed mixture. Dissolve the soda in the hot water and add. Blend well. Drop by teaspoonfuls on greased cookie sheets and bake for 8 minutes at 400 degrees. Cool on racks.

While the cookies are cooling, make the filling. Combine the milk, powdered sugar, and vanilla. In a separate bowl, cream the shortening and flour together well. Combine with the milk-sugar mixture, then add the stiffly beaten egg whites and beat vigorously. Spread the filling on half the cooled cookies, then top with the other half.

Makes: 50 to 60 cookies

Mrs. William Yoder
Topeka, Indiana

CHOCOLATE DROP COOKIES

"This is a cakelike cookie that does not spread when baking, so they can be placed very close together."

1 cup brown sugar
1/2 cup shortening
1 teaspoon vanilla extract
2 eggs, beaten
1 1/2 cups sifted all-purpose flour
1/2 cup cocoa
1 teaspoon baking soda
1/2 teaspoon salt
1/2 cup milk
1 cup chopped nuts or shredded coconut

Cream together the sugar and shortening. Add the vanilla and beaten eggs and beat until fluffy. Sift together the sifted dry ingredients, then add, alternately with the milk, to the sugar mixture. Beat until the ingredients are well blended, then fold in the chopped nuts or shredded coconut. Put by spoonfuls on a greased cookie sheet and bake at 375 degrees for 10 to 12 minutes. Cool on racks.

Makes: 54 cookies

Mary Mast
Seymour, Missouri

PIE-CRUST COOKIES

"A tasty cookie—even husbands like them. For variety, add raisins, nuts, coconut, or dates."

4 cups sifted all-purpose flour
2 teaspoons baking powder
1 teaspoon baking soda
2 cups brown sugar
1 cup lard
2 eggs, broken into a measuring cup and milk added to fill 1 cup
1 teaspoon vanilla extract

Mix as you would pie dough, sifting together all the dry ingredients and cutting in the lard. Add the milk-egg mixture and vanilla and mix well. Drop by spoonfuls on cookie sheets and bake at 350 degrees for 8 minutes. Cool on racks.

Makes: About 60 cookies

Mrs. Eli Stutzman
Apple Creek, Ohio

AMISH DROP COOKIES

Every Amish baker makes these simple but excellent cookies. They can be sprinkled with sugar or a sugar-cinnamon mixture, and chocolate chips can also be added to some of the batter.

2 cups granulated sugar
1½ cups lard
2 eggs
1½ teaspoons grated nutmeg
2 teaspoons vanilla extract
3 teaspoons baking powder
1 teaspoon baking soda
1½ cups milk
6 cups sifted all-purpose flour

Cream the sugar and lard, then add the eggs, nutmeg, vanilla, and baking powder and mix well. Mix the soda with the milk and add, alternately with the flour, to the creamed mixture, mixing well after each addition. Drop with a soup spoon on ungreased cookie sheets and bake in a 350-degree oven for 10 to 12 minutes; do not overbake.

Makes: 60 cookies

Mary Ann Hostetler
Topeka, Indiana

BEST BUTTERMILK COOKIES

A basic, very-easy-to-make cookie recipe.

2 cups brown sugar
1/2 pound butter or margarine
2 eggs, well beaten
1 teaspoon vanilla extract
2 teaspoons baking soda
1 cup buttermilk
2 teaspoons baking powder
4 cups sifted all-purpose flour

Combine the sugar and butter and cream well. Add the beaten eggs and vanilla and blend well. Add the soda to the buttermilk, add the baking powder to the flour. Add the liquid and flour alternately to the creamed mixture, mixing well after each addition. Store in the refrigerator overnight.

The next day, drop by teaspoonfuls on greased cookie sheets and bake at 375 degrees for 10 minutes. Cool on racks.

Makes: 96 cookies

Mrs. Sam Hershberger
Apple Creek, Ohio

SOUR CREAM DROP COOKIES

A nut drop cookie with a confectioners' sugar frosting.

1/2 cup shortening
1 1/2 cups brown sugar
2 eggs, beaten
2 1/2 cups sifted all-purpose flour
1/2 teaspoon baking powder
1/2 teaspoon salt
1 teaspoon baking soda
1/2 pint sour cream
1 teaspoon vanilla extract
2/3 cup chopped walnuts

Frosting

6 tablespoons butter
1 1/2 cup confectioners' sugar
1 teaspoon vanilla extract
Hot water

Cream the shortening and sugar, then add the eggs, and mix well. Sift together the dry ingredients and add alternately with the sour cream, to the creamed mixture. Blend in the vanilla and nuts, then drop by teaspoonfuls on a greased cookie sheet and bake at 350 degrees for 10 to 12 minutes. Cool on racks.

While the cookies are cooling, make the frosting. Melt and brown the butter, then add the confectioners' sugar and vanilla. Blend in hot water by spoonfuls until the icing is of a spreading consistency, then frost the cooled cookies.

Makes: 48 to 60 cookies — *Mrs. Jake Schwartz*

BUTTERSCOTCH-NUT DROP COOKIES

Flavored with butterscotch and textured with nuts.

1/4 pound butter
1 1/2 cups brown sugar
2 eggs
1 teaspoon vanilla extract
2 1/2 cups sifted all-purpose flour
1 teaspoon baking soda
1/2 teaspoon salt
1/2 teaspoon baking powder
1 cup sour cream
2/3 cup chopped nuts
Confectioners' sugar icing of your choice and shredded coconut for decoration

Cream together the butter and sugar. Add the eggs and vanilla and beat well. Sift together the dry ingredients, then add, alternately with the sour cream, to the creamed mixture, mixing well after each addition. Stir in the nuts.

Chill the dough for at least 1 hour, then drop on greased cookie sheets by teaspoonfuls, about 1 1/2 inches apart. Bake at 400 degrees for 8 minutes. Cool on racks, then frost with confectioners' sugar frosting and sprinkle with coconut.

Makes: 66 to 72 cookies — *Mrs. Lester Yoder*
Millersburg, Ohio

MICHIGAN ROCK COOKIES

An Amish favorite date-nut cookie.

Butter
1 1/2 cups brown sugar
4 eggs
1 teaspoon vanilla extract
3 cups sifted all-purpose flour
1 teaspoon baking soda
1 1/2 teaspoons ground cinnamon
1 1/2 pounds nuts, coarsely broken
1 pound dates, chopped

Cream the butter and sugar until smooth, then add the eggs and vanilla. Sift together the flour, soda, and cinnamon; mix thoroughly with the creamed mixture. Stir in the coarsely broken nuts and chopped dates, then drop by teaspoonfuls on ungreased cookie sheets. Bake at 350 degrees for 10 to 12 minutes, then cool on racks.

Makes: 168 cookies

Janice Peachy
Belleville, Ohio

GLAZED PINEAPPLE COOKIES

This is a soft, cakelike cookie.

1 cup brown sugar
1/2 cup shortening
1 egg
1 teaspoon vanilla extract
3/4 cup crushed pineapple
2 cups sifted all-purpose flour
1/4 teaspoon baking soda
1/4 teaspoon salt
1 1/2 teaspoons baking powder

Cream the brown sugar and shortening, then add the egg, vanilla, and pineapple and mix well. Sift together the dry ingredients and stir into the batter well. Drop by teaspoonfuls on greased cookie sheets and bake at 350 degrees for 10 to 12 minutes. Cool on racks.

Makes: 60 cookies

Mrs. Ray Miller
Dundee, Ohio

CARROT COOKIES

A sweet, cakelike cookie with orange icing.

1 cup shortening
3/4 cup granulated sugar
2 eggs
1 cup cooked, mashed carrots
2 cups sifted all-purpose flour
2 teaspoons baking powder
1/2 teaspoon salt
3/4 cup grated coconut

Frosting

2 1/2 tablespoons butter, softened
1 1/2 cups confectioners' sugar
1 1/2 tablespoons orange juice

Cream the shortening and sugar, then add the eggs and beat well. Add the carrots and blend until smooth. Sift together the dry ingredients, then add to the batter and blend well. Add the coconut. Drop by teaspoonfuls on greased cookie sheets and bake at 400 degrees for 8 to 10 minutes. Cool on racks.

While the cookies are cooling, make the frosting. Blend the butter, confectioners' sugar, and orange juice until smooth. Use to frost the cooled cookies.

Makes: 60 cookies

Mrs. M. Shetler
Apple Creek, Ohio

HELEN'S SUGAR COOKIES

Not too rich—ideal for the low-calorie dieter who wants to indulge himself occasionally.

1 cup granulated sugar
1/2 cup shortening
2 eggs, well beaten
1 teaspoon vanilla extract
1/2 teaspoon baking soda
1/2 scant teaspoon salt
2 teaspoons baking powder
2 cups sifted all-purpose flour
1/2 cup sour cream

Cream the sugar and shortening, then add the eggs and vanilla and beat well. Sift together the dry ingredients and add, alternately with the sour cream, to the creamed mixture, mixing well after each addition. Chill the dough for several hours or overnight.

Cut the dough into pieces the size of walnuts and roll out into circles. Put in greased cookie sheets and bake at 350 degrees for 10 to 12 minutes. Remove the cookies with a spatula and cool on racks.

Makes: 60 to 72 cookies

Mrs. Andy Mast
Napanee, Indiana

GRANDMOTHER'S CHRISTMAS COOKIES

"This is a spicy sugar cookie that improves some with aging. I love to dunk these in cold milk."

1 1/2 cups brown sugar
1/2 cup shortening
4 to 5 cups sifted all-purpose flour
1 1/2 teaspoons baking powder
1 1/2 teaspoons baking soda
1/2 teaspoon salt
1/2 teaspoon grated nutmeg
1 cup sour milk or buttermilk
Colored sugar, nuts, or frosting for decoration

Cream the sugar and shortening and beat until fluffy. Sift together the dry ingredients and add, alternately with the sour milk, to the creamed mixture. Combine thoroughly, using enough flour to make a stiff dough. Roll very thin and cut into fancy shapes. Bake, on a lightly greased cookie sheet, at 375 degrees for 10 to 12 minutes. Remove with a spatula to a rack to cool, then sprinkle with colored sugar or nuts, or frost them.

Makes: 60 to 72 cookies

Mrs. Eli A. Raber
Millersburg, Ohio

JUMBLES (1880)

The basic Amish butter cookie.

1 pound butter
3 cups granulated sugar
1 egg, beaten
1 teaspoon vanilla extract or other flavoring
5 cups sifted all-purpose flour
1/2 teaspoon baking soda
Colored sugar (optional)

Cream the butter with the sugar, then add the beaten egg and flavoring and blend well. Sift together the flour and soda and add to the creamed mixture, small amounts at a time. Mix well, then roll out rather thin on a slightly floured board. Sprinkle with sugar and cut to desired shapes. Bake at 420 degrees for about 10 minutes, or until golden. Remove with a spatula to racks to cool. To add color, use colored sugar for topping.

Makes: About 90 cookies

Mrs. Cornelius Miller
Apple Creek, Ohio

OLD-FASHIONED GINGER COOKIES (LEBKUCHEN)

"This smells so good it brings back childhood memories."

1½ cups molasses
½ cup granulated sugar
½ pound butter
4 cups flour, more if necessary
½ teaspoon salt
1 tablespoon baking soda
1½ teaspoons ground ginger
1½ teaspoons ground cinnamon
1 cup buttermilk or sour milk
1 egg, beaten

Combine the molasses and sugar in a saucepan and heat. When sugar has dissolved, add the butter and stir until melted. Remove from the heat. Sift the dry ingredients together, then add, alternately with the sour milk, to the molasses mixture. Stir until a soft, smooth dough is formed. Work the dough with your hands for 5 minutes, then chill in the refrigerator for several hours.

Turn the dough out onto a lightly floured board and roll ¼ inch thick. Cut with a large round cookie cutter and place, 1 inch apart, on greased cookie sheets. Glaze with the beaten egg and bake at 350 degrees for 20 to 25 minutes. Remove with a spatula to racks to cool.

Makes: 60 to 72 cookies

Mrs. Venus Znercher
Millersburg, Ohio

KNEE BLATZ (KNEE PATCHES)

These taste best eaten warm.

3 tablespoons sour cream
1 egg, well beaten
½ teaspoon salt
1½ cups sifted all-purpose flour
Fat for deep frying

Add the sour cream to the beaten egg, then add the salt and mix well. Add the flour and knead well. Take pieces of dough the size of a walnut, no bigger, and roll paper thin. Fry in deep fat like doughnuts, then put on a dinner plate, one on top of the other, sprinkling each one with sugar.

Makes: 18 to 20 cookies

Mrs. Andy Mast
Shreve, Ohio

FET KUCHIE (LARD CAKES)

Crispy fried cookies—an Amish favorite, good served with coffee.

3 eggs, well beaten
1 cup cream
1 teaspoon baking soda
1 cup buttermilk
1 teaspoon salt
1 cup sifted all-purpose flour
Fat for deep frying

Combine the eggs, cream, and soda, then add the buttermilk, salt, and enough flour to make a dough stiff enough to roll out. Roll out to about 1/4 inch thick and cut in oblong pieces about 2 x 4 inches, then cut two or three slits three-quarters of the way through each piece. Fry in deep fat like doughnuts.

Makes: About 18 cookies

Mrs. Andy Mast
Shreve, Ohio

CHINA SWIRLS

Spicy raised, rolled, fried cookies.

3/4 cup milk
3/4 cup plus 1 tablespoon granulated sugar
1 teaspoon salt
1/4 cup vegetable oil
1 package active dry yeast
1/4 cup lukewarm water
1 egg, beaten
3 1/4 cups sifted all-purpose flour
1 teaspoon ground cinnamon
Fat for deep frying
Confectioners' sugar

Scald the milk, then stir in the 3/4 cup sugar, the salt, and oil. Let set until lukewarm.

Dissolve the yeast in the warm water. Stir in the milk mixture, egg, and half of the flour. Beat until smooth, then stir in the remaining flour. Cover and let rise until doubled in bulk, then roll out into a rectangle and sprinkle with the 1 tablespoon sugar combined with the cinnamon. Starting with a long side, roll the rectangle up, then slice off as for rolls. Allow to rise for about 30 minutes, then fry in deep fat. Glaze with confectioners' sugar.

Makes: 12 to 16 cookies

Mrs. Amos Miller

PINWHEEL COOKIES

Refrigerator cookie with chocolate and vanilla layers.

1/4 pound butter or lard
1/2 cup granulated sugar
1 egg yolk
1 1/2 cups sifted all-purpose flour
1/8 teaspoon salt
1 1/2 teaspoons baking powder
1 1/2 teaspoons cocoa
3 tablespoons milk
1/2 teaspoon vanilla extract

Cream the butter and sugar, then blend in the egg yolk. Sift together the flour, salt, and baking powder and add, alternately with the milk, to the creamed mixture. Mix well. Divide dough into two parts, adding cocoa to one part and vanilla to the other part.

Roll the white dough to a thin rectangular sheet and then roll out the cocoa dough. Place the white dough on the cocoa dough and press together. Roll up, like a jelly roll, into a tight roll 2 inches in diameter. Chill for 1 hour or longer, then cut into 1/4-inch slices. Arrange flat in a pan or on a cookie sheet and bake at 350 degrees for 8 minutes. Cool on racks.

Makes: About 40 cookies *Annie W. Bender*

DATE-NUT PINWHEELS

"Fine for freezing, good for box lunches."

1 cup shortening
1 cup brown sugar
1 cup granulated sugar
3 eggs
1 teaspoon vanilla extract
4 cups sifted all-purpose flour
1 teaspoon baking soda
1 teaspoon ground cinnamon
1/4 teaspoon salt

Date Filling

1 pound dates, chopped
1/2 cup granulated sugar
1/2 cup water
1 cup finely chopped nuts

Cream until fluffy the shortening and sugars. Add the eggs and blend well, then add the vanilla. Sift together the dry ingredients and add to the batter, mixing well. Chill while you prepare the filling.

Combine the dates, sugar, and water in a saucepan and cook, stirring occasionally, until a thick paste is formed. Stir in the nuts. Cool before using.

Roll out the dough on a floured surface to 1/4-inch thickness and spread with the date filling. Roll up jelly-roll fashion and chill until quite firm. Cut in thin slices and place on greased cookie sheets. Bake at 375 degrees for 10 to 15 minutes. Cool on racks.

Makes: 4 dozen cookies

Mrs. Aden Miller
Sugarcreek, Ohio

MACAROON OATMEAL COOKIES

"Family style." You can add raisins or chocolate chips to the recipe, too.

1½ cups sifted all-purpose flour
1 teaspoon baking soda
1½ teaspoons salt
1 cup vegetable shortening
1 cup granulated sugar
1 cup brown sugar
2 eggs, well beaten
1 teaspoon vanilla extract
3 cups quick-cooking oats

Sift together the dry ingredients. Cream the shortening, add the sugars gradually, and beat until light. Add the eggs and vanilla, then add the dry ingredients and blend thoroughly. Stir in the oats. Form into rolls, wrap in waxed paper, and chill. Slice and bake at 350 degrees for 10 minutes, or until golden brown. Cool on racks.

Makes: About 40 cookies

Mrs. Levi Raber
Millersburg, Ohio

OVERNIGHT COOKIES

A refrigerator cookie, nut flavored.

4 cups brown sugar
1 cup lard
4 eggs
¼ cup water
1 teaspoon vanilla extract
7 cups sifted all-purpose flour
1 tablespoon baking soda
¼ teaspoon salt
1 cup chopped nuts

Cream the sugar and lard well. Beat eggs, adding the water and vanilla, then add to the sugar-lard mixture and beat till smooth. Sift together the flour, soda, and salt. Add to the creamed mixture in small portions, blending until smooth after each addition. Blend in the chopped nuts. Work the dough with your hands until the dough is stiff, then form into three rolls about 12 inches long, wrap in waxed paper, and refrigerate overnight.

The next day, slice 1/4-inch thick and bake on greased cookie sheets at 350 degrees for 8 to 10 minutes. Cool on racks.

Makes: About 100 cookies *Mrs. John Miller*

BUTTERSCOTCH COOKIES

These have an odd, thick yet light, butterscotch flavor. It's hard to describe, but nice to the taste.

1/4 pound butter or margarine
2 cups brown sugar
2 eggs, beaten
1/4 teaspoon salt
1 teaspoon vanilla extract
3 cups sifted all-purpose flour
1 teaspoon cream of tartar
1 teaspoon baking soda
1 cup grated coconut (optional)

Beat the butter until lightly creamy, then add the brown sugar, one cup at a time, beating well after each addition. Add the beaten eggs, salt, and vanilla. Sift together the flour, cream of tartar, and soda and add to the butter-sugar mixture, one cup at a time. Mix well, then stir in the coconut, if desired.

Divide the dough into four parts and make each into a roll. Wrap in waxed paper and chill for 8 hours or more. Cut into 1/4-inch slices and bake on greased cookie sheets at 350 degrees until lightly browned (approximately 8 minutes). Cool on racks.

Makes: 60 cookies *Mrs. Ezra Deimar*
Sullivan, Illinois

ORANGE COOKIES

A light, shaped, orange-flavored cookie.

1/4 pound butter or margarine
3/4 cup granulated sugar
1 egg
1/4 cup milk
2 cups sifted all-purpose flour
1 teaspoon baking powder
1/4 teaspoon baking soda
1/2 teaspoon vanilla extract
1/2 teaspoon salt
1 teaspoon orange extract
1 teaspoon grated orange rind

Combine the ingredients in the order given, then chill. Form into small balls, flatten on greased cookie sheets, and bake at 350 degrees for 8 to 10 minutes, or until done. Cool on racks.

Makes: 60 to 72 cookies

Esther Miller
Millersburg, Ohio

THUMBPRINT COOKIES

Good especially for holidays.

1/4 cup shortening, softened
4 tablespoons butter
1/4 cup brown sugar
1 egg, separated
1/2 teaspoon vanilla extract
1 cup sifted all-purpose flour
1/4 teaspoon salt
3/4 cup finely chopped nuts
Chopped candied fruit, jelly, or tinted icing for decoration

Cream thoroughly the shortening, butter, and sugar, then blend in the egg yolk and vanilla. Sift together the flour and salt, then combine with the creamed mixture. Roll into 1-inch balls. Dip the balls in the egg white, beaten, and roll in the nuts. Place about 1 inch apart on ungreased cookie sheets and press your thumb into the center of each. Bake at 375 degrees for 12 to 15 minutes, or until set. If desired, place a bit of chopped candied fruit, jelly, or tinted icing in the thumbprint.

Makes: 24 cookies

Katie Miller
Middlefield, Ohio

SAND TARTS

A shaped cookie, very tasty, with a walnut center.

1/4 pound butter
1/2 cup shortening
1/2 cup granulated sugar
1 teaspoon vanilla extract
1/2 teaspoon baking powder
2 cups sifted all-purpose flour
1 cup walnut pieces
Confectioners' sugar

Cream the sugar with butter, shortening, and vanilla. Sift the baking powder with the flour and add to the creamed mixture, blending well. Form the dough into round balls the size of a walnut. Place on greased cookie sheets and put a walnut on each; do not press down.

Bake at 350 degrees for about 10 minutes. Cool on racks, and when thoroughly cooled, roll in confectioners' sugar.

Makes: 30 cookies

Mrs. Amos Zook
Stuarts Draft, Virginia

ANGEL FOOD COOKIES

Include these in your Christmas collection.

1 cup shortening
1/2 cup granulated sugar
1 egg, beaten
1 teaspoon vanilla extract
1/4 teaspoon salt
1 teaspoon baking soda
1/2 cup brown sugar
2 cups all-purpose flour
1 teaspoon cream of tartar
1 cup grated coconut

Cream the shortening and sugar till fluffy, then add the egg and vanilla and blend well. Sift together the dry ingredients and slowly add to the creamed mixture, blending well after each addition. Blend in the coconut last. Roll the dough, with floured hands, into small balls. Dip into water, then into sugar. Put on greased cookie sheets and bake at 375 degrees for 15 minutes. Cool on racks.

Makes: 48 cookies

Ray M. Yoder
Accident, Maryland

SNICKERDOODLES

"Very tasty, like an old-fashioned dunking cookie."

1 cup shortening, softened
1 1/2 cups plus 3 tablespoons granulated sugar
2 eggs, well beaten
3 scant cups sifted all-purpose flour
2 teaspoons cream of tartar
1 teaspoon baking soda
1/2 teaspoon salt
2 teaspoons ground cinnamon

Cream the shortening and the 1 1/2 cups sugar, then blend in the eggs and mix well. Sift together the flour, cream of tartar, soda, and salt and add gradually to the sugar mixture, blending well after each addition. Chill the dough, then roll into balls the size of walnuts. Roll in a mixture of 3 tablespoons sugar and 2 teaspoons cinnamon. Put on greased cookie sheets and bake at 400 degrees for 8 to 10 minutes, until lightly browned. (These cookies puff up at first, then flatten out with crinkled tops.) Cool on racks.

Makes: 60 cookies

Mrs. Alvin Miller
Shreve, Ohio

PUDDINGS

MAPLE SPONGE PUDDING

A maple-custard layered pudding topped with cream, bananas, and nuts.

1 envelope (1 tablespoon) unflavored gelatin
2 cups cold water
2 cups brown sugar
½ teaspoon maple flavoring
2 eggs, separated
3 cups milk
2 egg yolks
½ cup granulated sugar
Pinch of salt
1 tablespoon all-purpose flour
1 teaspoon vanilla extract
2 bananas, sliced
1 cup heavy cream, whipped
1 cup chopped peanuts

Soak the gelatin in 1½ cups of the cold water for 5 minutes. In a saucepan, combine the brown sugar, ½ cup water, and maple flavoring and boil for 10 minutes. Pour the syrup gradually into the soaked gelatin. Let cool, then fold in the egg whites, stiffly beaten. Combine the milk, egg yolks, granulated sugar, salt, flour, and vanilla in a saucepan and bring to a boil. Cool. Layer the pudding mixture with the gelatin mixture in a mold. Chill, then cut in chunks and top with banana, whipped cream, and nuts.

Serves: 6 to 8

Mrs. Melvin Miller
Fredericksburg, Ohio

CHOCOLATE SPONGE PUDDING

Light and not too sweet, and the chocolate flavor is subtle.

1/4 cup cocoa
1/2 cup hot water
1/4 cup granulated sugar
4 eggs, separated
1 3/4 cups milk
1 teaspoon vanilla extract
1 envelope (1 tablespoon) unflavored gelatin, softened in 2 tablespoons cold water
Pinch of salt
Ground nuts

Dissolve the cocoa in the hot water and add half the sugar. Beat the egg yolks and combine with the remaining sugar. Scald the milk in the top of a double boiler and slowly add the egg yolk mixture. Cook briefly over boiling water, then add the cocoa mixture and vanilla. Pour in the gelatin soaked in cold water and stir until smooth. Let cool. When cold, pour in the egg whites, stiffly beaten with the salt. Chill until set, then sprinkle with nuts and serve.

Serves: 6

Mrs. E. D. Troyer
Fresno, Ohio

APPLE SPONGE PUDDING

A cakelike pudding with a bottom apple layer.

1 egg, separated
1/2 cup granulated sugar
1/2 cup sifted all-purpose flour
1/4 teaspoon salt
1/2 teaspoon baking powder
1/4 cup water
1/2 teaspoon vanilla extract
3/4 cup brown sugar
2 tablespoons butter
4 medium apples, peeled and sliced

Beat the egg yolk, then add the sugar. Sift together the dry ingredients and add, alternately with the water and vanilla, to the egg yolk mixture. Fold in the egg white, stiffly beaten. Put the brown sugar in the bottom of a large, flat baking dish and dot with the butter. Add the apple slices and pour the batter over. Bake, uncovered, at 350 degrees for 45 minutes. Serve warm, with milk or cream.

Serves: 8

Mrs. Abe Mast

SPANISH CREAM

A light, sweet, creamy dessert.

1 envelope (1 tablespoon) unflavored gelatin
1 cup milk
2 eggs, separated
3/4 cup granulated sugar
1/2 teaspoon salt
1 teaspoon vanilla extract

Soak the gelatin in the milk for 10 minutes. Combine the egg yolks, sugar, and salt in a saucepan. Add the milk and gelatin and bring almost to a boil, stirring constantly. Remove from the heat and cool. Add the vanilla.

Beat the egg whites until stiff, then add to the gelatin mixture and beat at high speed. Pour into a serving dish and chill until firm.

Serves: 4

Verna Wenger

SPECIAL PUDDING

"This is also delicious in alternate layers with flavored gelatin."

2 eggs, separated
1 cup granulated sugar
1/2 cup milk
1 envelope (1 tablespoon) unflavored gelatin
1/3 cup cold water
1 teaspoon vanilla extract
1/2 pint cream, whipped
16 graham crackers, crushed
4 tablespoons butter

Combine the egg yolks, sugar, and milk in a saucepan and boil for 1 minute. Soak the gelatin in the cold water for a few minutes, then pour into the hot mixture. Cool until the mixture starts to set, then fold in the 2 egg whites, stiffly beaten, with the vanilla and the whipped cream. Combine the graham-cracker crumbs and butter. Layer the pudding and crumb mixture and chill.

Serves: 4

Mrs. Don Burkholder
Eureka, Illinois

YUMMY RICE PUDDING

A rich-tasting rice pudding with a meringue topping.

1 cup cooked rice
Salt to taste
1 teaspoon grated nutmeg
1 cup raisins
4 eggs, separated
$1^1/_2$ cups granulated sugar
1 quart milk
$1^1/_2$ cups confectioners' sugar

Combine the rice, salt, nutmeg, raisins, egg yolks, granulated sugar, and milk and stir carefully. Pour into a $1^1/_2$-quart casserole and bake at 350 degrees for 30 minutes. Beat the egg whites until frothy, then add the confectioners' sugar and beat until stiff. Top the pudding with the mixture and bake for 30 minutes longer.

Serves: 4

Clara Hershberger
Staunton, Virginia

DATE PUDDING

A quick-and-easy, cakelike pudding you can top with whipped cream if you want.

1 cup boiling water
1 teaspoon baking soda
1 cup chopped dates or prunes
$1^1/_2$ cups sifted all-purpose flour
1 cup granulated sugar
1 egg, beaten
$^1/_2$ cup chopped nuts
1 tablespoon butter

Filling

1 quart milk
1 tablespoon brown sugar
$^1/_4$ cup all-purpose flour
1 cup granulated sugar
1 teaspoon vanilla extract
$^1/_2$ pint cream, whipped

Combine the boiling water, soda, and dates and let stand till cooled. Meanwhile, combine the flour, sugar, egg, chopped nuts, and butter. Add to the cooled date mixture, mix well, and put into an 8-inch-square pan. Bake for 25 to 30 minutes at 350 degrees. Cool.

While the pudding is cooling, prepare the filling. Combine the milk and brown sugar in a saucepan and bring to a boil. Stir in the flour, granulated sugar, and vanilla and cook until thick. Cool, then stir in the whipped cream.

Cut the cooled pudding into 8 squares, split each square one or more times, and layer with the filling.

Serves: 8

Mrs. Moses Raber
Sugarcreek, Ohio

DATE-NUT PUDDING

This is more like cake than pudding, and tastes best warm.

1 cup granulated sugar
2 tablespoons milk
1 teaspoon baking powder
1 cup chopped nuts
2 eggs, separated
2 tablespoons all-purpose flour
1 cup chopped dates
Whipped cream

Combine the sugar, milk, baking powder, nuts, egg yolks, flour, and dates. Fold in the egg whites, stiffly beaten, then pour into an 8-inch-square baking pan and bake for 45 minutes at 350 degrees. Serve with a topping of whipped cream.

Serves: 6 to 8

Mrs. Ray Easton

GRAHAM CRACKER PUDDING

This looks like a modified soufflé, but tastes like cake.

16 graham crackers, rolled fine
3/4 cup brown sugar
1 teaspoon baking powder
1/4 teaspoon salt
1/2 cup raisins
3/4 cup milk, more if necessary
1/2 teaspoon vanilla extract
2 eggs, well beaten

Topping

1 cup water
4 tablespoons butter
1 cup brown sugar
1 tablespoon cornstarch dissolved in 2 tablespoons water
1 teaspoon vanilla extract

Combine the graham crackers, sugar, baking powder, salt, and raisins. In a separate bowl, combine the milk, vanilla, and beaten eggs, then stir into the dry ingredients. (If the batter is too thick add more milk; the batter should be like thick cake dough.) Bake in a 1-quart casserole at 350 degrees for 30 minutes.

Meanwhile, prepare the topping. Combine the water and butter in a saucepan and bring to a boil. Combine the sugar and dissolved cornstarch, then stir into the boiling liquid. Bring to a boil again, add the vanilla, and remove from the heat. Cool before spreading over the pudding.

Serves: 6 to 8

Mrs. Ben Borntrager
Clark, Missouri

CROW'S NEST PUDDING

"Spoon the sauce over the pudding just before serving individually."

1 cup granulated sugar
2 tablespoons butter, softened
2 eggs
1/2 cup milk
1 teaspoon baking powder
1 cup sifted all-purpose flour
Chopped hickory nuts

Filling

2 tablespoons butter
2 tablespoons all-purpose flour
3/4 cup brown sugar
2 cups cold water
1 cup cream
1 teaspoon vanilla or maple flavoring

Combine the sugar, softened butter, eggs, milk, baking powder, and flour and beat until smooth. Pour into a greased and floured 9-inch-square pan and bake at 350 degrees until light golden brown (about 30 minutes).

Meanwhile, prepare the filling. Brown the butter, then add the remaining ingredients, and cook until a sauce consistency. Cut the pudding into squares. Pour the filling over the top, sprinkle with hickory nuts, and serve warm or cold.

Serves: 9

Leona Miller
Kalona, Iowa

COTTAGE PUDDING

A cake dish with a sweet, vanilla-flavored syrup.

1 3/4 cups sifted all-purpose flour
2 teaspoons baking powder
1/2 teaspoon salt
1/4 cup shortening
3/4 cup granulated sugar
1 large egg
3/4 cup milk
1 teaspoon vanilla extract

Sauce

1 cup granulated sugar
2 tablespoons cornstarch
2 cups boiling water
4 tablespoons butter
2 teaspoons vanilla extract

Sift together the flour, baking powder, and salt. Add the remaining ingredients and beat with a spoon until smooth. Pour into a greased and floured 9-inch-square pan and bake in a 350-degree oven for 25 to 30 minutes.

Meanwhile, prepare the sauce. Combine the sugar and cornstarch in a saucepan. Gradually stir in the boiling water. Boil 1 minute, stirring constantly, then stir in the butter and vanilla. Keep hot till serving time, then pour over the pudding.

Serves: 9

Ester Marie Yoder
Centerville, Michigan

SUPREME DESSERT

A cakelike dessert with a cream and fruit topping.

6 egg whites
1/4 teaspoon cream of tartar
2 cups granulated sugar
2 cups rolled soda crackers
3/4 cup nuts
2 teaspoons vanilla extract

Topping

1 one-pound can pie filling
1 four-ounce envelope whipped topping mix

Beat the egg whites until foamy, then add the cream of tartar and beat until stiff. Add the sugar, the rolled cracker crumbs, and the nuts and vanilla. Pour into a greased 9-inch-square pan and bake at 350 degrees for 25 minutes. Cool, then refrigerate overnight. The next day, top the mixture with the pie filling and the whipped topping, prepared according to package directions.

Serves: 8 to 10

Mrs. Jacob Miller
Millersburg, Ohio

CHERRY PUDDING

A layered pudding with a cherry topping over a cakelike layer.

1 cup milk
1 cup granulated sugar
4 teaspoons butter
2 teaspoons baking powder
2 cups sifted all-purpose flour
1 one-pound can sour cherries, undrained
1/2 cup boiling water
1/2 teaspoon almond extract
1 tablespoon cornstarch dissolved in 1 tablespoon water

Combine the milk, 1/2 cup of the sugar, 1 tablespoon butter, the baking powder, and flour. Pour into an 8-inch-square pan and set aside while you prepare the cherry topping.

In a saucepan, combine the cherries, juice, boiling water, remaining butter, remaining sugar, and almond extract. Stir in the cornstarch and water, then bring to a boil and pour over the reserved batter. Bake at 350 degrees for 35 minutes.

Serves: 6 to 8

Ella Mae Martin

CINNAMON PUDDING

This is good with or without a whipped topping.

1 cup brown sugar
3/4 cup water
2 tablespoons butter, softened
1/2 cup granulated sugar
1/2 cup milk
3/4 cup plus 2 tablespoons flour
1 1/2 teaspoons baking powder
1 teaspoon ground cinnamon
1/4 cup chopped nuts

Combine the brown sugar, cold water, and butter in a saucepan and cook for 5 minutes. Meanwhile, combine the remaining ingredients and place in a greased $1^1/_2$-quart casserole. Pour the mixture in the saucepan on top, then bake at 350 degrees for about 45 minutes.

Serves: 8

Mrs. Eli B. Miller
Wooster, Ohio

SWEETHEART PUDDING

"Nice texture. Not too sweet."

$^1/_4$ cup all-purpose flour
6 tablespoons granulated sugar
2 eggs, separated
$2^1/_2$ cups milk
1 teaspoon vanilla extract

Crust

13 graham crackers, crushed
$^1/_3$ cup sugar
$^3/_4$ stick melted butter

Topping

2 reserved egg whites
$^1/_4$ cup granulated sugar

Combine the flour, sugar, egg yolks (reserving the whites for the topping), and $^1/_2$ cup of milk. Bring the remaining milk to a boil, then stir in the flour–egg yolk mixture. Cook for a few minutes, then add the vanilla. Cool while you prepare the crust.

Combine the graham-cracker crumbs with the sugar and melted butter. Put into a 1-quart pan or baking dish and pat in place. Pour the cooled pudding over the crackers and bake at 350 degrees for about 15 minutes. Prepare the topping by beating the egg whites with the sugar. Spread on the partially baked pudding and continue baking for 15 minutes.

Serves: 6

Mary Kinsinger
Meyersdale, Pennsylvania

CUP CUSTARD

The traditional Amish baked custard.

5 eggs
5 tablespoons granulated sugar
5 tablespoons brown sugar
1/4 teaspoon salt
1 teaspoon vanilla extract
1 quart hot milk

Combine eggs, sugars, salt, and vanilla, then beat in the hot milk. Pour into a 1 1/2-quart casserole and set, uncovered, in a pan of hot water. Put in a 250-degree oven for 1 hour, or until nicely browned on top. Do not let the water boil.

Serves: 4 to 6

Mrs. John H. Miller
Guthrie, Kentucky

POMPADOUR PUDDING

A good tasting, economical and very nutritious dessert for a family.

2 eggs, separated
2 cups milk
Pinch of salt
1 cup sugar
2 tablespoons cornstarch
1 square (1 ounce) unsweetened chocolate
2 tablespoons milk

Beat the egg yolks until lemon colored, then combine with the milk, salt, 1/2 cup of the sugar, and cornstarch in a saucepan. Bring to a boil and cook for a few minutes, stirring, then cool. Pour into a 1-quart casserole. Melt the chocolate with the remaining sugar and milk in the top of a double boiler. Let cool. Beat the egg whites till stiff, then pour the cooled chocolate mixture into the egg whites and blend lightly. Pour over the pudding. Set the casserole in a pan of hot water and bake in a 325-degree oven for 40 to 45 minutes, or until the chocolate puffs up and cracks open. Cool and serve.

Serves: 4 to 6

Elizabeth Fisher
Gordonville, Pennsylvania

CHOCOLATE PUDDING

"Not overly sweet."

2 cups plus 1 teaspoon milk
1/2 cup granulated sugar
2 tablespoons cocoa
1/2 teaspoon salt
1 tablespoon cornstarch
2 eggs, separated
1/2 teaspoon vanilla extract
1/2 cup grated coconut

Scald the 2 cups milk in a double boiler. Combine the sugar, cocoa, salt, and cornstarch and add to the milk, then cook for 15 minutes. Beat the egg yolks and dilute with the 1 teaspoon milk, then add to the milk and cocoa mixture and cook, stirring constantly, for 2 or more minutes. Remove from the heat, add the vanilla and coconut, and fold in the egg whites, stiffly beaten. Chill and serve with whipped cream.

Serves: 4

Mrs. Rudie Yoder
Catlett, Virginia

BANANA PUDDING

Use the same day you make it.

3/4 cups granulated sugar
2 tablespoons all-purpose flour
1/4 teaspoon salt
2 cups milk
3 egg yolks
1 teaspoon vanilla extract
30 vanilla wafers, approximately
6 bananas, sliced

Combine 1/2 cup of the sugar, the flour, and salt in the top of a double boiler. Stir in the milk and cook over boiling water, stirring constantly until thickened. Cook, uncovered, for 15 minutes longer, stirring occasionally. Beat the egg yolks, then gradually stir in the hot mixture. Return to the double boiler and cook for 5 minutes, stirring constantly. Remove from heat, add the vanilla, and let cool.

Line the bottom of a 1 1/2-quart casserole with the vanilla wafers, then top with a layer of sliced bananas. Pour some of the custard over the banana. Continue making alternate layers of wafers, bananas, and custard until all the ingredients are used, ending with custard on top.

Serves: 6

Annie Stoltzfus
Christiana, Pennsylvania

CHOCOLATE BREAD PUDDING

A cocoa-flavored pudding made with chunks of bread.

3/4 cup granulated sugar
1 tablespoon all-purpose flour
1/4 teaspoon salt
1/4 cup cocoa
3 cups milk, scalded
6 eggs, beaten
1 teaspoon vanilla extract
3 thick slices bread, cut in 1/2-inch cubes

Combine the sugar, flour, salt, and cocoa. Stir the hot milk into the mixture, stirring until smooth. Add the eggs and vanilla, then pour into a 2-quart casserole. Layer the bread cubes over the top before baking in a 375-degree oven for 25 to 30 minutes, or until firm. Serve hot, with sweetened milk.

Serves: 8

Evelyn Fender
Baltic, Ohio

OLD-FASHIONED BREAD PUDDING

"Can be baked in a loaf pan so servings can be sliced."

4 cups bread crumbs
2 cups milk
4 tablespoons butter
1/2 cup granulated sugar
2 eggs, lightly beaten
1/4 teaspoon salt
1/2 cup raisins
1 teaspoon vanilla extract
Ground cinnamon

Place the bread crumbs in a 1 1/2-quart baking dish. In a saucepan, scald the milk, then add the butter, sugar, eggs, salt, raisins, and vanilla. Blend well, then pour the mixture over the crumbs. Sprinkle with cinnamon and bake at 350 degrees for 30 to 35 minutes, or until the top is golden. Serve warm or cold.

Serves: 4

Evelyn Fender
Baltic, Ohio

TAPIOCA IN PINEAPPLE JUICE

"Makes a parfait of tapioca and cream, layered."

1/4 cup tapioca
1/4 to 1/2 cup granulated sugar
1/4 teaspoon salt
2 1/2 cups pineapple juice

Combine all the ingredients in a saucepan and let stand for 5 minutes, then bring to a full boil over medium heat, stirring constantly. Remove from the heat and let stand for 20 minutes before serving.

Serves: 8

Edna Mae Miller
Guthrie, Kentucky

TAPIOCA CREAM

"This is a simple, nourishing dessert, easy to make." It is best eaten warm.

1/2 cup tapioca
3 eggs, separated
1/3 cup plus 2 tablespoons granulated sugar
5 1/2 cups milk
1/8 teaspoon salt
1 teaspoon vanilla extract

Boil together the tapioca, egg yolks, 1/3 cup sugar, milk, salt, and vanilla. Fold in the egg whites, stiffly beaten with the 2 tablespoons sugar, and serve.

Serves: 8

Mrs. John J. Burkholder
Dundee, Ohio

ICE-BOX DESSERTS

DELUXE PINEAPPLE CHEESE CAKE

A baked cheese cake with a sweet pineapple topping and graham-cracker crust.

2 cups fine graham-cracker crumbs
1/4 pound butter
1 cup granulated sugar
3 eight-ounce packages cream cheese
3 eggs
1 teaspoon vanilla extract
1 twenty-nine-ounce can crushed pineapple
1 envelope (1 tablespoon) unflavored gelatin

Combine the graham-cracker crumbs, butter, and sugar, then press firmly on the bottom and sides of a spring-form pan. Thoroughly beat the cream cheese, eggs, sugar, and vanilla, then pour into the graham-cracker crust. Bake at 375 degrees for 30 minutes, then chill.

Drain the pineapple, reserving the juice. Sprinkle the gelatin over the juice in a saucepan, then place over low heat, stirring until the gelatin dissolves. Cool until slightly thickened. Spoon the drained pineapple over the cake top and spread with the gelatin glaze. Chill thoroughly.

Serves: 12 to 16

Mrs. Eli Anderson
Holmesville, Ohio

CHERRY REFRIGERATOR CAKE

A no-bake cheese cake with cherry topping and a graham-cracker crust.

1 cup crushed graham crackers
1/4 cup melted butter
1/4 cup granulated sugar
2 four-ounce envelopes whipped topping mix
1 eight-ounce package cream cheese
1 cup confectioners' sugar
1 one-pound can cherry pie filling

Combine the graham-cracker crumbs, melted butter, and sugar and pat into an 11 x 9 inch pan. Mix the whipped topping mix as directed on the package. Combine the cream cheese and confectioners' sugar together. Fold into the whipped topping and pour into the graham-cracker crust. Let set in refrigerator for at least 1 hour, then pour the cherry pie filling over the top and refrigerate overnight.

Serves: 12

Mrs. David Hershberger
Areola, Illinois

LEMON CHEESE CAKE

Has a light lemon flavor and a graham-cracker crust.

1 three-ounce package lemon gelatin
1 cup boiling water
3 tablespoons lemon juice
1 eight-ounce package cream cheese
1 cup granulated sugar
1 teaspoon vanilla extract
2 cups evaporated milk, stiffly beaten
2 cups graham-cracker crumbs
1/2 cup melted butter

Dissolve the gelatin in the boiling water, then add the lemon juice. Cream together the cheese, sugar, and vanilla. Add the gelatin and mix well. Fold in the stiffly beaten evaporated milk.

Mix the graham-cracker crumbs with the melted butter, reserving some for the topping, pack the remainder around the sides and bottom of a 13 x 9 x 2-inch pan or dish; add the filling and sprinkle the remainder of the crumbs on top. Chill for several hours.

Serves: 12 to 16

Mrs. Alvin Miller
Shreve, Ohio

RASPBERRY DELIGHT

Make it up the day before and add the topping just before serving. This can also be made with canned cherry pie filling.

3 cups graham-cracker crumbs
1 cup brown sugar
1/4 cup melted butter
1 eight-ounce package cream cheese
2 cups sweetened condensed milk
1/3 cup bottled lemon juice
1 teaspoon vanilla extract

Glaze

1 cup raspberry juice
2½ teaspoons granulated sugar
1 cup raspberries
2 tablespoons cornstarch dissolved in ¼ cup water

Combine the graham-cracker crumbs, sugar, and melted butter and mix well. Pat onto the bottom of a 9-inch cake pan as thick as desired. Chill for 1 hour. Meanwhile, combine the cream cheese, milk, lemon juice, and vanilla. Beat well, then spread over the chilled crumbs. Chill until firm.

While the dessert is chilling, prepare the glaze. Combine the raspberry juice and sugar in a saucepan and cook over low heat until the sugar is dissolved. Add the raspberries and bring to a boil, then add the cornstarch and water. Cook until thickened (about 3 minutes) and let cool. Spread on top of the chilled dessert, and chill again before serving.

Serves: 8

Esther Miller
Fredericksburg, Ohio

APRICOT DELIGHT

For a more finished look, add ½ cup chopped nuts.

3 three-ounce packages orange gelatin
2 cups crushed pineapple, juice reserved
1 cup miniature marshmallows
2 cups coarsely chopped apricots, drained but juice reserved

Topping

½ cup granulated sugar
3 tablespoons all-purpose flour
1 egg, beaten
½ cup reserved pineapple juice
½ cup reserved apricot juice
½ pint heavy cream

Prepare the gelatin according to package directions. When it begins to set, stir in the rest of the ingredients, pour into a serving dish, and chill until set.

Meanwhile, prepare the topping. Blend the sugar, flour, egg, and pineapple and apricot juice in a saucepan. Cook over medium heat until thick, then let cool. Beat the cream until stiff, then fold into the cooled mixture. Spread over the chilled gelatin, and keep chilled until ready to serve.

Serves: 8 to 10 — *Tillie Hostetler*

STRAWBERRY SWIRL

Strawberry and pineapple layers, frosted with whipped cream.

1 six-ounce package strawberry gelatin
1 fourteen-and-one-half-ounce can crushed pineapple, drained
1 ten-ounce package frozen strawberries
Miniature marshmallows (optional)

Topping

1 eight-ounce package cream cheese
1/2 pint heavy cream
3 tablespoons sugar

Prepare the gelatin according to package directions, then chill until partially set. Fold in the strawberries and pineapple and, if you like, miniature marshmallows. Pour into a serving bowl and chill until completely set.

Cream the cheese, then fold in the cream, whipped with the sugar. Spread over the gelatin and keep chilled until ready to serve.

Serves: 8 — *Mrs. Aaron T. Stutzman*
Middlefield, Ohio

PINEAPPLE DAPPLE

A cheese pie with a pineapple or lemon flavor in a graham-cracker crust.

Crust

1 cup graham-cracker crumbs
2 tablespoons granulated sugar
1/4 cup melted butter

Filling

1 eight-and-one-half-ounce can crushed pineapple
1 three-ounce package orange-pineapple gelatin
1 1/4 cups boiling water
3 tablespoons sugar
1 three-ounce package cream cheese, softened
1/4 teaspoon grated orange rind
1/2 teaspoon vanilla extract
1/2 pint heavy cream, whipped

Make the crust by combining the graham-cracker crumbs, sugar and butter. Press into an 8-inch-square pan and chill.

To prepare the filling, drain the pineapple and save the juice. Dissolve the gelatin in the boiling water, add the reserved pineapple juice, and cool. Combine the sugar, cheese, orange rind, and vanilla. Combine half the cooled gelatin with the pineapple and set aside. Add the remaining gelatin to the cream-cheese mixture. Fold in the whipped cream, pour into the graham-cracker crust, and chill until firm. Spoon the reserved pineapple mixture on top and chill once more.

Serves: 8 *Sarah Troyer*

STRAWBERRY DELIGHT

A nicely fluffy gelatin dessert.

2 three-ounce packages strawberry gelatin
3/4 cup cream, whipped with 1/2 cup granulated sugar
1/2 cup sweetened fresh or frozen strawberries
Whole strawberries for garnish

Prepare the gelatin according to package directions. Chill until partially set, then beat with an electric mixer till fluffy; the mixture will almost double in volume. Fold in the sweetened whipped cream and the sweetened strawberries and spoon into parfait glasses. Top each with a whole strawberry.

Serves: 6 *Mrs. Simon Miller*
Millersburg, Ohio

LEMON OR LIME FLUFF

Fluffs, always tasty, are standard Amish fare. If desired, you can line the pan with vanilla wafers before the fluff is poured in.

1/2 cup cold milk
1/2 teaspoon vanilla extract
1 four-ounce envelope whipped topping mix
1 three-ounce package lemon or lime gelatin
2 tablespoons granulated sugar
1/2 teaspoon salt
1 cup hot water
2/3 cup drained crushed pineapple
1 cup pineapple juice and water, mixed

Combine the milk, vanilla, and whipped topping mix. Whip and chill. Dissolve the gelatin, sugar, and salt in the hot water. Add the juice and water and chill until slightly thickened, then beat until fluffy and thick. Fold in the chilled whipped topping and pineapple and chill until firm.

Serves: 8 to 10

Mrs. Elmer Hershberger
New Paris, Indiana

GRAHAM-CRACKER FLUFF

The most common and best-tasting Amish fluff.

1 envelope (1 tablespoon) unflavored gelatin
1/2 cup cold water
2 eggs, separated
2/3 cup milk
2/3 cup plus 3 tablespoons granulated sugar
1/2 pint heavy cream
1 teaspoon vanilla extract

Crust

3 tablespoons butter
12 graham crackers, crushed

Soak the gelatin in the cold water. Beat the egg yolks, then put in the top of a double boiler with the milk and 2/3 cup sugar and cook over boiling water until slightly thickened. Pour the dissolved gelatin into the hot mixture and stir until smooth, then chill until partially set. Beat the egg whites until stiff, then the cream, and fold both into the gelatin mixture, along with the vanilla.

Combine the melted butter, 3 tablespoons sugar, and graham-cracker crumbs. Put into a serving dish in layers with the gelatin mixture and chill until ready to serve.

Serves: 8

Rebecca Stutzman
Baltic, Ohio

SNOW ON THE MOUNTAIN

A gelatin dessert served as a syrup over angel food cake.

2 three-ounce packages cherry or strawberry gelatin
3 cups water or fruit juice
2/3 cup granulated sugar
3 to 4 bananas, sliced
1 can drained crushed pineapple
3 to 4 marshmallows, cut up
3/4 cup chopped pecans
1/2 pint heavy cream, whipped
Angel food cake

Combine the gelatin and water or fruit juice and cool until the mixture starts to set. Fold in the sugar, the sliced bananas, pineapple, marshmallows, 1/2 cup of the pecans, and the whipped cream, then spoon the mixture on top of broken pieces of angel food cake. Sprinkle the remaining pecans on top.

Serves: 8

Beth Verden
Eureka, Illinois

PINEAPPLE DELIGHT

This is a very rich but excellent dessert.

1 cup crushed graham crackers
1 1/2 sticks butter
2 eggs, beaten
2 cups confectioners' sugar
1 one-pound can crushed pineapple, well drained
1/2 pint heavy cream, whipped
2 teaspoons granulated sugar
1/2 cup chopped nuts

Melt ½ stick of the butter, then combine with the graham-cracker crumbs. Spread half the crumbs on the bottom of a 9-inch-square baking dish. Set the remainder aside.

Combine the beaten eggs, remaining butter, and the confectioners' sugar and beat for 5 minutes. Sprinkle on the reserved graham crackers.

Gently combine the pineapple, whipped cream, granulated sugar, and half the nuts. Pour this over the second layer and top with the remaining nuts. Refrigerate for at least 6 hours or overnight.

Serves: 12 *Mrs. Lewis Martin*

BOYSENBERRY DELIGHT

You can use blueberries as well, for a nice change.

15 graham crackers
¼ cup melted butter or margarine
25 to 30 large marshmallows
1 cup milk
½ pint heavy cream, whipped
1 twenty-ounce can boysenberries
2 tablespoons cornstarch
¼ cup granulated sugar
1 tablespoon lemon juice
½ cup chopped nuts

Crush the graham crackers and mix with the melted butter. Put part of the mixture on the bottom of an 11 x 7 x 1½-inch pan, reserving enough for the top.

Melt the marshmallows with the milk in the top of a double boiler. Cool and fold in the whipped cream. In a separate saucepan, cook berries with the cornstarch, sugar, and lemon juice. Let cool.

Spread half the marshmallow mixture over the crumbs in the pan, then add berries. Top with the rest of the marshmallow mixture, then sprinkle the reserved crumbs and the nuts over the top. Refrigerate overnight.

Serves: 8 to 10 *Alta Mae Yutzy*
Hutchinson, Kansas

CHERRY MALLOW DESSERT

A cream filling in a vanilla wafer crust, topped with cherries.

30 marshmallows
1/2 cup milk
1 1/2 cups vanilla-wafer crumbs
1/2 cup melted butter
1/2 pint heavy cream, whipped
1 one-pound can cherry-pie filling
1/8 teaspoon almond extract

Melt the marshmallows in the milk over medium heat, stirring often. Cool and set aside. Combine the vanilla wafer crumbs and butter. Reserving 1/4 cup, press the remaining mixture in the bottom of a 9-inch-square baking pan or dish. Fold the whipped cream into the marshmallows, then add the almond extract. Spread over the crumbs in the pan, and over that spread the pie filling. Sprinkle the reserved crumb mixture on top. Chill until ready to serve.

Serves: 8 to 10

Mrs. Eli Anderson
Holmesville, Ohio

CHOCOLATE-MALLOW DESSERT

A chocolate-mallow cream filling in a graham-cracker crust.

32 large marshmallows
1/2 cup milk
1 six-ounce package chocolate chips
1/2 pint heavy cream, whipped
1/4 cup chopped nuts
2 cups graham-cracker crumbs

Soften the marshmallows in the milk in the top of a double boiler. Add the chocolate chips and let melt. Let the mixture cool until thickened, then fold in the whipped cream and nuts. Spread half the graham-cracker crumbs in a baking dish. Pour the chocolate mixture into the dish, then cover with the remaining crumbs. Chill until ready to serve.

Serves: 8

Mrs. John Beechy
Topeka, Indiana

NO-BAKE HOLIDAY CAKE

This is a rich and creamy dessert.

1 pound graham crackers, crushed
1 pound figs, chopped
1 cup nut meats
1 pound raisins
1/2 cup maraschino cherries
1 pound marshmallows, cut up
1 pint heavy cream, whipped

Combine the graham crackers, figs, nut meats, raisins, cherries, and marshmallows. Fold this mixture into whipped cream, then pile onto a serving plate. Chill until ready to serve.

Serves: 8 to 10

Mrs. Moses A. Coblentz
Sarasota, Florida

YUMMY FRUIT ROLL

A creamy roll with bananas, marshmallows, and dates.

1 cup heavy cream
1 1/2 cups chopped dates
1 cup chopped nuts
1/2 pound finely cut-up marshamallows
3 bananas, diced
8 graham crackers, crushed

Whip the cream. Fold in the dates, nuts, marshmallows, and bananas. Shape into a roll 3 inches thick. Spread the graham-cracker crumbs on waxed paper and roll the fruit roll in them. Chill overnight, then slice and serve.

Serves: 8

Mrs. Andy Miller
Fredericksburg, Ohio

ICE CREAM DESSERT

A highly nutritious dessert of ice cream, cereal, nuts and coconut.

1/4 cup melted butter
1/2 cup ground nuts
1/2 cup coconut
1 cup brown sugar
1 cup crushed Rice Chex
1 quart softened ice cream

Combine the butter, nuts, coconut, brown sugar, and crushed Rice Chex. Reserving some of the mixture, spread the remainder 1/2 inch thick in an 8-inch-square pan, then spread on the softened ice cream and cover with the remaining crumbs. If not to be served immediately, place in the freezer.

Serves: 8

Mrs. Jonas Detweiler
Fairview, Missouri

ORANGE ICE CREAM

Amish ice cream flavored with orange gelatin. Any other flavored jello may be used, or course, or unflavored gelatin with vanilla added.

2 cups granulated sugar
5 eggs
2 cups heavy cream
2 three-ounce packages orange gelatin
1 cup boiling water
Whole milk

Beat together the sugar, eggs, and cream. Dissolve the orange gelatin in the boiling water. Combine the two mixtures, stir well, and pour into a 1-gallon ice cream freezer. Stir in enough whole milk to fill the freezer to within 2 inches of the top. Freeze in the usual way.

Serves: 8

Mrs. Levi E. Yoder
Topeka, Indiana

OTHER DESSERTS

BAKED APPLES

These have a cinnamon and sugar syrup.

4 cooking apples
1 cup brown sugar
1 teaspoon ground cinnamon
$^{1}/_{2}$ cup water
2 tablespoons all-purpose flour
Pinch of salt

Peel, halve, and core the apples. Place in a baking dish, cut side down. Combine the brown sugar, cinnamon, water, flour, and salt in a saucepan and cook until thickened. Pour over the apples and bake at 325 degrees for 30 to 40 minutes, baste two or three times during the cooking with the syrup.

Serves: 4 to 8 *Mrs. Enos Chupp*

APPLE CRISPETT

For extra zip, try sprinkling the apples with cinnamon.

4 cups, peeled, sliced apples
$^{1}/_{2}$ cup water
1 cup sifted all-purpose flour
$^{3}/_{4}$ cup granulated sugar
$^{3}/_{4}$ cup brown sugar
5 tablespoons butter

Place the apple slices in a 13 x 9 x 2-inch pan. Pour the water over them. Sift together the flour, sugar, and brown sugar; cut in the butter. Spread the mixture on top of the apples (do not mix together) and bake at 350 degrees for 45 minutes. Cool and cut into squares. Serve with whipped cream.

Serves: 12 to 16 *Mrs. P. Miller*
Dalton, Ohio

APPLE BROWN BETTY

Sweetened, baked apples and bread crumbs.

- **1/3 cup granulated sugar**
- **1/2 teaspoon ground cinnamon**
- **1/4 teaspoon salt**
- **2 cups fine, dry bread crumbs**
- **4 tart apples, peeled and diced**
- **3 tablespoons melted butter**

Combine the sugar, cinnamon, and salt and set aside. Put a layer of bread crumbs in a greased baking dish, cover with a layer of apples, and sprinkle with sugar mixture. Continue layering until all the ingredients are used, ending with a layer of crumbs on top. Pour the melted butter over the crumbs, then cover and bake at 375 degrees for 40 minutes. To brown the top, remove the cover for the last 10 minutes of baking.

Serves: 6

Mrs. Elmer Wengerd
Fredericksburg, Ohio

OATMEAL BROWN BETTY

This a good for a different and extra-hearty dessert.

- **1 cup whole-wheat flour**
- **1/2 teaspoon salt**
- **1/2 cup brown sugar**
- **1/2 teaspoon baking soda**
- **1 cup rolled oats**
- **1/4 pound plus 3 tablespoons butter**
- **2 1/2 cups sliced apples**
- **1/4 cup raisins (optional)**

Combine all the dry ingredients, then cut in the 1/4 pound butter until the mixture is crumbly. Spread half the mixture in an 8-inch-square baking dish and cover with the apples and raisins. Put the remainder of crumbs on top, covering the apples and raisins. Dot with the 3 tablespoons butter and bake in a 350-degree oven for 35 minutes, or until the top is brown and crusty. Serve with milk or cream.

Serves: 6 to 8

Mrs. Melvin S. Miller
Millersburg, Ohio

AMISH APPLE ROLL

Apples baked in a biscuit roll and served with syrup.

2 cups sifted all-purpose flour
1 tablespoon baking powder
6 tablespoons granulated sugar
1/2 teaspoon salt
3 tablespoons butter
1 egg
3/8 cup milk
4 to 5 apples, peeled and finely chopped
3/4 teaspoon cinnamon
1 tablespoon melted butter
1 1/2 cups brown sugar
3/4 cup hot water

Sift together the flour, baking powder, and 2 tablespoons of the sugar, then add the milk, egg, and butter, mixing well. Roll out into a 1/2-inch-thick rectangle. Arrange the chopped apples on the dough and sprinkle with the remaining sugar, the cinnamon, and melted butter. Roll as for a jelly roll and cut off as for cinnamon rolls.

Combine the brown sugar and hot water and spread in a 9-inch cake pan. Lay the rolls in this syrup and bake at 350 degrees until done (about 35 minutes).

Serves: 8

Lydia Mae Bontreger
Jamesport, Missouri

AMISH APPLE FRITTERS

Another traditional Amish delight.

1 cup all-purpose flour
1 1/2 teaspoons baking powder
1/2 teaspoon salt
3 tablespoons granulated sugar
1/3 cup milk
1 egg, beaten
2 apples, peeled and sliced
Fat for deep frying

Prepare the batter by combining the flour, baking powder, salt, confectioners' sugar, milk, and egg. Dip the apple slices into the fritter batter, then drop into hot deep fat and fry until brown. Drain on paper towels and serve with a syrup.

Serves: 4

Carrie Miller

APPLE KUCHEN

Apples with a distinctive flavor baked in a cakelike dough.

1/2 cup shortening
1 1/4 cups granulated sugar
2 eggs, separated
1 cup sifted all-purpose flour
1 teaspoon baking powder
1 teaspoon vanilla extract
6 apples, peeled and cut in wedges
Ground cinnamon
2 tablespoons butter

Cream the shortening and 1 cup of the sugar, then beat in the egg yolks. Sift together the flour and baking powder and add to the creamed mixture, then add the vanilla. Fold in the egg whites, stiffly beaten. Pour the batter into a greased and floured 9-inch-square pan and top with the apple wedges. Sprinkle top with the remaining sugar and some cinnamon, and dot with the butter and bake at 325 degrees for 30 to 35 minutes. Serve hot, with milk or whipped cream.

Serves: 8 to 10

Mrs. Pauline Burger
Baltic, Ohio

APPLE GOODIE

Sweetened apple with a cakelike topping—a classic Amish dish.

3/4 cup granulated sugar
1/8 teaspoon salt
1 tablespoon all-purpose flour
1/2 teaspoon ground cinnamon
4 to 5 apples, peeled and sliced

Topping

1/2 cup sifted all-purpose flour
1/8 teaspoon baking soda
1/2 cup brown sugar
1/8 teaspoon baking powder
4 tablespoons butter

Sift together the dry ingredients and combine with the apples. Mix well, then place on the bottom of a greased casserole.

To make the topping, sift together the dry ingredients and cut in the butter to make crumbs. Put crumbs on top of the apple mixture and bake at 375 degrees for 30 to 35 minutes, no more than 40. Serve hot or cold, with rich milk.

Serves: 6

Mrs. Christ Yoder

GREAT LAKES BLUEBERRY COBBLER

A very easily assembled and rich dessert. Served warm, with whipped cream or vanilla ice cream.

1 pint blueberries
1/3 cup granulated sugar
1 teaspoon grated lemon rind
3/4 cup water

Cobbler Batter

1 cup sifted all-purpose flour
1/2 teaspoon baking powder
1/4 teaspoon salt
4 tablespoons butter or margarine
1/2 cup granulated sugar
1 egg, well beaten
1/2 cup milk
1 1/2 teaspoons vanilla extract

Combine the blueberries, sugar, lemon rind, and water. Bring to a boil, stirring constantly until the sugar dissolves, then reduce the heat and simmer for 5 minutes.

Cream the butter or margarine until soft, then add the sugar gradually, beating after each addition until light and fluffy. Sift together the flour, baking powder, and salt; combine the eggs, milk, and vanilla. Add the dry ingredients alternately with the egg mixture, beating well after each addition; the batter will be thin.

Pour the hot blueberry mixture into a greased 2-quart casserole, then spoon on the cobbler batter. Bake at 375 degrees for 30 minutes.

Serves: 6 *Fanny Bontrager*

PEACH COBBLER (DELUXE)

"You can also substitute cherry or apple fillings in this recipe."

3 cups sweetened, sliced fresh or frozen peaches
1 teaspoon vanilla extract
2 1/2 tablespoons quick-cooking tapioca

Cobbler Batter

1 1/2 cups sifted all-purpose flour
1 teaspoon baking powder
2 teaspoons salt
6 tablespoons butter or margarine
1 egg, beaten
1/3 cup milk

Glaze

3/4 cup granulated sugar
1/2 cup water
3 tablespoons butter or margarine

Combine the peaches, vanilla, and quick-cooking tapioca, then put into a greased 2-quart casserole. Sift together the flour, baking powder, and salt, then cut in the butter till the mixture resembles coarse crumbs. Add the beaten egg and milk and stir just enough to moisten, then drop by spoonfuls on top of the peaches.

Make the glaze. Combine the sugar, water, and butter in a saucepan and bring to a boil, then pour over the batter. Bake at 375 degrees until the topping is brown (about 30 minutes). Serve hot or cold.

Serves: 6

Mrs. Joe Stutzman
Blountstown, Florida

JAM PUFFS

A sweetened, biscuitlike treat. They can be garnished with grated coconut or chopped nuts.

1 package active dry yeast
3/4 cup warm water
1/4 cup granulated sugar
1 teaspoon salt
2 1/4 cups sifted all-purpose flour
1 egg
1/4 cup shortening, softened
1/2 cup thick red jam

Dissolve the yeast in the water, then add the sugar, salt, and about half the flour. Beat thoroughly for 2 minutes. Add the egg and shortening, then gradually beat the rest of the flour in. Beat until smooth.

Fill 16 to 20 greased medium-sized muffin cups half full with the batter. Let rise until doubled in bulk (about 50 to 60 minutes), then bake for 15 minutes at 375 degrees. When done, spread with the jam.

Makes: 16 to 20 puffs

Mrs. Steve P. Miller
Halleday, Tennessee

CREAM PUFFS

"Use a quick, rapid filling in this."

$^1/_4$ pound butter
1 cup boiling water
1 cup sifted all-purpose flour
3 eggs
Filling as desired

Add the butter to boiling water, then, while still boiling, stir in the flour. Remove from the heat and cool. Stir in the eggs, one at a time, and beat well. Drop by spoonfuls on greased baking sheets and bake in a 350-degree oven until lightly browned. When done, each will have a hollow center. Fill with any type of filling and bake at 375 degrees for 30 minutes.

Makes: 18 cream puffs

Mrs. Aden Miller
Dundee, Ohio

CANDY

SEAFOAM

Very fluffy, sweet, and tasty peaks.

2 cups brown sugar
$^1/_4$ cup granulated sugar
1 cup cold water
$^1/_4$ teaspoon cream of tartar
2 stiffly beaten egg whites
1 teaspoon vanilla extract

In a saucepan, combine the brown sugar, granulated sugar, cold water, and cream of tartar and boil until the syrup spins a fine thread. Pour it over the stiffly beaten egg whites, then add the vanilla and beat until the mixture stands in peaks. Drop on waxed paper and let cool completely.

Makes: About 24 pieces

Mrs. Ida Miller
Arthur, Illinois

CORN FLAKE CANDY

A crunchy candy made of corn flakes, coconut, and peanuts.

1 cup granulated sugar
1 cup light corn syrup
1/2 cup heavy cream
4 cups corn flakes
1 cup grated coconut
1 cup peanuts

Cook the sugar, corn syrup, and cream to the soft-ball stage, then stir in the corn flakes, coconut, and peanuts. Mix well, then drop by spoonfuls on waxed paper. Let cool completely.

Makes: About 24 pieces *Saloma Mullet*

FIVE-MINUTE BLACK WALNUT FUDGE

Very creamy, with a taste like milk chocolate.

2/3 cup undiluted evaporated milk
1 2/3 cups granulated sugar
1/2 teaspoon salt
16 marshmallows, diced
1 1/2 six-ounce packages semi-sweet chocolate chips
1 teaspoon vanilla extract
1/2 cup chopped black walnuts

Combine the evaporated milk, sugar, and salt in a saucepan and heat to boiling, then cook for 5 minutes, stirring constantly. Remove from the heat and add the marshmallows, chocolate chips, vanilla, and nuts. Place in a buttered 8-inch-square pan and cool at room temperature. Cut into pieces when cool.

Makes: About 60 pieces *Mrs. John Raber*
Orrville, Ohio

PEANUT BUTTER CUPS

These taste just like the store-bought kind.

1 pound butter
2 cups peanut butter
2 1/2 to 3 cups confectioners' sugar
3 tablespoons vanilla extract
1 pound sweet chocolate
Shredded coconut

Cream the butter and peanut butter, then add confectioners' sugar until the mixture is ready to form into balls. Add the vanilla and mix thoroughly. Shape into balls and flatten a little, then put the balls in the refrigerator to chill. Meanwhile, melt the chocolate over very low heat. When the balls are thoroughly chilled, dip them into the melted chocolate, then roll them in shredded coconut.

Makes: 8 dozen pieces

Katie Miller
Middlefield, Ohio

HOMEMADE TURTLE CANDY

These are just like the store-bought "turtles."

1/2 pound butter
1 cup brown sugar
1 teaspoon cream of tartar
1 cup light corn syrup
1 fourteen-ounce can condensed milk
1 pound shelled pecans
1 pound sweet chocolate
1 teaspoon shaved paraffin
1 teaspoon vegetable shortening

In a saucepan, combine the butter, brown sugar, cream of tartar, corn syrup, and condensed milk. Bring to a boil and cook for about 12 minutes, stirring constantly. Remove from heat and let cool.

Laying 3 or 4 pecans together in groups on waxed paper, add the brown sugar mixture by the spoonful to the nut clusters and let set. Meanwhile, very slowly melt the chocolate; add the paraffin and vegetable shortening. When the "turtles" are set, cover with the melted chocolate.

Makes: About 50 pieces

Mrs. William Hochstetler
Middlefield, Ohio

PEANUT CANDY BARS

Caramel-coated candy with peanuts and chocolate.

1 tablespoon butter
2/3 cup milk
2 1/2 cups granulated sugar
1 1/3 cups light corn syrup
1/3 cup peanut butter
1/2 cup brown sugar
1 to 2 cups chopped peanuts
1 pound sweet chocolate

In a saucepan, combine the butter, milk, granulated sugar, and 1/3 cup of the corn syrup. Cook till the soft-ball stage, then add the peanut butter and stir well. Let stand a few minutes, then stir till thick. Pour into a buttered pan and let cool. When firm, cut into 2 x 1-inch bars.

Cook the remaining corn syrup with the brown sugar until the mixture reaches the hard-ball stage. Dip the bars into this hot syrup and quickly roll in the chopped peanuts. Let cool. Melt the chocolate over very low heat and use to coat the cooled bars.

Makes: 30 bars *Mrs. Dan Yoder*

PEPPERMINT PATTIES

Mint-flavored patties coated with chocolate.

2 1/4 cups granulated sugar
1/2 cup water
1/4 cup light corn syrup
1 stiffly beaten egg white
4 drops peppermint oil
1 twelve-ounce package semi-sweet chocolate chips, melted

Combine the sugar, water, and corn syrup in a small saucepan with straight sides, wiping the sides with a damp cloth to prevent the formation of sugar crystals. Bring to a gentle boil and cook, covered, for 6 minutes, then uncover and insert candy thermometer. Cook, without stirring, to 235 to 238 degrees, or the soft-ball stage. Cool until just warm. Beat with a wooden spoon until the mixture gets cloudy, then add the beaten egg white, a little at a time; add the oil of peppermint and beat until milky white. Cool, shape into 1 1/2-inch patties and dip in the melted chocolate.

Makes: 80 patties *Katie Miller*
Middlefield, Ohio

CARAMEL POPCORN

This is a crunchy, sweet way to serve popcorn.

1 cup unpopped popcorn
2 cups granulated sugar
1 cup dark corn syrup
1/4 pound butter
1/2 teaspoon baking soda

Pop the corn. Combine the sugar, corn syrup, and butter in a saucepan and cook until the syrup spins a thread. Add the soda to puff the syrup up, then add enough popped corn to consume the syrup. Stir until all the corn separates and serve.

Serves: 6 to 8 *Mrs. John Knissley*

POPCORN CAKE

Caramel popcorn shaped into a large block.

1 pound brown sugar
1 cup corn syrup
1/4 pound butter
1/4 teaspoon baking powder
1/4 teaspoon salt
2 cups unpopped popcorn

Cook the brown sugar and syrup until it almost burns (about 7 minutes), then add the butter, baking powder, and salt. Pop the corn and put into a large kettle. Pour the syrup over the corn and stir well with a large spoon to coat the corn thoroughly. Press the corn into a large cake pan. Cut it into pieces when ready or break off chunks as needed.

Serves: 10 to 12 *Cora Byler*

Putting Up

The Amish can hundreds of jars of fruits and vegetables and often use salicylic acid with no apparent ill results. As a matter of caution we have eliminated such practices from this book and recommend following the excellent canning instructions given in the publications of the U.S. Department of Agriculture. These can be obtained by writing to the U.S. Department of Agriculture, Washington, D.C.

OVEN-MADE APPLE BUTTER

A delicious traditional combination is apple butter and cottage cheese on homemade bread.

1½ quarts sweet cider
6 pounds apples, preferably Grimes, peeled and quartered
2½ to 3 pounds granulated sugar

Put the cider in a large kettle, cook it down to about 3 cups, and skim. Cook the cider and apples together until the apples are soft, then put them through a sieve. Put the sieved apples into a large kettle, add the sugar, and cook in a 300-degree oven for at least 3 to 4 hours, stirring occasionally. Pour into sterilized jars and seal.

Makes: About 7 pints *Sara Raber*

RHUBARB PRESERVES

This is a great topping for ice cream and other desserts.

6 cups finely cut-up rhubarb
3 cups granulated sugar
1 three-ounce box strawberry gelatin

Cook the rhubarb with the sugar until very tender, then remove it from the heat and stir in the strawberry gelatin.

Makes: 2 quarts — *Mrs. Jonas Schrock*

PINEAPPLE PRESERVES

Use as a dessert topping or a spread.

1 quart crushed pineapple
1 quart light corn syrup
8 cups white sugar

Combine the ingredients in a kettle and bring to a boil. Boil for 10 minutes, then pour into sterilized jars and seal.

Makes: About 4 pints — *Mrs. Alvin P. Miller*

GRANDMOTHER'S PEACH JAM

A nice, thick, full-flavored jam.

1 quart peeled, chopped peaches
2 cups white sugar
1 tablespoon epsom salts

Combine the peaches and sugar in a large saucepan. Bring to a boil, then add the epsom salts and cook until thick (about 5 to 10 minutes). Pour into sterilized jars and seal.

Makes: About 2 pints — *Mrs. Perry Stutzman*

WHITE SUGAR SMEAR

Doubles as a topping or a spread for bread.

2 quarts light corn syrup
2 cups brown sugar
1 quart marshmallow topping or 4 cups granulated sugar
Fresh fruit or fruit jam (optional)

Combine the corn syrup and brown sugar in a saucepan and heat until the sugar dissolves. Stir in the marshmallow topping. Add fresh fruit or fruit jam, if desired.

Makes: About 3 quarts *Mattie Schlabach*

MAPLE SPREAD FOR BREAD

A sweet spread, very tasty on toast.

2 cups granulated sugar
2 cups brown sugar
2 cups water

Boil the sugars and water in a covered saucepan until a soft ball forms in cold water. Let stand, still covered, until cool, then stir until the mixture changes color. If too thick, add warm water.

Makes: About 1 quart *Mrs. Ben Miller*

CORN-COB MOLASSES

"I use this on pancakes as syrup."

1 dozen new corn cobs
1 gallon water
4 pounds brown sugar

Boil the corn cobs in the water for 30 minutes. Strain, then add the brown sugar to the liquid and cook like syrup.

Makes: 1½ quarts *Alta Schlabach*

QUINCE HONEY

This makes a fine topping for other desserts.

5 pounds granulated sugar
1 quart water
6 large quinces

Dissolve the sugar in water and let boil. Paring and grating 1 quince at a time, stir it into the boiling syrup until all 6 quinces are used. The honey will be done 5 minutes after the last quince is stirred in. Pour into sterilized jars and seal.

Makes: About 5 pints *Mary Brenneman*

HOLMES COUNTY GRAPE JUICE

Real homemade grape juice.

5 heaping cups grapes
3 quarts water
2 1/2 cups granulated sugar

Bring the grapes and water to a boil. Cook until the grapes are soft, then strain and discard the grapes. Add the sugar to the liquid and bring to a boil again. Pour into sterilized jars and seal.

Makes: About 3 quarts *Mrs. Lester B. Miller*

ROOT BEER

This will be ready to drink when cold.

1 3/4 cups granulated sugar
4 teaspoons root beer extract
1 package active dry yeast
Warm water

Put the sugar in a gallon jug and add the root beer extract. Dissolve the yeast in a little warm water and add this to the mixture already in the jug. Fill the jug with warm water and put it in the sun or a warm place for 4 hours. Then put it in a cold place to cool. Make sure the mixture remains cool; if the yeast is reactivated, the mixture may explode.

Makes: 1 gallon

Mrs. Menno A. Erb
Sugarcreek, Ohio

CANNED TOMATO JUICE

This is good either as a juice drink or as soup.

1 peck tomatoes, chopped
2 bunches celery, chopped
1 bunch parsley, chopped
3 medium-sized onions, chopped
3 green peppers, chopped
1 cup sugar
1/4 cup salt
1/4 teaspoon pepper

Combine the tomatoes, celery, parsley, onions, and green peppers in a kettle and cook until soft. Put through a sieve, then add the sugar, salt, and pepper. Bring to a boil, then pour into hot sterilized jars and seal.

Makes: About 5 quarts

Mrs. Alvin J. Miller
Sugarcreek, Ohio

PICKLED BEETS

These have a slightly sour taste.

1 gallon cooked, cut-up tender, young beets
1 1/2 cups vinegar
2 cups granulated sugar
Pickling spices
1 1/2 cups water
4 teaspoons salt

Combine the vinegar, sugar, pickling spices, water, and salt. Bring the beets to a good rolling boil in this vinegar solution, then pack in sterilized jars and seal.

Makes: About 8 pints

Mrs. Al Raber

SAUERKRAUT

Homemade kraut, Amish style.

Shredded cabbage
Salt

Pack the shredded cabbage into sterilized quart jars. Make a hole down through the middle of the cabbage with a wooden spoon or similar utensil and put in a teaspoon of salt, more if desired, to each quart. Fill the jars with boiling water and seal them tightly at once. The sauerkraut will be ready to use in 4 to 6 weeks.

Mrs. J. Troyer
Fredericksburg, Ohio

PEPPER RELISH

Standard fare in all Amish homes—quite a spicy relish.

24 peppers
12 onions
1 quart vinegar
5 cups granulated sugar
2 tablespoons salt
2 ounces mustard seed

Grind the peppers and onions with a food chopper. Cover with boiling water and let stand for 15 minutes, then drain and put in a large kettle. Add the vinegar, sugar, salt, and mustard seed and cook for 20 minutes. Pour into sterilized jars and seal hot.

Makes: About 4 pints

Mrs. Benjie Schlabach
Millersburg, Ohio

SPICED GREEN TOMATOES

A favorite relish.

4 quarts green tomatoes
Salt
1 cup granulated sugar
1 quart vinegar
Whole cloves
Cinnamon sticks

Slice the tomatoes and sprinkle with salt, letting stand overnight. Then drain and cook in the vinegar and spices for half a day on the back of the stove.

Makes: About 3 quarts

Mrs. Roman Raber

CORN RELISH

Another popular relish.

- 5 cups fresh whole-kernel corn
- 4 large onions, chopped
- 2 green peppers, chopped
- 2 cups diced celery
- 3 cups shredded cabbage
- 2 tablespoons salt
- 3/4 teaspoon turmeric
- 3 cups granulated sugar
- 2 cups vinegar
- 2 tablespoons dry mustard

Put all the ingredients into a large kettle and heat well, without boiling. Pour into sterilized jars and seal.

Makes: 4 to 6 pints *Mrs. Levi Christner*

CHOW CHOW

This is a famous Amish recipe.

- 1 quart green beans
- 1 pint yellow beans
- 1 pint pickles
- 1 pint lima beans
- 1 pint carrots
- 1 head cauliflower
- 1 pint fresh whole-kernel corn
- 3 to 4 stalks celery
- 6 green tomatoes, salted
- 6 mangoes (3 red and 3 yellow)
- 3 quarts vinegar
- 5 cups granulated sugar
- 2 onions
- 1 tablespoon mustard seed
- 1 tablespoon celery seed

Chop the vegetables to a uniform size. Cook the beans, pickles, limas, carrots, cauliflower, corn, and celery until not quite tender, then salt and drain. Add the chopped, salted green tomatoes and the mangoes and mix well.

In a saucepan, bring to a boil the vinegar, sugar, onions, mustard seed, and celery seed. Add the vegetables to the boiling syrup, then pour into sterilized jars and seal.

Makes: About 6 quarts *Lizzie Helmuth*

COMPANY BEST PICKLES

A long pickling process, but well worth it.

10 medium cucumbers
8 cups granulated sugar
2 tablespoons mixed pickling spices
3 teaspoons salt
4 cups cider vinegar

Cover the whole cucumbers with boiling water and allow to stand overnight. Drain, then repeat this procedure on the next three mornings. On the fifth day, drain and slice the cucumbers into 1/2-inch pieces.

Combine the sugar, spices, salt, and vinegar in a saucepan and bring to a boil. Pour over the cucumbers and let stand for 2 days. On the third day, bring to a boil and seal in hot sterilized jars.

Makes: 7 pints

Mrs. Elmer M. Yoder
Dundee, Ohio

OLD-FASHIONED BREAD-AND-BUTTER PICKLES

A long-time favorite.

18 medium cucumbers
Salt
6 cups sliced onion
1 1/2 cups white vinegar
1 1/2 cups brown sugar
1 teaspoon mustard seed
1 teaspoon celery seed
1 teaspoon turmeric

Slice the unpeeled cucumbers and put in a weak salt solution overnight in an enameled dish, stone jar, or bowl. Drain off the water, then place the cucumbers in an enameled saucepan or kettle. Add the onions, vinegar, sugar, spices, and salt to taste and simmer for 20 minutes. Place in hot sterilized jars and seal tightly.

Makes: 6 to 7 pints

Mrs. Elam Burkhart

ROSY WATERMELON PICKLES

A popular by-product of summertime eating.

2 pounds watermelon rind
1 quart water
6 inches stick cinnamon
1 tablespoon whole cloves
2 cups granulated sugar
1/2 teaspoon salt
1 1/2 cups vinegar
1 1/2 cups light corn syrup
1/2 cup maraschino cherries

Trim off the dark green and pink parts of the rind, then cut the white part of the rind into 1-inch cubes. Cover with water and simmer until tender (about 20 minutes), then drain thoroughly. Put the spices in a bag and combine in a kettle with the sugar, salt, vinegar, syrup, and cherries. Simmer for 10 minutes, then add the watermelon rind. Heat to boiling, remove the bag of spices, and simmer until the rind is transparent (about 40 minutes). Seal in hot sterilized jars.

Makes: 2 pints *Mrs. Clarence Troyer*

AMISH SANDWICH SPREAD

Wonderful for any sandwich occasion.

1 dozen sweet red peppers
3 dozen medium-sized green tomatoes
2 cups water
5 cups granulated sugar
3 tablespoons salt
2 cups vinegar
2 cups prepared mustard
1 quart mayonnaise
2 tablespoons celery seed

Grind the vegetables and drain off the liquid, then boil the vegetables with the water, sugar, salt, and vinegar for 10 minutes. Add the mustard, mayonnaise, and celery seed and boil until the mixture thickens. Pour into sterilized jars and seal.

Makes: About 1 quart *Mrs. Eli Yoder*

HOMEMADE CATSUP

Far better, of course, than the store-bought product.

1 tablespoon allspice
1 tablespoon cinnamon
1 tablespoon mustard seed
5 quarts tomato juice
1 cup vinegar
2 cups sugar
2 tablespoons cornstarch
2 cups cooked, sieved onion

Tie the spices in a cloth, then combine in a kettle with all the other ingredients except the cornstarch and onion. Bring to a boil and cook, stirring, until the mixture begins to thicken. Moisten cornstarch with water and add, along with the onion. Bring to a good boil again, then pour into sterilized jars and seal.

Makes: About 5 quarts

Mrs. Jacob B. Weaver
Washington, Indiana

CHICKEN BAR-B-Q SAUCE

A simple, yet tasty marinade and sauce for outdoor cooking.

2 cups vinegar
2 cups water
1/2 pound butter or 1 cup vegetable oil
1/4 cup salt
1 tablespoon Worcestershire sauce

Combine all the ingredients.

Makes: Enough sauce for 8 to 10 chickens

Mrs. Lloyd Yoder

PICKLED PIGS' FEET

These are even better if refrigerated for several days before serving.

4 pigs' feet
1 onion
6 whole cloves
1 tablespoon salt
3 cups vinegar
12 whole peppercorns
1 bay leaf

Split the pigs' feet, scrub thoroughly, and cover with cold water. Add the vinegar and bring to the boiling point. Skim, then add the remaining ingredients and simmer for 2 hours. Cool in liquid and serve cold.

Serves: 4 to 8 *Mrs. Dan C. Schwartz*

AMISH PUT UP STEAK

Refer to Department of Agriculture instructions when canning meat.

10 pounds beefsteak
1 cup brown sugar
1 scant cup salt
1 gallon water

Cut the steak into chunks. Combine the sugar, salt, and water in a saucepan and bring to a boil. Let cool, then divide this liquid among fourteen pint jars. Add the steak, one piece at a time, until it comes up to the neck of the jar. (Do not pack the steak in the jar solidly, as the brine should come up to cover the meat.) Put on lids and cold pack for 2 hours.

Makes: 14 pints *Mrs. Ben Miller*

STINK CASE

The finished product is a lot like a special cottage cheese. Famous in all Amish areas.

1 gallon whole milk, at room temperature
1/2 cup buttermilk
1 tablespoon butter
1 teaspoon baking soda
Salt
Cream or milk to taste

Into the whole milk, stir the buttermilk, then set aside in a warm place (70 to 72 degrees) until clabbered (about 12 to 14 hours).

Put the clabbered milk in a large saucepan and heat, stirring constantly, until you can press curds together. Put the milk through a cheesecloth or any material thin enough to divide the curds from the whey. After the whey is thoroughly pressed out, melt the butter in a skillet and add the curds, baking soda, and salt to taste. Stirring with a potato masher, cook until smooth. Add cream or milk to achieve the desired thickness, then pour in a dish; it's ready to eat.

Serves: 6 to 8

Mrs. E. L. Yutzy
Winesburg, Ohio

Recipe Testers

Rose Abdou, Margaret Africa, Mrs. Jerry Ahlegean, Renee Albert, Mrs. G. M. Allen, Ann Alterio, Ruth Althans, Barbara Armstrong, Mrs. George Baratko, Dorothy Barney, Lillian Bartsch, Mrs. William Baughman, Juanito Baylon, Mrs. Manfred W. Berger, Mrs. Frank Bilicic, Virginia Bivin, Mrs. Wilfred Blakley, Phyllis Blau, Ann Boughton, Patricia Breszinsky, Barbara Brillinger, Nancy Brisbin, Clara B. Brown, Syd Brown, Louise Buckley, Mrs. Thomas Bulloch, Mrs. George Burd, Jean Busch, Mrs. Leonard Bushek, Pat Butler, Stefanie Buzek, Mary Buzzelli, Helen Cake, Diane Cantwell, Martha Carey, Dawn Cermak, Mrs. Jack Chalabian, Mrs. Joseph Cistone, M. J. Clough, Eleanor Clymer, Evelyn Collier, Nola A. Cook, Mrs. Tillman Cooper, Gail Cowalan, June Cratty, Mrs. Henry B. Curtis, Edna M. Davis, Mrs. William DeFord, Elena DiFrancisco, Joe DeGirolamo, Kay Del Regno, Joyce DePamphilis, Evelyn DiBello, Dorothy Dornberg, Alice Dram, Mrs. George K. Driscole, Katherine Eastman, Mrs. William L. Edwards, Linda Emigh, Mrs. Mary Erskine, Pat Fagan, Nancy Faron, Mrs. Ralph Felice, Mrs. Larry Filka, Mrs. H. Firsten, Ruth Fitch, Mrs. David Fleming, Beverly Fordyce, Shirley Fortner, Mrs. William Fraunfelder, Mrs. Ray Fredman, Cecilia French, Mrs. Ralph Frick, Mrs. Richard Froehlich, Anne Frygier, Mrs. Nicholas Fumic, Florence Hubbell Gagnon, Veronica Gallo, Janice Garber, Marie Gayer, Sara George, Frances Gibbons, Lucille Gilpin, Nancy Gilpin, Terry Gilpin, Helen Gluck, Florence Goekjian, Ellen A. Good, Elaine Goss, Doris Gregory, Irene Grey, Ruth Griebel, Lois Gross, Mrs. Regis Haas, Mrs. Bill Hansen, Mrs. Thomas B. Hardy, Betty Harris, Hattie B. Harris, Mrs. Charles Haynosch, Mrs. David Herman, Mrs. Thomas Higgins, Jessie F. Hlad, Mrs. Douglas Hoag, Mrs. Michael Hoffman, Mrs. Michael Hoffner, Nancy Hollis,

Mrs. Miliard M. Horace, Mrs. Ron Hulee, Sue Hulligan, Helen Huss, Mrs. C. K. Issel, Mrs. Floyd Jackson, Carol Janiewicz, Mrs. Robert Jankowski, Betty Jedan, Madeline Johnson, Elsie Jonas, Carol Juniewicz, Lois Kapis, Jennie Kapoudjias, Carol Kasper, Carolyn Kasprzak, Irene Kavin, Mrs. Thomas Klasik, Mrs. Ralph Klemm, Mrs. Rudolph Klincko, Mrs. R. M. Knight, Mrs. David Koelewyn, Jewel Koesy, Elaine Kosdrosky, Betty Kovach, Mrs. Albert Kovalik, Mrs. G. C. Krause, Elsie Kres, Ileen L. Kroh, S. J. Kucinski, Mrs. Eugene Kuhn, Mrs. Herman Kurz, Kay Kusnirek, Mrs. Wayne Le Blanc, Ruth Lambert, Mrs. Robert Lambie, Mrs. Leonard Laskin, June Laurence, Kay Lehman, Edythe Leighton, Mrs. Victor Leo, Dorothy Licht, Mrs. Raymond Lisowski, Mrs. David Little, Sharon Lodge, Helen Longville, Tina Lichniak, Jane Lutheran, Mary Lyons, Arlene Mack, Carol Maichrye, Mrs. Russell Manzatt, Ken Marcin, Mrs. Kenneth Marcin, Mildred Marski, Lucille Maruskin, Mary Mastnardo, Mrs. R. J. Matij, Margaret McCarthy, Mrs. Charles H. McCrobir, Mollie McCrolie, Mrs. Joseph McDonald, Dorothy McDonnell, Ruth McDonough, Dorothy McDowell, Mrs. Richard McKee, Diane Mealey, Mrs. Roger Meckes, Sharon Mehler, Virginia Metyk, Mrs. Arthur Meyer, Dr. Ronald Michota, Alice Milite, Mrs. James Minard, Irene Monkowski, Olga Montonini, Mrs. David H. Moore, Pat Morgano, Mrs. Earl Munson, Mrs. Arthur J. Murton, Mrs. Melvin T. Neill, Mrs. William D. Nicastro, Jean Nicholson, Peggy Nowacki, Joan O'Brien, Mrs. D. Oliver, Alice Oram, Mrs. Charles S. Orban, Mrs. Frank Oswald, Yvonne Packard, Diane Paolucci, Wanda Patton, Frances Payne, Rita Pence, Margaret Pepoy, Helen Pfeffer, Helen Phillips, Helen Phoneuf, Ruth Pickering, Mrs. Stephen Pilat, Mrs. Earl W. Piper, Mrs. Norman E. Placak, Mrs. Donald Poduska, Mary Poplstein, Louise Preebe, Anne Pribula, Madelyn R. Prince, Mrs. W. E. Quinn, Mrs. William Randle, Sr., Mrs. Charles Rawson, Marchia Razayeski, Mrs. Homer Redmond, Mrs. Philip Reichert, Mrs. James Reigle, Wanda Reiss, Helen Reitman, Mrs. George Rickelman, Mrs. Thomas Riley, Mrs. Ray Robeck, Mrs. Alan Robbins, Joyce Robinson, Ruth Roeble, Pamela Roosa, Arlyne Rosen, Mrs. Robert Rossilli, Mrs. Jerry Roth, Mrs. Neil Ruben, Rose Ruggiero, Judy Saraceme, Marie S. Sawyer, Carol J. Schell, Kay Schmidt, Mrs. Fritz Schnabel, Phyllis Schnell, Pat D. Schrader, Mrs. Donald Schneider, Mrs. Karl Schreiber, Bernyce Scott-Krogg, Terri Schulte, Mrs. Joseph Sefchick, Mrs. Joseph Seil, Joan Semenik, Peggy Shaw, Zelma Shepherd, Mrs. William J. Sigler, Vicky Simcic, Georgette Simon, Patricia Sinclair, Arlene Slimmer, Georgia Smith, Eileen Snider, Mrs. Nicholas Solar, Mrs. A. G. Somerville, Mrs. W. P. Spath, Sara Sterling, Victoria Sterling, Henrietta Stevenson, Yvonne Stokowski, Mrs. Walter Stromski, Billie Burke Stubbs, Margaret Suhanic, Mrs. William Svoboda, Mrs. Jack Swed, Lilliam P. Szakacs, Helen Takacs, Penny Tarkany, Mrs. Ronald Thomas, Andrea Tiktin, Mrs. Joseph Tillo, Jr., Elaine Timko, Sharon Tressler, Dorothy Valerian, Mrs. Mircea Valescu, Mrs. C. J. Van Duyn, Virginia Vernon, Mrs. T. Vertal, Mrs. Robert Visk,

Diana Vlach, Mary Wachter, Frances Walkowski, Nancy L. Walsh, Jacqueline Keeling Watters, Mrs. James Weiland, Elaine Weiner, Frances Wesley, Susan Wesley, Mary Wessell, Mrs. Robert Wiencek, Marianne Wiley, Donna Willis, Eileen Wilson, Darlene Winters, Mrs. Melvin Wise, Marlene Wisniewski, Janet Yoppolo, Joyce Yaronczyk, Joyce Yates, Mrs. Louis Zabarsky, Barbara Zavasnik, Mrs. John W. Zeager, Mrs. Joseph Ziegler

Subject Index

Recipe Index